NOTHING BUT THE GOSPEL

NOTHING BUT THE GOSPEL

Can We be Saved through Creation, Other Religions, or Human Philosophy?

Nothing but the Gospel: Can We be Saved Through Creation, Other Religions, or Human Philosophy?

Published by Action Faith Books Press

Copyright © 2014 Floyd Talbot. All rights reserved.

ISBN 0-692-23682-6
ISBN 0-692-23682-1

No part of this manuscript may be reproduced, stored in a retrieval system, or transmitted in any form or by any means, electronic, photocopy, mechanical, scanned, or by any other means except by brief notations, without prior written permission of the author. All rights reserved.

Scripture taken from the New King James Version®. Copyright © 1982 by Thomas Nelson. Used by permission. All rights reserved.

Scripture quoted by permission. Quotation designated (NET) are from the Holy Bible: The NET Bible® (New English Translation[TM]). Copyright© 2001 by Biblical Studies Press, L.L.C. www.NetBible.com. All Rights Reserved.

First Edition 2014

Printed in the United States of America

DEDICATION

God receives all the glory from beginning to end for His unfailing love. He remains faithful in spite of all the waywardness of the human heart and guarantees complete deliverance to His glorious Kingdom where all of those who trust Him in this life will find their final peace and comfort in His presence.

To my wonderful wife, Vickie, for all her efforts in reading the manuscript and highlighting corrections and offering thoughtful suggestions.

ACKNOWLEDGMENTS

I would like to thank Rev. Lamar Allen, Dr. Mark Platt, and Richard Taillefer for their reviews and endorsements. A special thanks to Rev. Rick Haan for his encouragement and taking the time to read the manuscript and to provide useful theological feedback. This book could not have materialized without the greatness of God's grace through all the years of my life.

Table of Contents

About This Book 9
1   How Shall Those Not Hearing Believe? 15
2   Inclusivism's Challenges to the Gospel 25
3   Compromising the Gospel and God 37
4   Christ and the Exclusivity of the Gospel 61
5   Center of the Gospel: God's Righteousness 85
6   Centrality of Christ 113
7   Christ in the Scope of Salvation 131
8   Case for Explicit Faith in Christ 157
9   Fairness and God's Justice 183
10   Destiny of Those Not Knowing Jesus Christ 199
11   A Wider Mercy: A False Hope 223
12   Implications for Missions and Evangelism 235
Bibliography 261
Index 267
About the Author 271

ENDORSEMENTS

"Nothing but the Gospel" addresses the issue of the eternal destiny of those who have never heard the Gospel. The core message of his effort is that God and His actions are not determined by the logic and understanding of man but rather by a traditional interpretation of the teaching of the Bible. Creation and nature reveal to mankind a clear understanding of God's character but "salvation comes only through explicit faith in Jesus Christ." He reminds us that it is only the Bible that reveals an accurate and adequate teaching on God's righteousness, fairness, mercy and justice. Man is not to determine how those attributes are to be expressed but rather to recognize that the Bible and not the explanation of man is the faithful followers' source of truth.
-- Lamar Allen, Pastor, Calvary Church, Los Gatos, CA

"Floyd Talbot's book would be a wonderful addition to your Christian apologetics library. This book logically and biblically refutes those who would add to the Gospel and foment heresy. Then, this book copiously footnotes and corroborates these arguments from the Scriptures and theologians down through the centuries. Jude 1:3 urges Christians "to contend for the faith that was once for all entrusted to the saints." Floyd's book will help you do just that!"
--Mark Platt, Next Chapter Transitions

"Those who are looking for a direct response to inclusivism and open theism will find Floyd Talbot's book helpful. Talbot looks at the inclusivism and open theism of Pinnock, Sanders, and others, and finds them in direct contrast to the clear teaching of the gospel. The arguing is clear and strong, and the book is essential reading for all who want to keep their eyes on the gospel of God through which Talbot demonstrates God provides His righteousness."
--Rick Taillefer, Master of Divinity

About This Book

This book arose from involvement in a community Bible study. During the course of the study, the issue arose concerning those who had never heard the gospel. Was it fair for them never to see God and go to heaven because the gospel never got to them? Is there another way for them other than the gospel? While my position before engaging in writing this book was that God would insure the gospel got to everyone He saved, I had not performed an in depth study on the topic. Discussions that arose in this group prompted me to search the one authority that could give answers – the Bible.

As I delved more into the subject, the more I learned about just how crucial it is for the preservation of the faith we as Christians know and embrace. Getting the message right is not only essential for our faith but also for insuring that God receives all the glory for salvation. The apostles Paul, Peter, and John warned their readers about false teachers creeping into the congregation of Christians and bringing with them a foreign and unsettling message contrary to the Scriptures. Getting the message wrong has numerous negative consequences personally and for missions. The greatest of these consequences are that it dilutes the authority of Scriptures, reduces Christ's preeminence in salvation, and focuses on the individual rather than on God.

This book addresses more than those who have not heard the gospel. Rather, it is about knowing the message and the God behind it. This message and compassion for God and the lost raise our urgency to reach those who do not know Him. This book focuses on a number of truths fundamental to the gospel. Read this book if you desire to know more about:

1. Living by and sharing your faith
2. Knowing the character and nature of God
3. Understanding the righteousness of God
4. Coming to grips with the Trinity in saving the lost
5. Understanding how one comes to know God

ABOUT THIS BOOK

6. Sharing the gospel with the unchurched who may have never heard the gospel
7. Understanding the meaning and application of justification by faith
8. Gaining a greater understanding of Christ in salvation
9. Answering those who believe God has another way or message than the gospel for those who have not heard it
10. Giving answers about God's fairness concerning people whose destination is separation from God eternally although they have never heard the gospel

A tug of war continues to exist over two positions within Christian circles:

1. Exclusivism – One who does not know God must encounter the proclaimed gospel to come to a saving knowledge of him.
2. Inclusivism – Those who have never heard the gospel can come to a saving knowledge of God without hearing the gospel. Rather, they can go to heaven by responding to the light from creation, other religions, human reason, or philosophy.

One of the major consequences of these two positions concerns the person and nature of God. This book engages in a lengthy discussion about how each position treats God and the difference such treatments of Him make. It addresses such questions as "Is God fair? Can we trust Him? Is God in control of the future, specifically our destiny, or does He share control and power with His creation, specifically humanity?"

Today's Christians live in a religiously pluralistic and diverse environment. Pluralism is a hot topic in our post-modern society. That is, we receive pressure to be all-inclusive and to embrace diversity. This pressure does not stop with culture, race, or specific behaviors. Religious pluralism is also included in this list. Such pluralism suggests that we should be accepting of other religions and their teachings as well as embracing more than one way to God and His salvation. Otherwise, we are labeled intolerant and narrow-minded. However, must we accept this mindset? This book tackles these challenges.

The environment of inclusivism has an increasingly negative influence on evangelical churches and whole denominations, leading many astray. It is of utmost importance for Christians to understand influences speculative philosophy and false teachings have on faith. Many teachings redefine God, biblical teachings, and salvation while subtly applying biblical language. One area where false teachings have negative influence is with the gospel and the unsaved.

This book explores the tug of war between the two positions, one a long held one and one a more recent one. The long held position is that salvation comes only through explicit faith in Jesus Christ. There is no other way (John 14:6) and no other name by which one comes to know God and His salvation (Acts 4:12). People must know the gospel for salvation. Exclusivism defines this position.

The other position called inclusivism uses the same Scripture to claim that Jesus is indeed the Savior of the world. However, according to this position, people do not need to know about Jesus for salvation. That is, Jesus as Savior is incognito or behind the scenes saving people through other means than the gospel. Moreover, God provides such means other than the gospel for salvation for those who may never hear it. Those means include the knowledge from the light given them through creation or through other religions (pluralism). Inclusivists differ concerning the amount of knowledge necessary and the contribution of other religions. They must also revise the nature and person of God to arrive at their conclusions.

Faith is critical to salvation and Christian practice. The knowledge of the gospel is essential to true faith. The Bible succinctly declares,

> *"But without faith it is impossible to please Him, for he who comes to God must believe that He is and that He is a rewarder of those who diligently seek Him"* (Hebrews 1:6).

ABOUT THIS BOOK

Faith is our marker that affirms who and what we believe. The *"who"* is the triune God. The *"what"* is that which testifies to God's nature, acts, and disclosure of Himself to humanity. The issue of salvation to the lost, whether they have heard the gospel or not, depends on how we understand the nature and acts of God, and more specifically His disclosure of Himself.

This book also affirms that only the gospel *"is the power of God unto salvation for everyone who believes"* (Romans 1:16). Salvation requires the right power. The Scriptures declare that the source of that power is in the gospel, and it begins with the righteousness of the triune God. Getting the God of our faith right insures that we come to an accurate understanding of salvation. This book discusses these two essential attributes of God, His power and righteousness, for salvation.

How do the Scriptures address the destiny of the lost? Where do we discover any question concerning those who have not heard the gospel? What answer do the Scriptures give? The two positions identified above have starkly different views on these questions. Does searching the Scriptures vigorously give an answer or do we rely on speculation and read into what the Scriptures teach? These two approaches lead to widely diverse answers. This book explores how the Scriptures provide an answer rooted in God's faithfulness to His promise and how His faithfulness gives the only hope for a secure destiny in His hands.

What is wrong with many ways for salvation? This question goes to the heart of the Christian life, evangelism, and missions. Accepting many ways to God diminishes the heart of the Christian life: the centrality of Christ. The centrality of Christ strikes at the heart of God's fairness. It replies to the following questions: "Would it be fair of God to judge those who have not heard the gospel not worthy of salvation? Would it not be fair for Him to provide another way for them apart from the gospel? What is it about the gospel that makes its explicit proclamation the only way to relating with God? What incentives do we who hold the Christian faith have for preaching the gospel to the lost? What content leads to truthful practice of faith?"

The exploration of these questions allows us to gain a greater passion for God and the lost. If we have many messages, they dilute our passion for God and others. Answers to these questions also motivate us to carry out Jesus' final command to His disciples and us with them in reaching a world in darkness and sin. If God makes a promise, would He not have the power and the provision to keep it? If God gives the message, would He not fulfill it? The answer to these questions is a resounding and unconditional YES. This book promotes that YES.

Both Christians and those who are seeking for answers concerning their eternal destiny will benefit from reading this book. For Christians who seek answers for sharing the gospel, this book will provide a wealth of information on the gospel and communicating it to others. It helps answer questions about the destiny of those who have not heard the gospel and how to address questions related to this issue. This book offers several launching steps to begin sharing the gospel. It helps to reply to those who have questions about God's fairness and justice concerning the destiny of the lost. This issue is a major roadblock for many. This book also provides points of departure for all that the gospel addresses: sin, grace, faith, Christ, the Trinity, and a number of other related issues.

For those unsure about whether they have a saving knowledge of God and seek answers about their destiny after death, this book gives replies. It consists of in depth discussions about Jesus Christ, the meaning of faith, justification by faith, salvation, the meaning of living by faith, and the Trinity's role in saving people from eternal death. In essence, this book explains what it means to be a Christian and to relate to God. In addition to a clear explanation of the gospel, this book provides accompanying Bible passages related to the discussion at hand.

1 How Shall Those Not Hearing Believe?

The challenge of those who have not heard the gospel continues to press the Christian Church to action. The question concerning God's fairness concerning those who never hear the gospel has surfaced a number of times over a few centuries. The challenge of His fairness has arisen with greater intensity over recent decades. Some question whether God could be fair in permitting people to go to hell without hearing of Christ. This issue has splintered present-day Evangelicalism and has led many to another gospel. The Apostle Paul initially raised the question about those who have not heard the gospel in his letter to the Church at Rome. Paul addressed those who doubted faithfulness in the promises God made to Abraham that they would be His people. In a series of his own rhetorical questions for addressing these doubters, Paul asked, *"And how shall they believe in Him of whom they have not heard"* (Romans 10:14)?

Many today question Paul's gospel message and diminish it by introducing other ways to salvation.[1] They raise the issue that many went to their graves without ever hearing about Jesus, thereby question the sufficiency of the gospel. If the gospel of Jesus Christ is the *"power of God to salvation to everyone who believes"* (Romans 1:16), is it fair of God to cast judgment of eternal separation from Him for those never hearing about Jesus?[2] Does God provide another way or message for those who have never heard the gospel? Must we hear or read the gospel to realize salvation?

The message of the gospel is the message of salvation. The mission of the church is the strategic umbrella for those without the gospel or to whom many refer as the unevangelized.[3] When considering the gospel message, the Philippian jailer's desperate question to the Apostle Paul echoes from the distant past: *"What must I do to be saved"* (Acts 16:30)? Paul's answer was

HOW SHALL THOSE NOT HEARING BELIEVE?

straightforward and to the point, *"Believe on the Lord Jesus Christ and you will be saved"* (16:31).

Paul was on a mission with the message of salvation resulting from a vision. Little did Paul know that God had other plans. God directed his course, because He gave him the vision. Casting out a demon from a little girl resulted in jail time for Paul and his companions. An earthquake shook the jail and freed all in it from their chains. Knowing that a prisoner escape meant immediate death for him, the jailer turned to suicide. The Apostle Paul yelled at him to stop at which point the jailer cried out his question, *"What must I do to be saved?"* The message was clear. God ordains the message, the missionary, and the mission. Should He not be trusted for salvation of the lost?

This jailer had never heard the gospel. From the text, we receive no clue of his interest in his eternal destiny. His only interest at that moment concerned his physical life. In the middle of his desperation, Paul gave him the gospel of hope. No question existed in Paul's mind about the content of the message he gave the jailer. He knew it as the message for eternal life. It involved faith. Christ was its centerpiece.

Two ways exist for asking the question concerning the lost. One could ask, "What about those who have never heard the gospel?" Is it fair for them to go to hell if they never had an opportunity to hear it? Another way of asking the question is the way the Apostle Paul asked it, *"How shall they who have not heard believe in Him"* (Romans 10:14)? These two questions are quite different and command a starkly different outlook and response.

PRESUMED SALVATION APART FROM THE PROCLAIMED GOSPEL

The first question from many arises out of doubt and challenges those who hold to an exclusive approach to salvation. Many sincere people raise this question out of concern for those in the most remote parts of the world away from modern civilization. In these far away locations, isolated tribes offer up worship and sacrifices to idols they created. They fashion rituals and practices of their own out of superstitions crafted from their imaginations. Such practices have occurred throughout the centuries even in modern civilizations. Nothing is new. However, almost immediately following this question comes more questions that seem to pass judgment on God.

John Sanders raises such subsequent questions in an illustration taken from a discussion he had with a student at a university seminar:

> *"The philosophy club at the local state university was sponsoring a discussion on the nature of God. My interest was piqued, and I decided to attend. Several of the students present were Christians I knew, and some outspoken self-professed atheists attended as well. I listened attentively, but said nothing, as the conversation flowed back and forth between the Christians and the atheists. Finally Matt, one of the atheists, said, "I just can't see how anyone could believe in God." Sensing an opportunity, I jumped into the fray, asking, "Which God don't you believe in, Matt? There are many different understandings of God on the market. Which one is it that you don't believe exists?" Matt retorted, "The God who damns to hell all those who never hear about Jesus."*[4]

Can God be fair? Is He simply vengeful and arbitrary? These questions are quick to pronounce judgment on God as being unfair and unjust. The issue of fairness immediately raises the questions Sanders cites in his illustration. That is, if God sends people to hell because they fail to hear the gospel, he must be a very cruel and merciless God. Such an indictment creates doubt about God and His ways.

However, must we accept this as the only conclusion apart from recognizing a way of salvation other than hearing the gospel? This book stresses that we must not accept an *either-or* trap. That is, do we impugn God for sending people to hell although they have not heard the gospel? Do we accept another way for those who have not heard the gospel? The first choice makes God out to be evil and cruel while the second choice shows Him presumably to be wide in mercy. Are these the only choices available? The subsequent chapters in this book give an unambiguous no. We must not only allow the Scriptures to speak truth but also to identify faulty interpretations and reasoning that give way to error.

THE PROCLAIMED GOSPEL OF SALVATION

The second question raises hope because of the preceding and subsequent questions Paul asks in Romans 10:14-15 and his conclusions:

> *"How then shall they call on Him in whom they have not believed?* **And how shall they believe in Him of whom they have not heard?** *And how shall they hear without a preacher? And how shall they preach unless they are sent? As it is written, 'How beautiful are the feet of those who preach the gospel of peace, who bring glad tidings of good things'"* (Romans 10:14-15).

At the beginning of his answers to this series of questions, Paul raises a stunning conclusion:

> *"But they have not obeyed the gospel. For Isaiah says, 'LORD who has believed our report?' So then faith comes by hearing, and hearing by the word of God"* (10:16-17).

People remain disobedient in spite of God's outstretched hand. While he appears to address the Jews in terms of his Scriptural citations of Isaiah and Nahum, Paul makes it clear that he also includes the Gentiles (10:11-13) among those toward whom he directs the gospel and its declaration. In this conclusion, he connects obedience and faith to the gospel as the means of arousing them. That is, faith arises from hearing the gospel in the word of God. To restate this conclusion, the word of God provokes faith so that such faith is God's doing.[5]

That is, the Scriptures assert that individuals receive salvation only when they believe the proclaimed gospel. The second question from Romans 10:14 suggests a greater hope. Following this question in the passage, Paul poses two more, *"And how shall they hear without a preacher? And how shall they preach unless they are sent"* (10:14-15). Paul points to the words of the prophet Isaiah as a declaration of the greater hope. That is, God will send the preacher who will preach the good news of the gospel.

This book addresses these questions and offers a fresh perspective from the view of who God is, His character as a righteous God, and the nature of mediation. Any other mediation, especially inclusivism's advocacy of creation, falls far short and wholly inadequate. In fact, such other mediation is nothing more than another gospel, and it should be rejected. Inclusivism stands opposite Evangelical exclusivism and the Bible as the means of salvation. Inclusivism proposes that a person can receive salvation apart from the proclaimed gospel of Jesus Christ. That is, knowledge from what one perceives through nature, reason, or even other religions mediates salvation. All one must do is place faith in God perceived through this general revelation (creation).

However, such mediation through general revelation is a compromise and an alternate to the true gospel found in the Scriptures. Such a compromise concerning God invariably leads to compromise with the nature and character of God. Millard Erickson makes the case that because of the organic nature of doctrine, a doctrinal position in one area necessarily affects other biblical doctrines.[6] He cites as examples the Incarnation, the Trinity, God's character, biblical authority, and salvation. These examples are core to the gospel message and point to the key component underlying each example – the righteousness of God.

The righteousness of God advances and promotes the explicit proclamation of the gospel to the lost who have never heard of Christ. It assumes that all people are among the unevangelized. In His righteousness, God takes an active and powerful role in ensuring the proclamation of the gospel to those whom He will save (Matthew 1:21, Romans 1:16-17). This proclamation does not mean that everyone who hears the gospel receives salvation. The argument centered in the righteousness of God also addresses the so-called "fairness" issue with God.

That is, is God fair to permit untold millions to face eternity in hell without ever hearing the gospel? Clark Pinnock refers to this view as the "fewness doctrine."[7] According to him, those who hold to exclusivism advocate that only a few will gain salvation. This book proposes that such a position is erroneous and leads to false conclusions about the means and message of salvation. Such a view of fairness pivots toward compromise of God and His word. It cannot help but do so, because Pinnock begins by assigning his own meaning to fairness.

Regardless of labels from those opposed to the explicit proclamation of the gospel, the mission of the church and the message of the gospel find their defense and comfort in the righteousness of God. Not only is the argument of the righteousness of God in the proclaimed gospel of Jesus Christ the most dominate in Scripture, but it is the strongest and most persuasive. Chapter five addresses how the righteousness of God stands as core to addressing the unsaved. It concludes that God is righteous in all His works and judgments because it surfaces from His very nature. Additionally, because He is righteous, His grace reaches into all humanity through the mediation of the Incarnation of Christ and provides redemption to those who by faith believe the proclaimed gospel.

Mediation is core to the salvation of the lost. The Bible speaks of Christ as the only Mediator between God and humanity (1Timothy 2:5). As Mediator, He shoulders the full weight of sin's burden. He also upholds God's promise of eternal life since He fulfilled the terms of the covenant God made with Abraham through His death on the cross (Hebrews 9:15; 12:24). Chapters six through eight explore the mediation of Christ in detail. The office of mediation is more than one of advocacy and intermediary. Rather, as James R. White notes, mediation is an intercession of a better covenant, superior sacrifice, glorious ministry, greater hope, and faithful promises.[8]

One cannot treat mediation lightly since it involves the second person of the Trinity who stands apart from creation as divine. Nothing or no one else can compare to Christ the

Mediator, not creation or anything else raised as a substitute. While inclusivism attempts to appropriate creation as some sort of mediation, it falls far short, as short as the difference between the finite and the infinite.

Pinnock does refer to Jesus as the only mediator,[9] yet in practical and actual terms, he treats creation as another by citing it as a medium through which a person may receive salvation.[10] This treatment places Christ as prima facie (on its face) mediator but not one in de facto (in fact). That is, according to statements Pinnock makes, Christ is the stated mediator, but he turns to the general revelation of creation as that which the "unevangelized" actually recognize salvation. Of course, Pinnock claims that it takes faith in God, and accordingly the mediation of creation actually drives that faith to Him. Consequently, according to inclusivism, general revelation mediates faith and replaces Christ as the one and only Mediator.

THE GOSPEL AND THE CHURCH'S MISSION

The issue of the lost stands as a core mission of the Church. Jesus commanded His disciples,

> *"Go, therefore, and make disciples of all the nations, baptizing them in the name of the Father and of the Son and of the Holy Spirit, teaching them to observe all things that I have commanded you; and lo, I am with you always, even to the end of the age"* (Matthew 28:19-20).

This command comes from Jesus' mouth and therefore carries God's authority. Jesus said He had all authority in heaven and earth (Mathew 28:18). He sent His disciples on His mission with His message. If Jesus possessed this authority and gave His disciples such a command, the power to accomplish what He commanded invariably follows.

This authority is especially true given the latter part of this mission Jesus gave concerning His continued presence with them (28:20). God will accomplish what He sets out to do with the power vested in His Son in whom and through whom He works out His redemptive purpose. It is a certainty because Jesus promised the success of His mission through the work of the Holy Spirit. Consequently, the triune God is the grounds for the success of the gospel: the Father's promise from the beginning of time, the Son's provision from all eternity, and the Holy Spirit's power now until the end of the age.

NOTES

[1] Fackre, Gabriel, Ronald H. Nash, and John Sanders, *What About Those Who Have Never Heard: Three Views on the Destiny of the Unevangelized* (Downers Grove: InterVarsity Press, 1995), 1588-1604, 1654-1669.

[2] Ibid, locations 614, 922, 1008.

[3] Pinnock, Clark, *A Wideness in God's Mercy: The Finality of Jesus Christ in a World of Religions* (Grand Rapids: Zondervan Publishing House, 1998), 149-180.

[4] Fackre, Kindle locations 165-169.

[5] Cranfield, C. E. B., *Romans: A Shorter Commentary* (Grand Rapids: William B. Eerdmans Publishing Company, 1985), Amazon Kindle Edition, Kindle location 3830.

[6] Erickson, Millard, "The Fate of Those Who Never Hear," *Bibliotheca Sacra*, Volume 152:605 (January 1995): 5-6.

[7] Pinnock, 17, 30, 38, 42, 153-156.

[8] White, James R., "The Newness of the New Covenant," *Reformed Baptist Theological Review*, Volume 01:2 (July 2004): 145, 151-153, 157-160, 162.

[9] Pinnock, 13, 49.

[10] Ibid, 22, 157-158.

2 Inclusivism's Challenges to the Gospel

Inclusivism creates for itself a number of theological and practical challenges it seemingly ignores in favor of establishing straw man arguments. A straw man argument is attributing a position to a person or group that such entities do not hold. The person using this argument then begins to launch criticism against this false position with the intent of invalidating the other's actual stance. Inclusivism takes this action with a number of its attacks on Evangelical exclusivism and by implication and subtly against the Scriptures and its claim of the proclamation of the gospel only for salvation.

For example, inclusivism criticizes Evangelicals for holding to what Clark Pinnock calls a "fewness doctrine." That is, only a few or minority of people will enter the gates of heaven, and the rest will be damned. As discussed in chapter nine, this "fewness doctrine" is the same argument the Jews used in accusing Paul of rejecting the Jews in favor of the Gentiles. In the opinion of inclusivists, this view restricts God's mercy and turns God into a cruel entity. Another argument he uses is in his use of "the wideness of God's mercy." This statement implies that Evangelicals do not find God as merciful as inclusivists, because, according to Pinnock, they allow so few to get into heaven. This argument relies on a numbers game and speculation instead of the authority of Scripture. It also makes heaven a final destination rather than God as the Christian's destiny.

This chapter examines how the proponents of inclusivism as Clark Pinnock and John Sanders create untenable and precarious positions that:

- contribute to doubting God's word
- judge God
- engage speculative thinking

These positions tend toward hurting them and others who follow them. They impede, suppress, and potentially kill faith. Toward the end of his book, *The Wideness in God's Mercy*, Pinnock appears to reflect such an impediment to his own faith when he writes, *"If I have fallen into errors, may the Lord have mercy, forgive, and shed light on my path."*[1]

DOUBT OF GOD'S WORD: IMPEDING FAITH

From the beginning of humanity with our first parents, doubt casts a dark cloud over the gospel. Doubt raises questions about God and is one of the core issues challenging believing and receiving the gospel message. When Satan approached Eve in the Garden of Eden, he posed the first question that instilled doubt, *"Has God indeed said?"* (Genesis 3:1) When Jesus encountered Satan in the wilderness, Satan attempted to derail Him with doubt about His heritage and His father's care and providence. Satan endeavored to get Jesus to question His own identity by posing a statement, *"If you are the Son of God, command this stone to become bread"* (Luke 4:3). Satan also tried to entice Jesus to doubt His Father's oversight, *"If you are the Son of God, throw Yourself down. For it is written, 'He shall give His angels charge over you," and 'In their hands they shall bear you up lest you dash your foot against a stone'"* (Matthew 4:6).

When Peter saw Jesus walking on the water and asked Jesus to command him to come to Him, he faltered due to doubt of Jesus' word (Matthew 14:28-31). After Jesus rose from the dead, He came to His disciples to give them proof. Some doubted (Matthew 28:17). Doubting seeks other answers in alternatives to faith in Christ through speculative conjectures from the view of the temporal world. Doubt conjures up the opposite of faith by proposing sight leads to believing. Thomas said he would not believe unless he actually saw the nail imprints. Doubt looks at what is in the created order and clings to hope in it because it seems to offer greater substance – something seen, touched, or handled.

However, the biblical message is faith leads to seeing. Faith is in the evidence of the unseen (Hebrews 11:1),[2] so that we may have our spiritual eyes opened. Placing faith in the created order, some light given to the unevangelized, or religion is false faith because it looks at the visible rather than what is invisible. While inclusivist John Sanders speculates about a "faith in God revealed to them [the unevangelized] through creation or providence,"[3] it remains faith by sight.

The Bible teaches us that faith in the created order is not sufficiently trustworthy due to sin. Rather those mentioned in Hebrews held on to the divine witness or the promise of God. Hebrews stresses the promise of God made to Abraham and confirmed to his heirs and the prophets. That promise stood as the reality of their hope. Their faith in it confirmed that the ultimate object of faith rested in Jesus Christ (Hebrews 12:1-3) and not in any alternate.

Since Jesus informed His disciples that He would be with them, we can have confidence that the truth will guide the mission. Why then would some question the Apostle Paul's message? Why would those like John Sanders, Clark Pinnock, and Gregory Boyd surface God's fairness concerning the destiny of those who have never heard the gospel of Jesus, if they go to hell when, according to them, they had no opportunity to hear of Jesus?[4]

Are God's presence, promise, and power to reach the lost through the gospel not sufficient? Does God not have the power and will to reach the unevangelized when Jesus promised that He would be with those on His mission with His message of the gospel? If the gospel held such an importance with Jesus so that He commanded His disciples to take it to all nations, why would He consider any other way? If He did consider other means, why did He not mention them to His disciples?

Additionally, is the issue of fairness real? Did God provide another message specifically for those who have not heard the gospel of Jesus Christ? Some who seek a way out of holding God accountable for His lack of fairness do believe God provided another message or means for salvation. If God did provide another message or means, does this change the mission? Such assumptions about God's fairness and that many unevangelized go to their graves without hearing the gospel opens the door for another message or means for salvation. By opening this door to another way, one shuts the only door for eternal life with God – Jesus Christ (John 10:1-9). Jesus makes clear that no other way exists for entry to God and eternal life. He is the door of life.

PRESUMED JUDGMENT: SUPPRESSING FAITH

Human judgment can stand as an impediment to faith. It is finite and fallen. Individuals have need of reconciliation with God to understand the things of God. Paul states,

> *"The natural man does not receive the things of the Spirit of God, for they are foolishness to him; nor can he know them, because they are spiritually discerned"* (1 Corinthians 2:14).

While we can understand certain things about God through nature, Paul insists that the mind must receive enlightenment through renewal to come to grips with spiritual realities. Individuals can observe creation day and night, but unless the Holy Spirit gives birth to individuals, no hope exists for knowing God. Rather individuals alienated from God reject spiritual truths and follow their own paths. Robert Pyne renders the phrase *"does not receive"* [NKJV] in 1 Corinthians 2:14 as *"not able to know."* He goes on to write,

> *"This seems considerably stronger. It is simply a consequence of the rejection mentioned in the first part of this verse...It seems that one's rejection of 'the things of the Spirit of God' is because of inability to 'know' them...The unsaved person does not accept God's truth because it seems foolish to him and he is not able to 'know' it."*[5]

Such an assessment also applies to human judgment. The incapability that leads to rejection of the word of God impairs judgment with those who do not know God. Even those who do know Him can make faulty judgments because of the finite state of our humanity. Combine that with the matter that sin continues to hinder us in grasping truth, we often fall short in our appraisal of God and His ways. Therefore, when we encounter difficult challenges about God and His ways, we easily stumble and take the course of least resistance. That course is judging Him or His actions.

Consequently, when the fate of the unevangelized or the lost arises, we want to believe God will be fair in opportunity. This belief is a valid concern. However, God calls us to trust Him in such matters rather than to doubt His faithfulness.

However, speculation is an easier route, because it permits what appears to be the freedom to read between the lines of Scripture or to engage in guesswork about what may be missing rather than in the pursuit of truth concerning the destiny of the lost. Speculation arises because of our finiteness and the hindrance of sin that remains with us. Therefore, it is important for us to think God's thoughts. The way that happens is fourfold:

1. Subjection to His judgments by faith that leads to our acceptance of Him as our Creator and Redeemer
2. Acceptance of His word as we give ourselves to the study of it
3. A constant reminder that He rules the world in righteousness and wisdom and that our thoughts are not His thoughts
4. Acceptance that we are not in the position to pass judgment on Him

These four principles will aid in removing impediments to faith and enable us to trust Him by faith to deal with those whom He saves. Paul reminds us that God's judgments are unsearchable and that His ways are beyond our capacity to comprehend them without His help (Romans 11:33). He discloses His word to us for our benefit so we may understand how we live by faith. He rules the world and we do not. While He places us as stewards over it, He holds all of it together (Colossians 1:16-17). He is infinite and we are finite. Consequently, we have no ability to judge Him.

All judgments of God cease with faith in Christ. Those who reject this faith also reject the only way to God. This faith looks to Jesus and receives His word rather than the speculative words of men. His word also reminds us that He is sovereign and we are finite. Faith embraces His sovereignty and faithfulness.

SPECULATIVE THINKING: KILLING FAITH

The Apostle Paul warned the church in Rome that speculation is foolish. He referred to it as futility of thinking (Romans 1:22). It is misplaced trust in the thoughts and conjectures of people rather than having its source in the word of God. When Paul went to Athens, he discovered philosophers sharing their ignorance over various worldviews (Acts 17:22-30). He brought them back around to the source of true knowledge – God Himself. Through His self-disclosure, God makes known His will and provides the basis for it and the way of salvation in His word. Paul also pointed out to these Greek philosophers that God is not far from each person (17:27), for He created all humanity in His image (17:29). Consequently, speculation about the things of God is not the means of seeking after God, because it tends toward idolatry (17:29). Faith alone through His disclosure to us in the Scriptures alone connects us to the God who is near, for through faith in Christ alone we come to know Him.

Speculation about God

What does this topic have to do with the destiny of those who have never heard the gospel? The question concerning their destiny often surfaces speculation concerning the lost. Speculation, as Paul demonstrates in Acts and Romans, tends to create a caricature of God by either projecting false attributes on Him or making Him to be something He is not. False attributes may include or combine something true and untrue, thus creating that which is false. When such attribution occurs, it results in false judgments about Him and His acts with humanity and His entire creation.

Such is the case with Harold Kushner's assessment of God. He entitles one of the chapters in his book "God Can't Do

Everything, But He Can Do Some Important Things." In it, Kushner builds his case for this stated title through continuous speculation. In one section, he writes,

> *"I can't believe that God chooses to hear the prayers of some and not of others. There would be no discernible rhyme or reason to His doing that. No amount of research into the lives of those who died and those who survived would help us learn how to live or how to pray so that we too would win God's favor."*[6]

Kushner sets up this conflicting scenario to illustrate that if God replied in the affirmative to one person, He would be ignoring another on the other end of the same issue or problem. His assessment places God in conflict with Himself. Accordingly, the only way out for this situation is to conclude that God cannot do everything.

However, this and similar situations Kushner poses intentionally limits alternatives for God to attempt to press Him into a corner of finitude and powerlessness. By beginning with speculation and faulty logic, Kushner shackles God and ignores His disclosure of Himself to humanity through the authority of His word.

We must take care that we do not enter a similar trap. It is much easier to engage in speculation about God than to seek the authority of His word in the Bible. Numerous circumstances we encounter in our lives leave us puzzled and nag at us concerning God's involvement or perceived lack of action in our favor. Quite often, we mull over the death of a loved one or the occurrence of a large disaster such as a hurricane or a 15-car pileup that kills several people. Sometimes our first reaction is to judge God for permitting such circumstances or to posit inability on His part to prevent them. Speculation becomes the rule rather than the exception.

INCLUSIVISM'S CHALLENGES TO THE GOSPEL

Speculation about Biblical Truth

Christians have two options in approach to faith: having it grounded in biblical truth or having it carried along by speculation. Biblical truth has its source in God Himself. Speculation has its source in human reason and imagination around the Bible. While we rely on human reason for reasoning and drawing conclusions from divine truth as it applies to our walk of faith, it alone cannot be our ultimate resource and authority for knowing truth. We need God to inform us about who we are and how we relate to the world, others, and God. His word disclosed in the Scriptures acts as the authority for guiding us. It trumps speculation, because the Scriptures require faith for knowing God. Our finite condition and alienation from God illustrates our need for God for direction in our lives and reconciliation with Him.

John Warwick Montgomery appropriately states that unbelief and speculation lead to hopelessness in this world and the next.[7] This is not to say that speculation in itself is wrong or evil. We engage in hypotheses and theory frequently concerning the world in which we live for coming to grips with the environment and our world. When separate from and not subject to divine revelation concerning God, His rule over creation, and spiritual things, speculation tends toward doubt of God's providence, unbelief, and human-centeredness. He points to the areas of philosophy, science, theology, literature and the arts, and law and society as those where secular speculation has made its detrimental marks.

Theological speculation is of particular relevance concerning the present topic of the destiny of the lost. In reference to scholars in the "higher criticism" camp, Warwick states,

> "Once the biblical documents have been dismissed as unhistorical, theological doctrine inevitably becomes a matter of speculation as well."[8]

Higher criticism tends to ignore or assign to secondary importance the grammatical-historical approach to the Scripture and the author's intent for textual meaning. Rather, it assumes that certain editors of the biblical documents pieced them together from a number of sources. While Pinnock and Sanders do not subscribe to higher criticism, they do engage in similar speculation with Scripture in coming to their conclusion that the view of inclusivism as God's way of salvation. They assume a parallel approach with higher criticism in that they seem to dismiss author intent and cite selective passages to support their position. From such an approach, they then conclude that the proclaimed gospel of Jesus Christ is not the only way individuals receive salvation.

John Sanders raises speculative questions that appear on the surface to appeal to God's trustworthiness in His word and His genuine effort toward inclusivist redemption. He states,

> *"Hence it is not surprising that some theologians simply deny that God wants all to come to repentance. But if God does not make salvation available to all people, then should these biblical texts be taken seriously? If God makes no genuine attempt to save the unevangelized, should it be said that God wants them to come to faith?"*[9]

He writes within the context of countering some for their attempts to water down the Scriptures while he himself waters down the Scriptures by engaging in speculation. The point of raising these rhetorical questions is to engage in speculation rather than call out the author's intent and meaning within their given contexts. Rather than rely on the biblical authors' messages to their audiences, Sanders engages in flawed premises. He establishes a conditional situation by assuming that God somehow deprives people of the way of salvation and does not attempt to save the "unevangelized." His series of rhetorical questions draws a false conclusion from flawed premises. He bases his premises on speculation and not on the authority of Scripture.

For example, Sanders draws upon the Exodus event to make his claim (Exodus 7:5, 17; 8:10). In his speculative approach, he treats Pharaoh just the opposite of the author's intent in the biblical text. Not only does he speculate around the text, but he also reads into it to support his position. He erroneously concludes that God sought to show Pharaoh His redeeming love and grace and applies the word *"know"* from the text to refer to *"relational and redemptive knowledge."*[10]

While the Hebrew word could imply redemptive knowledge, it most certainly does not carry that meaning within this context. The biblical text does not show any inclination that God desired to redeem Pharaoh. This is sheer speculation on Sander's part and misleading to the reader. Sanders' speculation leads to misinterpretation of the biblical text to support his position of God's radical love. This explanation is only one of many places where Sanders engages in speculation leading to erroneous application.

Speculation is misleading and can upset faith, especially when it comes to a misreading of the Scriptural text. It raises many more questions than it answers concerning the nature and activity of God in the world, especially among those who reject Him. In addressing the Sanders' speculative claims, A. B. Caneday states,

> *"It is commendable for Christians to "theologize" and not "adopt an agnostic stance before we have made a thorough investigation," just as it is right to provide answers to detractors of Christianity, even concerning the issue of the destiny of the unevangelized. However, theological structures must be built upon the solid foundation of biblical exegesis. Though it is both necessary and proper to attempt to fit texts into a comprehensive and intelligible system, what is inadmissible is to do this without permitting the text of scripture to speak for itself. Sanders not only fails to do biblical exegesis with sensitivity to context, his "control beliefs" (his term) misguide his efforts."*[11]

Caneday offers the defense that the Bible is not a book for speculation. He contends that a difference exists between "theologizing" and theological speculation. One grounds interpretation in having *"scripture speak for itself,"* (theological investigation) while the other (theological speculation) goes beyond Scripture and attempts to read into it something other than what it says. As Christians, we must check our approach and allow biblical interpretation to begin with the author's intent in communicating God's word.

Speculation shifts authority for faith from God to the speculator and grounds Christian living in presumption. This in turn makes hope fragile and shaky. Reaching the lost pivots on a clear message for those living in darkness and blind to the ways of God. When a person obscures the message with speculation, those who depend on that message for knowing the redemptive work of Christ get lost in a maze.

Doubt impedes faith by entering in and raising questions about Christ as the center of faith and the gospel. Being quick to pass judgment on God lends to suppressing faith. Such judgment leads to enmity just as it did when Satan brought charges against God's truth with Eve and Jesus. Questioning God's fairness concerning His redemption of the lost interrupts our trust of Him and registers in our minds another god of our imaginations. Speculation is a faith killer. It allows doubt to take root and permits it to substitute the created order for the glory of God (Romans 1:21-23). Without faith in revealed truth, we rely on our own reasoning and an alternate to the gospel.

INCLUSIVISM'S CHALLENGES TO THE GOSPEL

NOTES

[1] Pinnock, 183.

[2] Baugh, S.M., "The Cloud of Witnesses in Hebrews 11:6," *Westminster Theological Journal*, Volume 68:1 (Spring 2006): 118-119.

[3] Fackre, 76.

[4] House, Paul R., "Biblical Theology and the Inclusivist Challenge," *Southern Baptist Journal of Theology*, Volume 2:2 (Summer 1998): 3. *See also* Pyne, Robert A., and Stephen R. Spencer, "A Critique of Free-will Theism – Part Two," *Bibliotheca Sacra*, Volume 158:632 (October 2001): 397-403.

[5] Pyne, Robert A., "The Role of the Holy Spirit in Conversion," *Bibliotheca Sacra*, Volume 150:598 (April 1992): 205-206.

[6] Kushner, Harold S, *When Bad Things Happen to Good People* (New York: Knopf Doubleday Publishing Group, Kindle Edition, 2004), location 1446.

[7] Montgomery, John Warwick, "Speculation Versus Factuality: An Analysis of Modern Unbelief," *Bibliotheca Sacra*, Volume 168:669 (January 2011): 33.

[8] Ibid, 41.

[9] Fackre, locations 209-210.

[10] Ibid, location 226.

[11] Caneday, A. B., ""Evangelical Inclusivism" and the Exclusivity of the Gospel: A Review of John Sanders's No Other Name," *Southern Baptist Journal of Theology*, Volume 01:4 (Winter 1997): 27.

3   Compromising the Gospel and God

Why does this book address doctrinal compromise of truth and the gospel? The Bible is the Christian's authoritative source for truth and the true gospel. Jesus Himself declared, *"I am the way, the truth, and the life. No one comes to the Father except through Me"* (John 14:6). Jesus encompasses all of these three characteristics in the gospel message as Mediator for us with the Father. Compromise is a train wreck for biblical truth, the gospel, and faith. The truth matters with the gospel, for without truth the gospel would not exists. The Christian community knows the truth about God's redemptive plan through the gospel and it only. For in it, we discover the way to the Father, the truth, reconciliation with God, and eternal life. Additionally, only in the gospel does the power toward salvation exists (Romans 1:16-17).

From the first century forward, other gospels have arisen and deceived many because they compromised the way to God, the truth, and the meaning of eternal life. Many false gospels continue to this day not only among new cults but also within mainstream Christian churches. Compromise of the gospel is the starting point for those a) who find certain biblical truths not to their liking, b) who by compromise presuppose biblical revelation is insufficient, or c) who pose questions that raise doubts concerning revealed truth. The Apostle John warned about false teachers who come with an unfamiliar message (1 John 4:1).

This chapter addresses what happens when compromises occur and how they apply specifically to inclusivism. First, the ripple effect runs its course and shreds other truths. Second, compromise leads to the rejection of the proclaimed gospel and the introduction of new ones. Third, compromise has a direct line leading back to God. That is, the revision of truth takes its ultimate course in creating God in the image of man so that He assumes some characteristics of humanity. It compromises His nature, message, or means of salvation.

For example, in discussing the vulnerability of God in human relationships and our prayers to Him, Clark Pinnock states,

> *"Echoing similar sentiments, Donald Bloesch writes that through prayer "God makes himself dependent on the requests of his children." This dependency and openness of God result from the fact that the divine love does not force its will on the creatures. Instead, according to Gabriel Fackre, God makes himself vulnerable by taking the risk of being rejected."*[1]

In another place, Pinnock writes,

> *"Though ontologically strong, God can be vulnerable because of the decision to make a world like this. The Lord of the universe has chosen to limit his power by delegating some to the creature. God gives room to creatures and invites them to be covenant partners, opening up the possibility of loving fellowship but also of some initiative being taken away from God and creatures coming into conflict with his plans. God gives us room to rebel against him, and when that happens patiently waits for the prodigal to return."*[2]

Pinnock projects human traits on God, such as dependency, vulnerability, and rejection. In doing so, he creates God in the image of the creature. Furthermore, by creating God in the image of the creature, inclusivism places limits on Him. He is limited by being dependent on humanity, which has its limitations. He is also limited by virtue of delegating His own power to humanity. Nowhere do the Scriptures inform us of God's delegation of His power to individuals.

While some Scriptures may give that impression, such as certain people performing miracles, that is not delegating His power as much as it is empowering some to accomplish His work

(Romans 15:19; 2 Corinthians 4:7). The power by which He works through individuals does not belong to those individuals but to God. It is not innately theirs but God's power. Through His empowerment, God retains His power and does not give it up to the extent of taking away initiative from God when human plans and God's plans conflict. Consider how much initiative God would have to relinquish to human rebellion. All rebel and resist. That would leave God hopelessly and helplessly waiting for any prodigals to return to Him. God would have to relinquish all of His power to the degree of making individuals gods and reducing God to the level of creation.

By being dependent on individuals, God shows greater limitation than those within creation. By making Himself vulnerable, God exhibits weakness. He is at risk to the whims of human free will. Why then would a Christian trust or depend on such a God?

Additionally, such vulnerability no longer makes God omnipotent, thus making it possible for the entire earth to spin out of His control because of the actions of those on whom God shows dependence *"on the requests of His children."* In their foolishness, individuals could request something in prayer that God realizes would not be wise for them or would bring harm to them. Does God take the risk of answering such prayers that may lead to their harm? Such an approach would seem to go contrary to Paul's assessment of God of whom he writes,

> *"And we know that all things work together for good to those who love God, to those who are the called according to His purpose"* (Romans 8:28).

How could the god of inclusivism work all things for good when humanity can circumvent His purposes through their free will or by His dependency on them in the manner described? Such a god is one at variance with the Scriptural presentation of Him.

Challenges related to compromise, especially compromises with the nature and identity of God, lead us farther from the Scriptures and God. The farther removed we become from the Scriptures, the less authority it has for us. Such movement gives us greater liberty to engage in speculation. The most serious compromise of them all is the compromise of God Himself. The more we compromise with God, the less we come to accept the biblical portrait of Him. The less we accept the biblical God, the more we turn to accept a god of our own creation. This leads to turning away from Him toward idolatry.

COMPROMISE AND SPECULATION

Speculation is the death of divine inspiration and authority of Scripture. It calls into question the Holy Spirit's movement among those who wrote as He led them. Speculation attempts to change divine truth into the doctrines of men. Speculation assaults faith and turns it into presumption through such words as "may," "could," "suppose," "assume," and "possible." Speculation raises questions that provoke doubt and unbelief in what God says. Satan raised such a speculative question with Eve when he asked, *"Has God indeed said...?"* (Genesis 3:1). It makes tentative what God makes certain. Where speculation sees an open door, it considers such a door an invitation. It brings with it all sorts of philosophies and opinions of men and attempts to integrate them with divine truth to create another "truth."

COMPROMISE OF BIBLICAL THEOLOGY

Ron House proposes that speculative questions relative to the Christian faith occur not only external to it but also from within the circles of *"orthodox belief."*[3] He points to the inclusivism view of salvation as one of those internal challenges. He continues to say,

> *"What is relatively new, and troubling, is that a few key thinkers from traditionally evangelical circles, such as Clark Pinnock, Richard Rice, and John Sanders, have joined them. Though no one of good will can accurately question the*

> *motives of these individuals, their arguments for inclusivism are faulty on methodological, theological, and practical grounds."*[4]

When speculation becomes the approach to theology, the realm of biblical interpretation and doctrine come under attack. It shifts interpretation from sound exegesis (calling out the meaning of the biblical text) to eisegesis (reading into the biblical text). It also shifts authority from the biblical authors and the Holy Spirit to the reader.

House points to questionable interpretive practices and the redefinition of biblical terms as results of these shifts. Theology suffers. Speculation behind these shifts makes theology into the philosophy of men rather than the truth of God. House also identifies the failure to consider integrated biblical theology. Gordon Lewis and Bruce Demarest outline integrative theology as involving six stages:[5]

1. Problem identification in coming to terms with the biblical text
2. A review of solutions brought forth through history
3. The review of relevant Scriptural teaching related to the issue
4. The organization of pertinent biblical teachings and their relation with other teachings
5. The defense of a doctrinal position relative to opposing teachings in theology, philosophy, and other religions
6. The application of the specific biblical teaching to life

Lack of integration fails to see how various doctrines complement one another to encompass the whole of truth. Integrative biblical theology also helps us see how the Old and New Testament work together to reveal the entire redemptive purpose of God.[6] The failure of integrative theology can also lead to Scriptural misapplication. Error in not considering the influence of one truth on others can lead to misinterpretation and misapplication. For example, if we fail to consider the gospel as grounded in the explicit confession of Christ, it would be easy to raise another gospel. House again suggests inclusivist proponents make application grounded in presumption while giving questionable hope for the unevangelized and undermining the gospel.[7]

COMPROMISE IN BIBLICAL INTERPRETATION

Inclusivist John Sanders advocates a speculative approach to the Bible and diminishes the authority of the biblical authors and the Holy Spirit speaking through them,

> *"If we did not speculate about subjects not directly revealed in the Bible, we would have very little theology; we would have no doctrine of the Trinity, no doctrine of Jesus having both human and divine in hypostatic union."*[8]

Sanders claims are not entirely accurate. He seems to confuse speculation with interpretation derived from inductive reasoning from the Scriptures. The manner in which he describes speculation in the above quote is interpretive inductive analysis as illustrated by the following,

> *"These articles of faith, hammered out over several centuries by the early church, are not explicitly explained in the Scriptures. They are theological formulations drawn from scriptural information to answer crucial issues raised in the intellectual (Hellenistic) context of the church at the time."*[9]

Gordon Lewis refers to the above example Sanders uses to support his speculative approach to Scripture as integrative theology using the inductive method.[10] Sanders bases his claim on implicit rather than explicit statements in Scripture about these doctrines. Just because the Scriptures make implicit statements (for examples the teaching of the Trinity) they do not lead to speculation to derive truth. The Councils of the early church did indeed conclude these doctrines to be true, and they grounded their conclusions on Scripture through inductive reasoning. Sanders affirms their use of Scriptures but overlooks the method of inductive reasoning the early Councils applied.

The early church saw clear Scriptural statements for the divine nature of the Father, Son, and Holy Spirit. They also recognized the Scriptures spoke of one God and not three. They surveyed the other alternate statements to determine if they squared with Scriptures. This process is not speculation but gathering from what all the Scriptures declare about God and drawing interpretive conclusions while allowing Scriptures to act as the authoritative source with the Holy Spirit's guidance.

If we accept Sanders' conclusion about the need for speculation to derive theological doctrine, then we must find Jesus, the Old Testament prophets, and the apostles also guilty of such speculation. Robert Allen informs us that Jesus often employed inductive method in His teachings.[11] He offers the example of how Jesus explained to the men on the road to Emmaus the Old Testament testimony to His Messianic appearance. Allen also points to Peter's sermon on Pentecost as inductive in that it gleaned Old Testament evidence for the coming of Christ and His death and resurrection and concluded that this evidence pointed to Jesus.[12]

Robert Lightner is also helpful on this point in supporting the inductive method as a means of deriving theology. He offers three sound principles for guiding it:[13]

1. Diligent and careful data collection
2. Comprehensiveness in scope
3. Derivation from the facts

The facts act as the basis while diligence, care, and comprehensiveness provide the parameters or borders for keeping interpretation in line with biblical truth. Sanders uses his confusion between speculation and inductive interpretation as a base for arriving at his inclusive approach to salvation.

REDEFINITION OF TERMS AND READING INTO SCRIPTURE

One of the most troubling aspects of theological challenges with inclusivism is the use of hyperbole. Hyperbole concerns methodology, because it returns to interpretive practices by either revising meaning or suggesting a different slant on truth. It could also borrow from human philosophy and integrate with Christian truth to make truth a hybrid of the human and divine or a compromise of God's disclosure of truth. Hyperbole can be persuasive and draw the listener or reader into a false hope.

Clark Pinnock applies hyperbole on a number of occasions in terms he uses. In the title of one of his books, *The Wideness of God's Mercy*, in which he defines his position of inclusivism, he frequently uses "Wideness" and "Finality." By these terms, he means to stress the greatness of God's mercy and the position Christ ("high Christology")[14] takes in God's redemptive activity.

The meaning he applies to them is absent in the Scriptures. Rather, they represent his attempt to redefine biblical terms or to make distinctions between other religious persuasions from the more liberal (pluralism) to conservative Evangelicals.[15] John Sanders also applies such terminology presumably to give a greater place for God's love in redemption. He emphasizes "God's radical love"[16] to stress the kind of love distinct from those holding the exclusive or restrictivist view of salvation. This "radical love" seemingly has greater scope. They mean for hyperbole to give credence to inclusivism as the more biblical view. Rather, what they actually do is alter theology by redefining biblical terms to mean other than what the biblical authors intended them to mean. They also make God one-dimensional by emphasizing certain of His attributes more than other attributes or ignoring some altogether.

For example, while placing emphasis on God's mercy and love, they de-emphasize or ignore God's righteousness and justice. Rather than giving these attributes equal standing, they use them negatively. They raise questions about God's justice if He is as the God Evangelical exclusivism proposes. In the

Introduction to his book, *A Wideness in God's Mercy*, Pinnock states,

> *"A majority of evangelicals today are hardline restrictivists in my estimation. The only possibility for encountering God and receiving salvation in this view is to exercise explicit faith in Christ in this earthly life. General revelation is not sufficient; all must receive God's revelation in Christ. Outside of this special revelation, there is near-total darkness. Other religions are error and falsehood and non-Christian with few exceptions are on their way to hell."*[17]

Not only does he marginalize a position opposed to his own, but he also portrays it in an uncomplimentary manner. They are *"hardline."* Additionally, why would anyone want to accept or embrace a God who desires to keep certain people in "near-total darkness?" To Pinnock, why would people worship a God narrow in His way who rejects a sincere seeker who sees Him through the eyes of another religion? Such a portrait of God causes Pinnock to conclude that one holding a view he opposes makes God unjust or unloving. With such a speculative approach, Pinnock creates straw man arguments by creating assumptions about the positions of Evangelicals and then attacking these assumed positions.

John Sanders also engages in similar tactics. He relates a story of a college student he engages at a university philosophy club meeting. This student decried the God of which the attending Christians spoke. He said to Sanders, *"I just can't see how anyone could believe in God."* When Sanders made further inquiry, this student replied, *"The God who damns to hell all those who never hear about Jesus."*[18] By highlighting this story, Sanders intended to illustrate how the God of Evangelical exclusivism is a very unjust God. Experience trumps divine disclosure.

His argument, like that of Pinnock, has its basis in straw man argumentation or wrongfully attributing a position to those who hold to an Evangelical exclusive position. This attribution takes it course with emotion and a skewed portrayal of God to support inclusivism. That is, a person raises a caricature of God, the God someone else supposedly holds when in fact that is not the position of the other person at all. Such an argument is nothing more than a distraction from the true disclosure of God in the Bible, one that neither Pinnock nor Sanders accurately represents. House states of this portrayal,

> *"Inclusivism as defined by Clark Pinnock... (and by others in various publications), bears neither the mark of full-orbed theology or of effective theological methodology."*[19]

One could add that inclusivism's depiction of God appears foreign to what the Bible truly discloses. Selecting certain traits of God and ignoring other Scriptural traits of God does not give God a reliable treatment. Such selectivity fails to consider context and the author's intent in the Scriptural authors' disclosure of God. It also lends to compromise of biblical truth. It does so not only of God but also of other biblical teachings, lending to a false hope and a faith based on speculative practice.

THE RIPPLE EFFECT OF COMPROMISE

When compromise occurs in one major doctrine, a compromise often causes a restatement of one or more other major doctrines. No sooner did the Church rise from birth after the resurrection of Jesus that it encountered a number of compromising heresies. The Apostle Paul warned the church in Ephesus about such heresies (Acts 20:28-31) as did the Apostle John (1 John 4:1) concerning the person and resurrection of Christ.

The heresies of the past about the nature of God and His activity and purpose in redemption have transformed into fresh battles. The tendency to redefine God, Christ, the Scriptures, and salvation continue to push and shove their way into churches and denominations, their leaders, and society. Being alert to these errors shuts the door to compromise.

The Ripple Effect with the Nature of God

Many contemporary views of God and salvation within Christendom are heretical. They have simply resurrected ancient heresies from the first three centuries of the Church. Many present denominations have entertained discussions concerning alternatives to the Trinity, the Incarnation of Christ, the nature of the Holy Spirit, and the means of salvation. Many are to what we refer as sects. Although they profess the Christian faith, they depart from what many Evangelical theologians hold as core Christian doctrines.

The church leaders of the first several centuries hammered out these doctrines in the Councils of the early Christian church. Such doctrines received confirmation by many later established creeds up to and through the Reformation to today. These core doctrines consist of the Trinity, the person of Jesus Christ, salvation by grace through faith, and the Scriptures.[20] Others appear more mainstream or receive acceptance as mainstream. Whole denominations reject the Trinity and consequently the Incarnation of Christ.[a]

Many teachers within purported Evangelical denominations have nuanced the Trinity in a way that denies parts of it or skews its statement and application. Clark Pinnock, John Sanders, and Gregory Boyd have done this. Pinnock and other inclusivists not only wrongly raise a straw man God, one that Evangelicalism does not hold, but also divorces God from the whole of biblical theology and holds Him to be somebody other than the God of the Bible.

Dr. Stephen Wellum suggests that these inclusivists established a division between the roles of Jesus Christ and the Holy Spirit. He states that by grounding the doctrine of Christ and the Spirit in their "wider-hope" theology, they split the roles and mission of Jesus and the Holy Spirit. That is, a person does

---

[a] The nonsectarian denominations professing Christian faith consist of Living Church of God, Oneness Pentecostals, Members Church of God International, Unitarian Universalists, and the United Church of God. Those denominations to which many evangelicals refer as sects include the Jehovah Witnesses, The Church of Jesus Christ of the Latter Day Saints, Christian Scientists, and Christadelphians.

not need to hear of Jesus Christ to realize the saving work of the Holy Spirit.[21] According to inclusivists, the Holy Spirit can work through the created order to bring people to salvation without even knowing Christ as the Savior.

This split contradicts the Apostle John's gospel of the Holy Spirit's witness to Jesus Christ in both glorifying Him and giving testimony of Jesus Christ's teachings (John 14:26; 15:26; 16:13). Wellum goes on to say Pinnock departs from the realization of faith and repentance toward an altogether different understanding of the Spirit's work. He points to what Pinnock refers as *"traces of Jesus in the world and people opening up to His ideals."*[22] Pinnock cites such characteristics as love, care, and justice as such "ideals."

These expressions are foreign to a biblical understanding of repentance and faith. They take the Christian mission into uncharted territory, a foreign land that bears no relationship with new life in Christ based on explicit acknowledgement of being a new creation in Him (Romans 6:1-14; 2 Corinthians 5:17). Ideals do not save or provide spiritual renewal. Only the proclaimed gospel of Jesus Christ has the power to bring salvation to its hearers (Romans 10:17).

When compromises occur with a core doctrine like God, it necessarily touches on the doctrine of Jesus Christ and the Holy Spirit. If one rejects the God of the Bible or creates a caricature of Him, it leads to a restatement of the person, work, and mission of Jesus Christ. If one redefines Christ in any of these terms, then one doing so necessarily redefines Him to fit another claim. This redefinition in turn follows a path of compromises in other Christian doctrines.

The Ripple Effect in the Unified Role and Mission of the Trinity

The doctrine of the Trinity stands as the essential core teaching of the Christian faith. It not only defines the nature and being of God but also God's role and mission in His redemptive purpose with humanity. That is, His expressed nature and activity are necessarily inseparable as the Triune God in creation and salvation. Millard Erickson states,

> *"In the doctrine of the Trinity, we encounter one of the truly distinctive doctrines of Christianity...The doctrine of the Trinity is crucial for Christianity. It is concerned with who God is, what he is like, how he works, and how he is to be approached."*[23]

While each member of the Trinity is distinct as to person, the three comprise one God. In like manner, each has a role with a unified purpose and mission with creation, interaction with it, and salvation for all creation, particularly humanity.

Gordon R. Lewis and Bruce A. Demarest are helpful at this point concerning the mission of God in redemption, the primary issue of this book,

> *"Most succinctly, in regard to the distinctive roles of each of the three persons in the work of salvation, God the Father planned it, God the Son provided it, and God the Holy Spirit applies it.*
>
> *Such harmonious functional activities of Father, Son, and Spirit reflect a deeper personal unity of conscious thinking, feeling, and willing. And that unity of mind and purpose reveals an even deeper essential oneness of being."*[24]

The vital importance of unity of persons and purpose arises in terms how the Church through time came to understand the interaction of God with humanity. The Apostle Paul spoke several times of God's singular purpose and how from eternity He worked it out in and through redemption (Ephesians 1:9; 3:11; 2 Timothy 1:9). All three persons of the Trinity participated together in this purpose. God the Father purposed it, the Son executed it, and the Spirit disclosed its mystery in the gospel. God chose His Son to be Savior and Mediator. The Son voluntarily laid down His life as a sacrifice for the sins of the world. The Holy Spirit reveals the eternal truths about this redemptive sacrifice and glorifies the

Son. There was never a departure from this purposeful unity by either one of the persons of the Trinity.

COMPROMISE WITH THE NATURE OF GOD

Compromise concerning God has occurred throughout history. Compromise is the leading agent toward a departure from Scripture or at worst idolatry. When God arises from the imaginations of the human mind, the divine assumes the image of the creation in the form of inanimate objects, animals, or humanity. Additionally, as theologians and teachers depart from the authority of Scripture, engage in speculation, or seek biblical interpretation through reading into the Scriptures, compromise of the doctrine of God finds its way through these avenues. Human imaginations and speculations reduce God to physical form or place on Him specific human emotions, feeling, or limitations.

One of the great battles of the early church arose over the nature of God. Just who is He? With Jesus entering the scene through the Incarnation, perplexity filled the minds of many in attempts to come to terms with Him who claimed divinity and equality with the Father. Jesus also spoke of the Holy Spirit whom He and the Father would send. His assertion perplexed many. The Council of Nicaea settled on the Trinity, as Athanasius became its champion.

The Trinity is the core of the Christian faith, because it defined the God whom Christians worship. The Trinity also became the linchpin for the teaching (doctrine) of salvation. The Father sent His Son into the world as Redeemer and Mediator. Peter declared, *"Nor is there salvation in any other, for there is no other name under heaven given among men by which we must be saved"* (Acts 4:12). Peter's context made clear that he spoke of the proclaimed Christ (4:10). In his letter to Timothy, Paul wrote, *"For there is one God and one Mediator between God and men, the Man Christ Jesus"* (1 Timothy 2:5). Again, context demonstrates that not only did God send the Son as Mediator, but also that salvation comes through proclamation of Him as Redeemer.

The Holy Spirit proceeded from the Father and Son (John 14:26; 15:26). He came to give God's sons and daughters comfort and assurance that God is with them and Jesus would never forsake them (Matthew 28:20). He would be their teacher and the one who guided them into all truth. Most of all, He would glorify Christ and show to all His preeminence above all creation, for through Him all things came into being (John 1:3).

Any compromise with the nature of God as Trinity necessarily leads to compromise with the purpose and mission of God in salvation. The Trinity has a unified purpose and mission in the redemption of not only humanity but also the entire creation. The persons of the Trinity are one in thinking and action in redemption. This means neither has separate plans or does anything apart from the others. Bruce Ware places the unified mission of the Trinity in perspective in the following way,

> *"So our sanctification is done by the triune God, with Father, Son, and Holy Spirit each participating in different but complementary ways. How wonderful is the unity and diversity of the trinitarian Persons. Rich harmony is heard from heaven as Father, Son, and Holy Spirit each sing their respective parts of one glorious and intricately unified composition."*[25]

The Trinitarian God accomplishes His entire scope of salvation in and through those whom He saves. The Father sent the Son into the world as Savior and Mediator. The singular purpose of the Son was to die on the cross and rise again as the Redeemer and to be the Mediator for the saved before the Father. The singular purpose of the Holy Spirit was and is to glorify the Son by placing Him front and center for the entire world, both living and dead, to recognize Him as Lord of all.

The Holy Spirit does this in the Church through the message of the gospel. He will do this at the end of all time when Christ comes again to gather all the redeemed to be with Him eternally in their new home with the triune God. The salvation of the lost depends on the purpose and singular mission of the triune God working together to bring about His plan of salvation.

EARLY DEBATES DEFINING THE TRINITY

The early church fathers struggled with the nature of God. The formulation of many Christian doctrines always seemed to find their way back to the being and nature of God in the Trinity. The issues of salvation, the gospel, and its core in Jesus Christ are no exceptions. The statement of the Trinity did not arise without a number of other heretical considerations. Many attempts to reconcile what appeared to be different portrayals of God in the Old and New Testaments prompted many to assign different ways of viewing God. From the first through the third centuries, several Church teachers attempted a number of ways of viewing God from a Trinitarian perspective as well as from a non-Trinitarian one.

They recognized God to be one from the Old Testament declarations of Him in the Shema: *"Hear, O Israel: The LORD our God, the LORD is one"* (Deuteronomy 6:4). When Jesus arrived on the scene through the Incarnation as the prophets earlier declared, He and others announced Him to be the Son of God (Mark 3:11; Luke 1:35; John 1:34; 3:16-18; 5:19) and equal to God. How then were they to reconcile the Shema with Jesus' claims of divinity and the recognition of the arrival of the Holy Spirit and His divinity? Darrell Johnson states the problem in the following manner:

> *"But they knew that something radical had taken place in the midst of history, in the life and ministry of Jesus of Nazareth, something that they could not ignore. They came to believe that in the man, Jesus, they had encountered the God who is one...And what, or who, is this divine reality called the Holy Spirit with whom and in whom, Jesus baptized His disciples? What is the relationship between the Spirit and Jesus and the Spirit and the Father? The challenge was to articulate who the one God is after Christmas and Pentecost, after the coming of the Son and coming of the Spirit."*[26]

If we understand the word *"radical"* correctly, we come to grips with the most far-reaching[27] encounter in all of history. The Creator met the created in the form of humanity in time and space. Such an encounter not only changed history but also the trajectory of all creation toward the culmination of restoration and reconciliation.

Encounter with God hinges on an accurate formulation of the Trinity, the role of each member of the Trinity, and the mission each member has in redemption of humanity. During the early Church period, His deity raised a quandary and numerous questions concerning the nature, expressions, and revelation of God. Jesus' identification of Himself with the Father surfaced charges of heresy from others (John 5:17-27). Decades and centuries after His death and resurrection, church leaders tried to make sense of the divine nature of God as Father, Son, and Holy Spirit. How could there be the divinity of the Father as well as the Son and Holy Spirit and still have one God?

A number of speculations arose in attempts to resolve the issue of the three divine persons of the Trinity. These philosophical speculations also tried to explain how the three persons of the Trinity interacted and expressed themselves in the world. Monarchianism claimed that Jesus became divine, the Word was not personal, and that Jesus Christ was not the Word.[28] Docetism, Apollinarinism, Arianism, Eutychianism, and several other early Church teachings attempted to redefine God and Jesus in ways that failed to attribute to God a Trinitarian nature and to the Son the divine second person of the Trinity. They did so by casting Him as fully divine (and not human), as fully man (and not divine), seeming to be one or the other (or an apparition), or part divine and part human.[29]

Early Deism that formally surfaced during the seventeenth and eighteenth centuries denied the divinity of Christ and viewed the Holy Spirit as an impersonal force.[30] Frederich Hegel (1770-1831) casts the Trinity as "merely a figurative expression" and described it in the following manner,

"A dialectic movement wherein the thesis (Father) and the antithesis (Son) are united into the higher unity of the Spirit or Absolute Love...This

> *God is an impersonal and immanental process of Self-Realization. As such the differentiation within the Godhead only represents simultaneous moments in its continuing being, of which the Son is mere finite existence and the Spirit a mere category of expression.*"[31]

Liberal Protestants treat God in a variety of ways, and most recently have broken down the gender barrier with God, no longer treating God as Father. Some make God dependent on human experience. That is, according to W. A. Brown, God in reality is not a Trinity but a "summary of the different ways in which one may know God in experience."[32] Experience trumps objective truth. Modern compromises continue through resurrecting and integrating many ancient heresies with secular philosophy. Many mainstream denominations deny the Trinity or the divinity of Christ.

Feminism has crept into the nature of God and revised the gender attribution of God the Father. The Re-Imagining Conference in 1993 brought together Presbyterians and Methodists to attempt to cast God into the image of feminism. It included contingents from the two denominations as well as participants from the Minnesota Council of Churches, forty-nine states, and twenty-two countries to present views on feminist theology and divinity.[33] The discussion of feminist theology involved Sophia, the goddess of wisdom, as representative of this gathering's depiction of its god for worship.

Many women holding senior positions in the Presbyterian USA denomination lost their positions resulting from their attendance at the Re-Imagining Conference. However, Re-Imagining did not go away. Rather, feminism and a feminist divinity became standard within the denomination. At its 220th General Assembly, the denomination convened its thirteenth annual Voices of Sophia breakfast. In addressing the attendees (July 3, 2012), Sylvia Thorson-Smith fondly recalled the Re-Imagining Conference and declared,

> *"Re-Imagining was chosen to point out that theological work is artistic work. God is imagined and re-imagined by many names."*[34]

This official arm of the Presbyterian Church USA voices that theology and God has its source and formulation in one's imagination. Theology becomes "artistic" rather than the discovery of God's authoritative will in the Scriptures.

THE IMPORTANCE OF THE NATURE AND MISSION OF GOD IN THE GOSPEL

Why is this review important? Those within mainstream Christian denominations and evangelicalism brought such thinking and activity forward through inclusivism and pluralism. The imagination of and speculation about God has taken its course in and through inclusivism. This, in turn, has opened the door to pluralism, that is, the redemptive knowledge of God also finds its way in other religions. Its proponents often read their own imaginations into Scripture to discover their theology of God and salvation. They formulate their own idea of God and seek Scriptural texts to support it. They also speculate about how God treats the lost, giving them a "wider hope" where such hope is presumptuous. Some revise God's attributes to cater to their "wider hope" or the "wideness of God's mercy." Consequently, they raise the prospect that those who never heard of Christ find their way into heaven anyway.

The rise of Open Theism with Gregory Boyd, Clark Pinnock, John Sanders, and others subtly introduces even more compromises. These compromises lend to a restatement of the gospel from one that includes Christ proclaimed to one with Him absent in it. This restatement or the essence of Open Theism rests on the dismissal of God as omniscient or a God who cannot know the future.[35] Pinnock refers to God as the "Most Moved Mover."[36] This portrayal presumably reveals Him as one with whom individuals can relate as a loving God who embraces them with that love and mercy. For God to be relational toward the humanity He created, Pinnock claims,

> "[He] *limits His power toward the world in order to have loving relations... For open theists, God self-limits for the sake of love.*"[37]

With a restatement of God also comes inclusivism's restatement of salvation. Robert Pyne shows how one's view of God naturally leads to a revised means of salvation. He states,

> "*The assumptions that are so central to free-will theism's doctrine of God will likely have a profound effect on one's doctrine of salvation. The implications go far beyond traditional distinctions between Arminianism and Calvinism. Different as those systems may be, they both affirm exhaustive divine foreknowledge and they both support an exclusivist understanding of world evangelism. Free-will theism, as its more vocal advocates demonstrate, is more compatible with soteriological inclusivism.*"[38]

Accordingly, God cannot know the future and individuals have free will sufficient to circumvent God's efforts. He simply moves with humanity and guides each person to Himself through the revelation He gave whether through the proclaimed gospel, nature, human reason, or the light of other religions. As these new ways of viewing the means of salvation surface, they influence significantly the message and mission of the church.

Just as the Trinity enables a more clear interaction between the members of the Trinity, an accurate picture of God provides us with greater assurance in our Christian faith and confidence in sharing the gospel and missions. If God is as inclusivism and its corresponding Open Theism express, what kind of assurance can we have in faith and missions? What hope does this perspective generate, and does such a hope have sound biblical grounding? The Scriptures inform us otherwise. When God speaks, He does so with authority and power. Paul claims,

"For all the promises of God in Him are Yes, and in Him Amen, to the glory of God through us" (2 Corinthians 1:20).

What God promises, He will fulfill. God does not helplessly wait for individuals to make a decision for Him. He works in human history saving people through the gospel proclamation and the powerful witness of the Holy Spirit working to give life. The Scriptures give witness to this God and not the one proponents of inclusivism create in their image.

NOTES

[1] Pinnock, Clark, Richard Rice, John Sanders, William Hasker, and David Basinger, *The Openness of God: A Biblical Challenge to the Traditional Understanding of God* (Downers Grove: InterVarsity Press), 1994, Kindle locations 1151-1153.

[2] Ibid, Kindle locations 1372-1375.

[3] House, Paul R., 3.

[4] Ibid.

[5] Lewis, Gordon R., and Bruce A Demarest, *Integrative Theology* (Grand Rapids: Zondervan, 1996), 7.

[6] Ibid, 4.

[7] Ibid, 4-5.

[8] Sanders, John, *No Other Name: An Investigation into the Destiny of the Unevangelized* (Grand Rapids: William B. Eerdmans Publishing Company, 1992), 17.

[9] Ibid.

[10] Lewis and Demarest, 12.

[11] Allen, Robert A., "The Expository Sermon: Cultural or Biblical?" *Journal of Ministry and Theology*, Volume 02:2 (Fall 1998): 216-217.

[12] Ibid, 218.

[13] Lightner, Robert, "A Case for Systematic Theology," *Conservative Theological Journal*, Volume 04:11 (April 2000): 37-38.

[14] Pinnock, 13-14, 50-51.

[15] Ibid.

[16] Fackre, Kindle locations 222-224, 494, 544.

[17] Pinnock, 12.

[18] Fackre, Kindle location 167.

[19] House, 5.

[20] Schaff, *Creeds of Christendom, Volume I: The History of the Creeds – Enhanced Version* (Grand Rapids: Christian Classics Ethereal Library, Amazon Kindle Edition), Kindle locations 1187-1193.

[21] Wellum, Stephen J., "An Evaluation of the Son-Spirit Relation in Clark Pinnock's Inclusivism: An Exercise in Trinitarian Reflection," *Southern Baptist Journal of Theology*, Volume 10:1 (Spring 2006): 5.

[22] Ibid, 13.

[23] Erickson, Millard, *Christian Theology, Second Edition* (Grand Rapids: Baker Books, 1998), 347.

[24] Lewis and Demarest, 280.

[25] Ware, Bruce A., *Father, Son, and Holy Spirit: Relationships, Roles, and Relevance* (Wheaton, Ill.: Crossway Books, 2005), 170.

[26] Johnson, Darrell, *Experiencing the Trinity* (Vancouver: Regent College Publishing, 2002), 39.

[27] _____, *Oxford American Dictionary and Thesaurus* (New York: Oxford University Press, 2003), 1234. The word *radical* often gets associated

with left-wing politics. However, its most fundamental meaning refers to returning to the basics. Hence, the word *far-reaching* expresses the extent toward which God goes to restore His creation and reconcile fallen humanity to Himself through Christ, returning it and them to their basic purpose.

[28] Erickson, 358-359.

[29] Schaff, Kindle locations 22,118, 35,357, 36,744, 36,761, 36,845-36846, 37,148, 50, 241.

[30] Lewis and Demarest, 252.

[31] Ibid, 253.

[32] Ibid, 255.

[33] Kersten, Kathy, "A New Heaven and New Earth," *First Things*, March 1994, http://www.firstthings.com/print/article/2009/03/002-a-new-heaven-and-a-new-earth-49, accessed November 7, 2013.

[34] Tuck, Janet, "Voices of Sophia Breakfast: Thorsen-Smith Reflects Back and Looks Forward," *News & Announcements*, Presbyterian Church USA, http://www.pcusa.org/news/2012/7/7/voices-sophia-breakfast-thorson-smith-reflects-bac, accessed November 7, 2013.

[35] House, Paul R., "The Battle for the Doctrine of God and a New Journal," *Southern Baptist Journal of Theology*, Volume 1:1 (Spring 1997): 5-6.

[36] Pinnock, Clark H., *Most Moved Mover: A Theology of God's Openness* (Grand Rapids: Baker Book House, 2001).

[37] _____, "Does Prayer Change Things? Yes, if you're an Open Theist," *Homiletics Interview: Clark H. Pinnock, Homiletics Online*, http://www.homileticsonline.com/subscriber/interviews/Pinnock.asp, accessed November 6, 2013.

[38] Pyne, Robert A., "A Critique of Free-Will Theism, Part 2," *Bibliotheca Sacra*, Volume 158:632 (October 2001): 397.

4 Christ and the Exclusivity of the Gospel

What is the destiny of those not hearing the gospel? The issue related to this question is the gospel itself. It is important to identify how the different approaches to salvation appraise the gospel and its contents. Is it the only message or one of many messages by which a person comes to a saving knowledge of God? Many authors have written about the different ways to salvation for the "unevangelized," especially the proponents of inclusivism. Most within the Evangelical Christian community uphold the exclusivist approach to salvation. That is, explicit faith in the proclaimed gospel of Jesus Christ is the only way to salvation. The exclusive approach to salvation takes the Apostle Paul at his face value when he makes the unambiguous claim, *"Faith comes by hearing, and hearing by the word of God"* (Romans 10:17). The word of God arouses faith in the hearer of the gospel.

According to the Scriptures the unsaved receive salvation by grace through faith in Christ (Ephesians 2:8-9), which are both revelations in the gospel. As opposed to inclusivism (or another form of inclusivism – pluralism) exclusivists hold to the biblical uniqueness of the gospel. The uniqueness of the gospel also includes the uniqueness of Christ and the uniqueness of Christ's claims as fundamental and necessary for salvation. Not only are they necessary, but a person must place faith explicitly in Christ. This chapter explains why explicit faith must be so.

THE UNIQUENESS OF THE GOSPEL

Paul brings together faith, the gospel, and salvation in his letter to the Romans when he writes,

> *"For I am not ashamed of the gospel of Christ, for it is the power of God to salvation for*

CHRIST AND THE EXCLUSIVITY OF THE GOSPEL

everyone who believes, for the Jews first and also to the Greek. For in it the righteousness of God is revealed from faith to faith; as it is written, 'the just shall live by faith'" (Romans 1:16-17).

In this passage from Romans, Paul makes several claims and raises the level of the uniqueness and preeminence of the gospel. It stands apart as the greatest revelation the world has ever known. Its uniqueness expresses itself in a number of ways that inclusivism and pluralism fail to recognize and embrace in their approach to salvation. While the proponents of the other positions mention the gospel, it is not in the same sense Paul gives it and its content. This chapter provides reasons why a person must explicitly place faith in Christ for salvation. In doing so, it shows how inclusivism falls short and plunges into serious theological errors.

The Claims of Inclusivism and the Gospel Message

Pinnock sees the gospel as a kingdom message of God's sovereign reign and an invitation *"to be caught up in its sweeping action."*[1] In this process, Pinnock sees God *"changing cultural entities we called religions into closer conformity with His purpose for the creation. God is not going to leave out anything as important as the religions from the work of transforming all things."*[2] Accordingly, we can just make assumptions from our observation of religions to derive truth. That is, he makes a subtle shift for authority concerning the means of salvation from the Bible to other religions.

He goes on to discuss the importance of religions and people's sincere search for God through them,

> *"People are searching for God, and they want to know the nature of transcendence. Although there is no present agreement about the answers (any more than there is in the sciences on numerous issues), people deserve to have their hypotheses about God taken seriously and not cavalierly dismissed. As Christians, we are*

> *convinced that God is revealing Himself to humankind; therefore, we take claims at having attained insight into his revelation seriously, and we weigh them in relation to our own understanding. The fact that religions differ ought not to discourage us or cause us to give up on the search for truth. Let us explore other people's opinions about God with enthusiasm."*[3]

So that there is no mistake in misinterpreting Pinnock's meaning concerning how he sees religions playing an authoritative role in God's redemptive plan, we need only read further. He speculates about God transforming the religions of the world. He notes that God is at work changing religions just as He changes cultures, and those religions play a positive role in society.[4] To him, they are not the source of idolatry but rather a positive transforming influence. While the Bible affirms the gospel as a kingdom message, it denies other religions as mechanism of expressing any mediatory capacity toward salvation. Contrary to Pinnock, Paul views religions apart from the gospel as idolatrous (Acts 17:22-29; Romans 1:21-25).

Pinnock claims that many religions are and have been bad and evil. However, through the influence of Christianity, they have reformed. Yet, he does not tell us the nature of this reformation. He argues world missions not only plant churches but also promote reform in these religions.[5] Because of his optimistic manner of viewing other religions, he does not see them in the same manner as the Apostle Paul. According to Paul, they arise from the imaginations of individuals who seek other gods after suppressing the truth and rejecting the God known to them (Romans 1:18-19).

While the Bible affirms Pinnock's assessment that other religions are bad and evil, the Bible cannot side with him or inclusivists concerning the purpose of missions to reform religions, especially without knowing what this reformation entails. Rather, we confirm with the Apostle Paul that the purpose of missions is to preach Christ so that the gospel through the Holy Spirit can bring about new life and faith in God (2 Corinthians 4:5-7; 5:17-20). This new life is inward spiritual transformation and not religious reformation. Such a mission is the true and genuine ministry of the Spirit. Pinnock and inclusivists must invariably reject Paul's assessment in favor of their own speculations. Inclusivism's mission is at variance with the Bible. God's purpose is not to reform religions but to transform the hearts of individuals through the renewal the Holy Spirit brings.

It is within the context of God's wider work in religions that Pinnock recommends bridging dialog with other religions for delineating truth claims and "truths" other religions may have discovered in their *"searching for God."* Several problems exist with Pinnock's assertions.

They go counter to Scriptural claims that no one seeks after God but rather engage in the suppression of truth (Romans 1:18-23; 3:11-12). To affirm Pinnock's statement about individuals seeking after God is to dismiss Scripture.

Pinnock also appears to dismiss the gospel as a settled issue by claiming, *"...there is no present agreement about the answers* [concerning the *"nature of transcendence"*]*."* If this were the case, why would Paul be so firm on the gospel so that the preaching of any other is a curse (Galatians 1:8)? He saw the gospel message as settled because God ordained it. There need not be an agreement among those in religions, cultures, or societies about their own religions or philosophies. If they depart from the gospel, they are vain. Rather, the only answer for the destiny of humanity and its estrangement from God is the gospel of Jesus Christ.

Pinnock wants us to believe that we should build a bridge through dialog to other religions, a bridge toward what Paul assails as idolatry. Pinnock invites Christians to explore enthusiastically the opinions of others about God. By asserting this claim, Pinnock shifts spiritual authority from the Bible to the opinions of other religions. While we respect what people say and should listen carefully to them, enthusiastically exploring the opinions of other religions without a standard or an authority can spell danger for us.

Listening to others enables us to determine their spiritual positions and needs so we can have a starting point for evangelism and show compassion. A listening ear develops empathy for individuals separated from God and in need of Christ. Christ calls believers to have compassion for the lost and to meet their condition with the only message of hope found in the gospel. Dialog without recognizing the authority of Scripture and the gospel in it as our starting point leaves us open to embracing error and fails to show compassion. Pinnock does not seem to acknowledge that other religions have their own gospels and by possessing one, they reject the gospel of Christ and embrace idolatry.

While speaking of the gospel within various contexts, Pinnock and Sanders also seem to place it in a secondary role. Like Pinnock, Sanders believes that people can come to salvation without knowing Christ or hearing the gospel.[6] He reaches this conclusion through what he terms his *"control beliefs"* or those beliefs that are *"extremely powerful in influencing what we 'see' in a text or the way we interpret our experiences."*[7] Sanders not only accepts this speculative approach to the Scriptures, but he also assumes that we can form our own doctrine and use it as a *"control belief"* and then go to the Scriptures to find support for it. Using these two principles together lend to reading into Scriptures what they may not teach.

Such an approach contributes to revisionism of core Scriptural teachings, one of which is the gospel itself. When the gospel does not receive the priority the Scriptures give it, its contents also are subject to revision. For example, Sanders states,

> *"Briefly, inclusivists affirm that particularity and finality of salvation only in Christ but deny that knowledge of His work is necessary for salvation. That is to say, they hold that the work of Jesus is ontologically necessary for salvation* [no one would be saved without it] *but not epistemologically necessary* [one not need be aware of the work in order to benefit from it]*."*[8]

Sanders poses two problems with this statement. First, he reads into Scripture what is not there, and second, he creates a division between Christ as Savior and Christ as Mediator. In the first instance, Sanders speculates in his use of *"particularity and finality."* The Scriptures nowhere use or imply such terms or teach any sort of notions as these concerning Christ. To ground biblical teachings of Christ in such speculation lends to error. It also steps outside of the authority of Scriptures to conjure up new doctrines and their applications related to the person and work of Christ and the Trinity. In claiming that salvation can come apart from hearing the gospel of Christ, he makes applications that arise from speculative teachings.

The Scriptures make Jesus Christ the object of faith (John 17:20; 2 Timothy 3:15; Hebrews 12:2; 1 Peter 1:8). We do not believe in God without believing in Christ the second person of the Trinity. If Sanders and Pinnock claim one receives salvation by simply believing in God, that must also include Jesus Christ, for He is God. To believe in God without believing in Christ is faith in another god altogether. To hide Christ is to hide the one true God and makes us susceptible to creating a god in the image of creation whether of humanity, animals, or sticks and stones. Consequently, Sander's speculating of *"particularity and finality"* rends Christ and God apart and creates a caricature of Him, a false god that exists in speculation.

Second, Sanders suggests an incognito Christ who is behind the scenes and silent, as noted with Pinnock in chapter two. Sanders and Pinnock identify Him as Savior but remove Him from the office of Mediator and replace Him with the mediation of the knowledge of general revelation. This portrayal is not the Savior and Mediator of the Scriptures.

The Gospel's Claims: Christ, Divine Power, and Righteousness

The gospel is unique in six ways. First, the gospel marks the difference between the Creator and creation. This distinction takes inclusivism to task for its reliance on general revelation or creation for salvation. Inclusivism blurs the line between the Creator and creation by looking to creation as a means through which one comes to God for salvation. The gospel has its source in the one who is distinct and separate from creation. Inclusivists also may say that the gospel has its source in God. However, inclusivism advocates a response of faith in the knowledge individuals have from general revelation (creation) as a means to salvation.[9] This advocacy of general revelation competes with the special revelation of the gospel. In other words, creation acts as a mediator for salvation rather than Christ. While creation is revelation, it lacks divine capability, such as power, righteousness, and love. Pantheism seeks to make creation divine for attributing these attributes to it. In a similar manner, inclusivism also seeks to blur the line between the Creator and creation to attribute the means of salvation to it.

Second, Christ is the center of the gospel. Having Him as its center makes it not only a divine message but also revelation of the divine. The gospel is about God in Christ mediating between humanity and God the Father and reconciling them to Him. Without Christ, there would be no gospel. Without the gospel, the unevangelized could not come to saving knowledge. Such knowledge comes by no other way.

Third, the gospel is the power of God for salvation. What makes the gospel the power of God is that God in Christ is the message and in the message. God Himself is the active agent for insuring the gospel reaches those He will save. Creation has no such power. It simply shows His eternal power and glorifies Him. Creation has no redemptive capacity, mediation, or power between God and humanity.

Fourth, the gospel is for all of the unevangelized without distinction. God does not discriminate between Jews and the rest of the world. Everyone is unsaved at one time or another. Everyone was at one time without the gospel. Everyone needs the gospel for salvation with no exception. To use a term like "unevangelized" is an attempt to distinguish between two groups of unsaved people, a distinction the Bible does not make.

Fifth, the gospel reveals the righteousness of God. The claim that the gospel reveals the righteousness of God carries the highest weight because it reveals the core character of God – His faithfulness to all generations. That righteousness, according to Paul finds its way to the cross as the righteous died for the unrighteous (1 Peter 3:18) that we might stand as righteous before God (2 Corinthians 5:21). Chapter five explores this claim in detail.

CHRIST AND THE EXCLUSIVITY OF THE GOSPEL

Sixth, the gospel is revelation from God. The gospel is special revelation while creation is general revelation. As God's special revelation, Jesus did not come incognito to anyone nor was He behind the scenes as the Savior in the wider world making it possible for those never hearing of Him to know salvation. Consequently, if Christ is behind the scenes, so also is God. How then could anyone place faith in the God who does not reveal Himself? God reveals His salvation through Christ, the second person of the Trinity.

Ronald Nash states,

> *"Evangelicals believe that Jesus is the only Savior. There is no other Savior and no other religion, we believe, that can bring human beings to the saving grace of God... I know no one who denies that evangelicals commonly understand verses like these to teach that since the death and resurrection of Jesus, explicit personal faith in Jesus is a necessary condition for salvation. Typically, evangelicals also believe that physical death marks the end of any human opportunity to receive the gift of God's salvation."*[10]

That is, not only is Christ the only Savior, but He is the explicit and recognized object of faith. He stands alone exclusively and distinct from anything else since He is wholly separate from creation as it Creator. Nothing or no one can come close to a stand-in for Him. While Pinnock, Sanders, and other inclusivists recognize Jesus Christ as the Savior, they cast Him aside as secondary to creation in their speculation related to the destiny of those who have not heard the gospel.

Source of Divine Authority: Scripture Alone

The authority for the exclusive view is the Bible. This book also takes that position. Destiny with God or otherwise separated from Him for all eternity depends on the gospel for all the unsaved. It is important that we get the message right so we do not communicate an uncertain, vague, or indefinable gospel about God's salvation. If those who hold to inclusivism also rely on the Bible for their position, how do we square these conflicting views from one book? One major difference between exclusivism and inclusivism on the means of salvation for the "unevangelized" is authority. Inclusivism does not recognize the full authority of the Bible whereas exclusivism affirms it.

By minimizing the gospel for those who hear it for salvation, inclusivists must necessarily claim two gospels. If we take the inclusivist argument to its logical conclusion, they must accept a dual gospel scenario. Those who hear it and believe existed beforehand as those who never heard it. Prior to hearing the gospel of Jesus Christ, they fell in the category of the "unevangelized." According to inclusivists, receiving salvation from faith in the knowledge a person gains from general revelation is a real possibility. All they would have to do is follow the knowledge gained from the light of creation. Such a person would not need the gospel, thereby minimizing its importance.

However, if a person encountered the gospel and discovered Jesus Christ as Savior and Mediator, then the knowledge of the light from creation would prove to be irrelevant, and if irrelevant then false. This would be the case unless of course that person gained salvation already from faith in the light of general revelation. Then the gospel would prove unneeded. The two gospels are mutually exclusive. That is, one is irrelevant and the other relevant or the opposite is true. With such a scenario, one would be true and the other false. The Bible itself confirms this scenario, that is, that there is only one gospel (Galatians 1:6-7).

Consequently, inclusivism finds itself in a quandary of finding at the same time two gospels and one gospel. If they are mutually exclusive because the Bible teaches one gospel, that leaves inclusivism with a choice. It must accept the authority of the Bible and affirm one gospel or engage in speculation and affirm a gospel for the "unevangelized" and a gospel for the evangelized. If inclusivism accepts the gospel only, it must dismiss its inclusive position and faith in the knowledge arising from general revelation.

If inclusivism accepts general revelation as a way to salvation, then it must rely on speculation (and human reasoning) as the final authority. In doing so, they must deny the biblical gospel of Jesus Christ and His central place in it. By accepting a gospel that finds its source in general revelation (creation), inclusivists must actually set aside the gospel of Jesus Christ. That is, inclusivism finds itself in conflict concerning authority. In one sense, it rests on speculation as its authority. In another sense, it goes to the Bible to support its claims but does so selectively and speculatively. These alternatives present inconsistency at the core of the belief in inclusivism.

The Apostle Paul makes the claim for the Scriptural authority of the gospel clear in his letter to the Galatians,

"But even if we, or an angel from heaven, preach any other gospel to you than what we have preached to you, let him be accursed"
(Galatians 1:8).

Behind Scriptural authority is divine authority. The Bible is God's word. Paul calls the gospel found in the Bible as the gospel of Christ (Galatians 1:7). It did not have its source in man (1:11-12). The forcefulness of his declaration about any other gospel shows in several ways. He makes this statement twice. He invokes any proclamation from God's very angels and any subsequent claim as false and a lie. The Apostle Paul leaves no exception.

The occasion for writing this letter served to alert the Galatians to a different message or their return to the practices of Judaism. Regardless of the circumstances, Paul made clear that the gospel he proclaimed accommodated all occasions, people, and opposing religious ideologies. In other words, there is no variation regardless of circumstances, culture, epoch, language, race, or nation. All who never heard the gospel need to hear and respond to it.

What is it about the gospel that leads exclusivism to reject any other approach to salvation? What makes inclusivism and pluralism unbiblical and not aligned with the gospel? The gospel is unique in several ways. First, it is unique in that it expresses and makes essential the righteousness of God as its core. Second, Christ makes the gospel unique. He takes second place to nothing else when it comes to salvation. Third, Christ's truth claims makes the gospel unique. Salvation hinges on His Incarnation, death, and resurrection. The first essential element of the gospel's uniqueness, God's righteousness, receives more lengthy discussion in chapter five. The remainder of this chapter addresses the other two unique components of the gospel: 1) the uniqueness of Christ and 2) the uniqueness of Christ's claims.

UNIQUENESS OF CHRIST

Christ stands unique in a number of ways. Primarily, He is God and the second person of the Trinity. The Trinity not only separates Christian faith from all other religions and their theologies, but it expresses the one and only God. We can make the claim that the Trinity and Christ as the second person of the Trinity make the Christian faith like no other. Additionally, we must also claim that no comparison exists between the truth and the falsehoods of all other religious expressions.

God stands apart from creation while all other religions find their source in creation or speculation arising from the human mind. Christ is not of the created order. Rather, He stands apart from the created order as God Himself, uncreated and as the eternal Son of God. Such a claim raises the question, "Was Jesus not part of the created order when He lived among humanity?" Sometimes language fails us in coming to grips with the Trinity and the distinctions between the created order and the divine. Darrell Johnson states,

> *"Yes, thinking about God as Trinity is hard work. But it's worth it. For when we enter into the intellectual process by which the church arrived at the Trinity, we very soon discover that we are not thinking human thoughts about God; we are thinking God's thoughts about God."*[11]

Contrary to what inclusivist John Sanders claims, thinking about the Trinity is not speculation. Johnson goes on the say,

CHRIST AND THE EXCLUSIVITY OF THE GOSPEL

> *"...the doctrine of the Trinity is not the result of philosophical speculation carried out in ivory towers, cut off from real life. It is the result of ordinary believers trying to make sense of the facts of God's self-revelation."*[12]

To add to this, the teaching of the Trinity arises from the Scriptures as those who penned them wrote as the Holy Spirit moved them (2 Peter 1:21). Furthermore, the Trinity is God's divine disclosure of Himself. Such truths of God place the Trinity beyond the reach and comprehension of the created order, especially humanity, unless God makes Himself known in ways He desires. God's disclosure or revelation of Himself occurred first from Him to humanity shortly after He created our first parents (Genesis 1:28; 2:16-17; 3:8-19).

Afterwards, He disclosed Himself to others and the prophets according to His will (Hebrews 1:1). Finally, He revealed Himself to the disciples and many within the early Church through His Son (Hebrews 1:2). God alone breached the gap between eternity and the temporal created order. Those to whom He revealed Himself did not speculate about the truth but wrote as the Holy Spirit moved them (2 Peter 1:20-21). They discovered what He revealed and declared what they learned from the revealed word of God in the Old Testament, through Jesus Christ, and by means of the Holy Spirit after Jesus ascended to His Father.

Consequently, the teaching of the Trinity results from reflecting on God's disclosure of Himself in and from the Scriptures. This insight also applies to the current discussion concerning the uniqueness of the gospel and Christ. The uniqueness of Jesus Christ and His incarnation sets Him apart uniquely as the God-man, the Son of God from all eternity. He entered into the created order voluntarily while sent from the Father. That is, He assumed the form of humanity without ceasing to be God the second person of the Trinity (Philippians 2:6-8). Although coming in the form of man, Jesus remained the uncreated divine Son of God. Jesus disclosed the triune God.

Such an argument is necessary for showing two very important truths about salvation. First, as separate from creation and as the Creator of all things, God in Christ does not partake of its sinful state. Furthermore, creation, especially humanity, is subject to the Creator and functions according to the way He created it. Humanity, through Adam and Eve, chose to go its own way and rejected the design of their creation. That is, humanity rebelled and became alienated from the God who created them. Because of sin, ruin and destruction came upon all creation (Romans 8:20-21). Humanity no longer stood in right relation with God but condemned before Him. The distinction of a holy God and a sinful humanity is a stark truth of reality. God provides salvation through Jesus who was without sin to fallen and sinful humanity existing in the created order.

Second, to provide such salvation, its means must also be separate from creation. That is, the solution to humanity's condemned and alienated state before God requires a divine solution or divinity itself. The Bible states that this solution finds its source in the Trinity, specifically in the second person of the Trinity, Jesus Christ. The position of Jesus as the second person of the Trinity and the one who stepped out of the timelessness of eternity into space and time in the incarnation makes Him uniquely qualified to mediate between the holy God and sinful humanity. Nothing else shares this unique position. He is God and is separate from creation. He entered into creation by taking on the created form of humanity in the incarnation. In doing so, He became the sinless Savior and Mediator. Nothing else could possibly equal this act. Millard Erickson says much the same thing but from the argument of uniqueness:

> *"There is just one true religious understanding and way of life, and there is a qualitative difference between biblical Christianity and all other faiths."*[13]

The incarnation is God dwelling with humanity, taking on Himself sinful flesh while sinless (2 Corinthians 5:21). He offered up Himself (Hebrews 7:27), and became the Source of salvation for all those who believe in Him. This qualitative difference combined with Erickson's argument of *"one true religious understanding and way of life"* establishes the distinction between Christian faith and all other religions. This distinction is one of reality and one of truth. The reality is that God is separate and distinct from all creation and marks a Creator and creation distinction. The truth is that Jesus made the claim that He was the truth, because He and the Father were one and the true God along with the Holy Spirit.

Why is it important to present this argument? Inclusivism fails to make these distinctions and thereby finds the mediation for salvation in finite, temporal, and fallen creation rather than in the Creator. Accordingly, for inclusivism, general revelation suffices as the mediation for salvation. Inclusivism claims faith in God. However, such faith arises from the knowledge found in general revelation. If such faith were true biblical faith, it would not separate Christ out from God. However, because inclusivism claims that a person could receive salvation through knowledge arising from creation, Christ is unknown or incognito. Consequently, creation substitutes for Him, the fallen mediating for the fallen rather than the divine for the fallen.

It is at this point that we must disagree sharply with Clark Pinnock. His bridge to and dialog with other religions cause him to depart from this distinction. His "pagan saint" analogy gives him impetus for bridging to other religions.[14] In this analogy, he gives sanction to other religions, because he speculates God's grace is at work in the wider world, and that includes other religions.[15] His and inclusivism's claims in this respect do not consider the full implications of the Trinity as discussed above.

UNIQUENESS OF CHRIST'S TRUTH CLAIMS

What makes Jesus' claims unique? John 14:6 declares one of the most startling claims Jesus ever made. It is easy to gloss over this claim in light of how the Apostle John begins this chapter. Jesus sought to comfort His disciples about His departure. He speaks of His return to gather them and others to be with Him in eternity and announces that they knew where He was going and how they were to get there. With perplexing words,

Thomas verbalized what the other disciples thought, *"...we do not know"* (14:5). Then Jesus made His stunning claim,

> *"I am the way, the truth, and the life. No one comes to the Father except through Me"* (14:6).

In this statement, Jesus claimed He was God three times. Later during His discussion with His disciples, He makes this claim unmistakably clear when He stated,

> *"He who has seen Me has seen the Father; so how can you say, 'Show us the Father'? Do you not believe that I am in the Father, and the Father in Me"* (14:9-10)?

He makes this latter statement twice (14:11). However, before reviewing this last statement concerning the Father and the Son, let us assess the three claims Jesus makes of Himself.

Jesus as the Way

Jesus claimed to be the way to God. Divinity alone shows the way to the Divine. The Bible informs us that the entire creation consists of space, time, and limitations. Humanity is incapable of reaching over the gap between eternity and the limitations of the temporal to discover the only true God. The finite cannot span the gap between the infinite God and the limitations of humanity. The expanse is far too great. Even the expanse or gap between eternity and temporal creation is incomprehensible to us. This gap is one between two realities – the reality of the eternal God and the reality of God's created order, which we can measure. We want to make things measurable. Measurements make our temporal world understandable.

However, the gap between the Creator and the created order has no measurement. They are simply distinct in the way they are. God is God and the measurements from the created order fail in measuring God or His eternal realm. The created order has shape, form, and dimensional limits. Those who live within the created order attempt to make sense of God with instruments used to measure dimensions, length, breadth, scope, and the width of things. No one can measure God by these devices.

For this reason, humanity can never reach God. He remains forever distinct from the created order as its Creator and Lord. He is unlike other so-called gods of the men who created them who dwell in polytheism, pantheism, or in individual imaginations. For this reason, God must cross that vast unmeasured expanse to humanity, and He did in Christ. When Christ crossed the gap between the Infinite and finite creation, He showed the way to God the Father. The Divine Son showed the way to the Divine Father. This alone makes Christ's claim unique. Consequently, neither the material world nor the imaginations of individuals can span the gap between God the Creator and creation.

Jesus as the Truth

Jesus claimed to be the truth. What is truth? Pilate asked this question when Jesus stood before him just before His crucifixion. Pilate quickly turned away without receiving an answer. Many today reduce truth to *"my truth may not be the same as your truth."* Such an assessment of truth cancels it out by reducing it to millions of individual opinions. In doing so, truth itself depends on humanity and not on God, and reduces it to non-existence. Such so-called truth relies on the limitations of finite beings living in a temporal existence and ignores the unknown. Jesus taught eternal truth beyond temporal existence and that which God declared. This truth rests on who He is, for He is its embodiment. As the Son of God, Jesus is also the truth because He characterizes its essence, that is, God.

Difficulties exist in describing truth relative to God, because of His distinctiveness and wholly separateness from creation. Like Pilate, we struggle with defining and applying truth. The reason for our difficulties rests with our finiteness and sinful state. We are separated from the sole source of truth, God Himself. That is the reason we need revelation, and Christ stands as the highest and most complete revelation we have from God.

We find in Him God Incarnate, the *"express image of His person"* (Hebrews 1:3). He is as David Crump states the *"heavenly reality."*[16] Crump goes on to say,

> *"As the revealer of truth, Jesus only teaches what the Father has given to Him. His eternal reality is ultimate reality. There are no external standards to evaluate His reality; according to John, His truth can only be accepted through faith in Jesus as the one who comes down from heaven...God the Father is the only standard by which all truth or falsehood, light or darkness are measured in the world."*[17]

As God, and the second person of the Trinity, Jesus can also declare clearly that He is the truth, the *"ultimate reality"* by which all judgments with humanity transpire. This means that love, mercy, grace, righteousness, faithfulness, and all other similar interactive characteristics that engage our rationale and feelings have their source in God's nature. Therefore, when we see Jesus in the Scriptures, we see truth. Furthermore, when the disciples saw Jesus, they saw God and all that constitutes Him.

His claim of being the truth finds its source in His divinity as the second person of the Trinity. He was from all eternity the Son of God reflecting the Father's exact representation of truth through a shared essence of being in the triune God. As such, Jesus shares all the qualities and characteristics of truth. He shines the light of truth in the darkness and *"gives light to every man coming into the world"* (John 1:9). The light of truth exposes all falsehood and the deceptions of those who try to suppress it through unrighteousness (Romans 1:18). Such a matchless characteristic is unique only to Christ so that His claim as the truth rests solely in who He is.

Jesus as the Life

Jesus claimed to be the life. This claim is stunning when seen from the viewpoint of His humanity. Humans die, and their bodies decay in the grave. Given that Jesus is not just human but

CHRIST AND THE EXCLUSIVITY OF THE GOSPEL

divine, He is eternal. He also conquered death through His resurrection to demonstrate the durability of His endless life (Hebrews 7:16). The claim Jesus makes that He is the life rests again on His divinity. As God, He has life within Himself in the same way the Father has life in Himself (John 5:26). This truth claim has significance beyond the life He possesses on His own that death cannot take away. Rather, this claim exhibits His absolute authority to give this same eternal life to those *"to whom He will"* (5:21).

Furthermore, since Jesus claims to be the life, all life in the created order has its source in Him. Paul makes this astonishing claim when he writes,

> *"For by Him all things were created that are in heaven and that are on earth...All things were created through Him and for Him. And He is before all things, and in Him all things consist"* (Colossians 1:16-17).

Consequently, since Christ is the source of all life, He alone determines the reality or truth for guiding it, as He is the source for that truth. This claim has no equal in creation but is unique beyond anyone in the created order could make.

Given that many other religions claim their way is the only way to truth, is it sufficient to claim the uniqueness of Christ for distinguishing the Christian faith from other religions? Ravi Zacharias notes that exclusivism arises from a truth claim, and every philosophy and religion have truth claims. He goes on to say,

> *"The clear implications of Jesus saying that he's the way, the truth, and the life are that, first, truth is absolute, and second, truth is knowable. His claim of exclusivity means categorically that anything that contradicts what he says is by definition false."*[18]

Geisler expands on Zacharias' statement concerning the truth of one religion and the falsehood of those standing opposite it. He asserts that truth must have correspondence to reality.[19] According to Christian faith, Jesus Christ is that reality. The fact that He is that correspondence to reality, He affirms not only the absoluteness and capacity to know truth, but also that the exclusivity of truth has its source in Him alone as He Himself claimed,

> "*I am the way, the truth, and the life. No one comes to the Father except through Me*" (John 14:6).

The Father Known through the Son

As though these three claims Jesus made of Himself were not enough for His disciples (and for us by way of them), He steps up to the next level of uniqueness with another astounding claim. He continues in His disclosure of Himself to His disciples after making the previous three claims by declaring,

> "*If you would have known me, you would have known the Father also; and from now on you know Him and have seen Him*" (14:7).

Stumped by Jesus' statement concerning Himself and the Father, Philip replied,

> "*Lord, show us the Father, and it is sufficient for us*" (14:8).

To Philip and the rest of the disciples, because He knew they all thought this way, He replied,

> "*Have I been with you so long, and yet you have not known Me Philip? He who has seen Me has seen the Father; so how can you say, 'Show us the Father'*" (14:9)?

Jesus taught them another claim that placed the other three in their proper perspective. When one looks upon Jesus, one sees God.

CHRIST AND THE EXCLUSIVITY OF THE GOSPEL

He alone is the exactness of the Father (Hebrews 1:3), for He alone is one with the Father (John 1:30).

Not only did His disciples struggle to understand this truth and claim, but many others also scratched their heads over what Jesus maintained. One of the major defenders of inclusivism, Clark Pinnock, brushes aside Jesus' claims to divinity by saying that He made no such claims for Himself. Pinnock erroneously states,

> *"Some Christians give the impression that they think Jesus went around saying point blank that He was God. Obviously he did not; it does not do our cause any good to pretend otherwise."*[20]

This statement denies Jesus' claims He made to His disciples as well as other like claims to others. To deny that Jesus did not go *"around saying point blank that He was God"* is to deny the whole point of what Jesus taught His disciples. It also denies that Jesus did in fact claim divinity in His confrontations with the Jewish leaders (John 3:16-18; 5:17-27; 11:4, 25-27). While Pinnock and inclusivists do not explicitly deny the triune God, they do not fully affirm Him. The language they use skirts around the Trinity for making God less than He is.

To minimize Jesus' own estimation of Himself as not only divine but the second person of the Trinity, Pinnock can also minimize His total role and specific sovereignty in salvation as the Apostle John Himself reveals,

> *"For as the Father raises the dead and gives life to them, even so the Son gives life to whom He will"* (John 5:21).

Who else but God can give life? His conclusions are inescapable: He is God. Life resides in the Son, and He has the sovereign authority to impart it according to His will.

Within the context of his statement about Christ not calling attention to Himself, Pinnock stresses the ushering in of the kingdom of God. He states,

> *"Jesus message was centered on God and the kingdom; therefore, the claims he made for himself arose from this context. He did not go around like a madman calling attention to himself. He was consumed by the message of the coming reign of God, and it is in relation to this announcement of the long-awaited divine intervention that the claims he made for his person and work have meaning... He does not strike one as an egoist."*[21]

While the point about Jesus' self-assessment as God may seem nit picking, it is a crucial and major one. Pinnock makes the kingdom the defining entity rather than the King. While the Scriptures narrate the strategic importance of the coming of the kingdom, Jesus' claim of divinity and the second person of the Trinity did not arise from that context. His claims and those of His disciples about Him were independent of the declaration of the kingdom. John spoke of Jesus as the pre-existing Word of God (John 1:1). The King must necessarily exist before the kingdom.

Although Matthew aligned Jesus with the coming of the kingdom of God, his emphasis with Jesus had to do not only with the coming King but also with Him as Savior (Matthew 1:21; 18:11; 19:24-26; 24:13-14). While the kingdom had yet to materialize, Jesus still reigned over all creation – the spiritual powers and all created earthly beings.

Furthermore, applying a pejorative, such as "madman," to Jesus' drawing attention to Himself takes away from His glory. It also stands at variance with how the Scriptures reveal Him and how He portrays Himself. For Jesus to speak truthfully about Himself does not signify the actions of a "madman." Rather, it discloses that He really knew who He was and that He wanted others to know that for two specific reasons. He wanted the world to know not only a) that the kingdom of God had arrived but also b) that the Redeemer had come to *"save His people from their sins"* (Matthew 1:21).

To minimize Jesus' assessment of Himself also minimizes how He saw Himself as the source of salvation. Inclusivism must necessarily minimize His person to permit an alternative way to salvation for the "unevangelized." For Jesus to disclose Himself as less than whom He really was, allows inclusivism to elevate an alternate gospel for the purpose of salvation. It also reduces the value of His claims and gives the impression to His disciples that He may not have been the true Messiah for taking away the sins of the world (John 1:29). If Christ did not disclose a true picture of Himself, why then should they? Furthermore, why would we look to Him or declare Him God if Jesus was reticent to make that claim?

Jesus never shied away from His self-disclosure as the divine Son of God. He was never embarrassed to call God His Father or to claim divinity. Why then should inclusivism attempt to marginalize Christ's claims of Himself? To marginalize something invariably leads to elevating something else in its place. That something inclusivism wants to elevate is general revelation as the mediation for salvation.

No amount of lofty inclusivist terminology works – such as *"high Christology," "Jesus, Savior of the World,"* and *"The finality of Jesus Christ"* – when it tries to marginalize Jesus' claims of Himself. Inclusivism cannot elevate Christ to His rightful position when it labels His divine self-disclosure to others as madness or as arising from egoism. Declaring the truth is not madness or egotistical. Otherwise, we must accuse Jesus of going to the extreme when He asked of His Father,

> *"Now, O Father, glorify Me with Yourself, with the glory which I had with You before the world was"* (John 17:5).

This request was rightful and altogether reasonable, for He was indeed the pre-existent Son of God from all eternity. Inclusivism misses this altogether in its judgments of Him.

The gospel pivots on the three major issues discussed in this chapter:

    1. The uniqueness of the gospel
    2. The uniqueness of Christ
    3. The uniqueness of Christ's claims

The gospel must stand as the one and only message for salvation for all or be relegated to a philosophy related to cultural, historical, religious, class, or racial bounds. Its significance will have no more than relativistic value like a message from any other religion. However, that is not the case. Its message spans creation and time, because it involves God bridging the gap between the divine and creation in the Incarnation with power and righteousness foreign to humanity. No message from the created order brings the solution of salvation to the dilemma of humanity's sinful state as the gospel. It has its source and authority in God Himself.

Christ stands as the one and only Savior and Mediator between God and humanity. His divinity as the second person of the Trinity makes Him the dividing line between truth and falsehood, for He is the truth. His uniqueness is unmatched because of who He is, the one true God separate from all creation. He alone spanned the gap between God and humanity as the one and only Mediator, not only as prima facie (on the face) but also as de facto (in fact). Only the divine could stand in for the divine.

Christ's claims stand unique among all the claims of any other. He alone could claim to be the way, the truth, and the life. God and creation has too great a gap to bridge for anything from creation to span it. Christ claimed He could do it. Sinful humanity does not understand truth and requires someone greater to reveal it. Since Christ is God, only He could reveal truth as realized in God. He claimed it and fulfilled that claim. Salvation hinges on the discussed biblical truths inclusivism misses in their fullness to its detriment. It must then seek another way and another gospel inferior to the divine message and the divine person in it. This different gospel leads many away from the true message of eternal life found only in Jesus.

NOTES

[1] Pinnock, *A Wideness in God's Mercy*, 117
[2] Ibid, 116
[3] Ibid.
[4] Ibid., 118-120
[5] Ibid., 125
[6] Sanders, *No Other Name*, 215
[7] Ibid., 31-34
[8] Ibid, 215
[9] Ibid.
[10] Fackre, 1121, 1130-1132.
[11] Johnson, Darrell W., *Experiencing the Trinity* (Vancouver: Regent College Publishing, 2002), 38.
[12] Ibid, 39.
[13] Erickson, Millard J., *The Word Became Flesh: A Contemporary Incarnational Christology* (Grand Rapid: Bake, 1991), 275-276 quoted in John H. Armstrong, *The Unique Christ and the Modern Challenge, Reformation and Revival*, Volume 2:02 (Spring 1993): 87.
[14] Pinnock, 92-93.
[15] Ibid, 93.
[16] Crump, David M., "Truth" in *Dictionary of Jesus and the Gospels*, Editors: Joel B. Green, Scot McKnight, and I. Howard Marshall (Downers Grove: InterVarsity Press, 1992), 859.
[17] Ibid., 861
[18] Strobel, Lee, *The Case for Faith: A Journalist Investigates the Toughest Objections to Christianity* (Grand Rapids: Zondervan, 2000), 150.
[19] Geisler, 3.
[20] Pinnock, 56
[21] Pinnock, 56-57.

5 Center of the Gospel: God's Righteousness

The center of the gospel is the righteousness of God. We cannot adequately discuss the righteousness of God without addressing the Trinity. God as God is righteous altogether. The Father expresses His righteousness in His faithfulness to His promises, especially concerning redemption and God's execution of it in Christ.[1] This righteousness finds its way into His pronouncement or declaration of righteousness toward those who express faith in Christ.[2] The Apostle Paul refers to this as justification by faith (Romans 5:1). The mantle of righteousness falls on Jesus as the Righteous One (Acts 7:52; 22:14; 1 John 2:1, 29; 3:7). As the Righteous One, Christ is the Advocate before the Father for those whom He accounts as righteous through His Son.[3]

As the one who completely and perfectly reveals God's righteousness, Jesus establishes the pattern of internal transformation to the will of God (Romans 12:2). Carey Newman states that Christ alone exhibits that pattern,

"Laying claim to righteousness involves a christoformic pattern of living."[4]

The knowledge of God's righteousness requires knowledge of and faith in the gospel and the centrality of Christ. Newman cites John's first epistle for this pattern of righteousness and explains how through faith believers reflect it (1 John 3:7). If individuals do not know Christ, they cannot know and reflect redemptive righteousness. If one does not practice righteousness found in Christ, that person is not of God but rather a child of the devil, for such a person is not born of God (3:8-10). John beforehand explained that this practice of righteousness shows that living it exhibits the Son and the Father (1 John 2:24). Given these truths, the Scriptures point to the Savior, Jesus Christ, as necessarily expressed and known as the One through whom one knows and embraces salvation.

Finally, the third person of the Trinity, the Holy Spirit, brings about the transformation of mind leading to righteousness (Romans 5:5; 14:17; Galatians 5:22-23; Titus 3:5). The Holy Spirit always points to the Son as the Son points to the Father so that the triune God works in and through the believer for partaking of the life of God. The triune God declares the gospel of power and righteousness.

UNASHAMED OF GOD'S POWER AND RIGHTEOUSNESS IN THE GOSPEL

In the opening of his letter to the church at Rome, the Apostle Paul writes,

> *"I am not ashamed of the gospel of Christ, for it is the power of God to salvation for everyone who believes, for the Jew first and also for the Greek. For in it the righteousness of God is revealed from faith to faith; as it is written, 'The just shall live by faith'"* (Romans 1:16).

In this passage, Paul states that the gospel is of Christ. He links it to the power of God and claims that it reveals God's righteousness. No other means does this. It is no coincidence that Paul includes the righteousness of God in the gospel. As we learn later in this letter, Paul explains that God displays that very righteousness in Christ Jesus.

Inclusivism spends few words discussing God's righteousness. Rather, it becomes a secondary discussion relating primarily to the means of the believer's standing before

God.[5] While inclusivism acknowledges God's justice or injustice, the biblical view of righteousness as the core of God's character receives little attention. There seems to be more of a discussion of God's justice (or lack of it) related to the "unevangelized." That is, if one assumes the position of exclusivism, God cannot be just by sending numerous people to hell who have never heard of Christ. This claim is a broadside attack on the gospel rather than support of inclusivism's position. As such, it is an attack without merit, because it establishes a caricature of the gospel and attacks that caricature.

The Bible places significant emphasis on God's righteousness. It stands as one of the major themes in salvation history spanning both the Old and New Testaments. From Noah and Abraham to the prophets, God revealed His righteousness. Its theme runs through the gospels (Matthew 3:15; 6:33; John 16:8-10) and Paul's letters. The psalmists uphold God's righteousness as the foundation of His reign in heaven and earth (Psalm 9:4, 8; 45:6; 97:2). They declare it as that on which all humanity depends (Psalm 4:1; 22:31; 35:24; 36:10; 71:2).

The gospel teaching of God justifying sinners by faith hinges on God's righteousness. That is, the believing sinner has right standing before God through faith in His Son. Of particular relevance to this discussion is Paul's letter to the church in Rome. Righteousness is the dominant theme of this letter, specifically not only with God but also concerning Jesus Christ. In this letter, Paul expands on the foundational teaching of justification by faith as an expression of God's righteousness (Romans 4:1-8; 5:1-2). God remained faithful to Abraham by fulfilling His promises to him before the Mosaic Law came (4:3). Forgiveness of sin finds its grounds in the righteous God who blesses apart from legal requirements (4:7). Peace with God comes through faith in Christ and not from works (5:1-2).

In glossing over the righteousness of God, inclusivist John Sanders makes a giant leap concerning the salvation of the lost or as he and other inclusivists state, the "unevangelized." This leap is from the proclaimed gospel of Jesus for salvation to a salvation for those who *"remain ignorant of special revelation* [the gospel] *without considering Jesus explicitly proclaimed."*[6]

CENTER OF THE GOSPEL: GOD'S RIGHTEOUSNESS

This leap is from faith in God through the meditation of Christ to faith in God through the medium of creation. In making this leap, inclusivists create two gospels. The first gospel is for those who have heard of Jesus through it. The second gospel is that Christ is the Savior of those who place faith in God without recognizing Christ.

In this second gospel, God's righteousness is a secondary matter and pertains only to God justifying sinners who place faith in Him based on the knowledge of the created order. It omits the explicit recognition of Christ as the expression of God's righteousness. In doing so, it dismisses the need to embrace Christ for righteousness and living it out. Therefore, inclusivism recognizes the theory but not the practice of salvation. Even in their theory, exclusivists falsify the gospel by denying the confession of God's righteousness in Christ.

If there is ignorance of God's special revelation in Christ, there is also an excused ignorance of God's righteousness and the necessity for it in salvation. Inclusivism fails to connect God's righteousness and the gospel, that is, the righteous act of Christ on the cross for justifying sinners before His Father. Such a failure allows an excused ignorance of God righteousness or the fulfillment of His faithfulness to His promises to save those who confess His Son. Inclusivists give little attention to the righteousness of God, especially when discussing justification by faith in Christ for salvation. This chapter shows how inclusivists, in marginalizing the gospel, also marginalize the righteousness of God. They make light of the proclamation of Jesus Christ as central to the gospel for salvation.

SPECIAL REVELATION VERSUS GENERAL REVELATION

When making the leap from the proclaimed gospel for salvation to another message that leaves Jesus out of it, Sanders and other inclusivists take this leap over a large chasm. On one side of this chasm is special revelation of Christ's incarnation or

His coming in the form of man. As explained in chapter three, this side of the chasm is external to the created order - the realm of God. It represents the proclaimed gospel that reveals the righteousness of God. God pierced time and space, entering the created order through Jesus Christ. Jesus is both the center of the gospel and the revelation of the righteousness of God.

On the other side of the chasm is general revelation of the created order or the realm of nature. This chasm makes it impossible for humanity to bridge the gap between the realm of God and the realm of nature. This impossibility arises because humanity dwells in the realm of nature. The dilemma for inclusivists is that they believe the knowledge gained from the natural world can bridge the gap for humanity to the divine realm of God.

The problem with such a belief is that human knowledge and understanding cannot reach beyond creation apart from the intentional will of God. No bridge exists of knowledge between the created order and the Creator unless God Himself bridges the gap. The Scriptures inform us,

> *"But the natural man does not receive the things of the Spirit of God, for they are foolishness to him; nor can he know them because they are spiritually discerned"* (1 Corinthians 2:14).

Therefore, God had to bridge the gap of knowledge and understanding of Himself when Christ penetrated the created order in the form of a baby.

The Scriptures inform us that creation indeed reveals God's invisible attributes. However, the created order as having its source in God requires spiritual discernment. We cannot comprehend it as being from God without Him giving us understanding. The writer of Hebrews states,

> *"By faith we understand that the worlds were framed by the word of God so that the things which are seen were not made of things which are visible"* (Hebrews 11:3).

CENTER OF THE GOSPEL: GOD'S RIGHTEOUSNESS

This passage highlights several truths. Faith imparts understanding about the source of the created order. God spoke, and the worlds came into being. The visible did not create the visible. We have extreme difficulty even understanding our observations of the created order let alone the unseen elements of creation. Therefore, only the Creator can reveal Himself, and He does so in Jesus, the second person of the Trinity and the only one through whom we can know God and His salvation.

The problem with Sanders' huge leap is that, like Pinnock's view, it keeps the divine Christ, the only one who reveals God, incognito or behind the scenes. With inclusivists, God's righteous act displayed with Christ on the cross has no bearing with the person expressing faith who has not heard of Christ. Rather, according to inclusivists, individuals are saved based on their response from a *"faith principle"* perspective to the light from the created order given them. In doing so, inclusivists fail to explain how any individual can cross the gap of the created order to understand God's righteousness or any of His other redemptive attributes (Romans 1:17).

If the gospel is the revelation of God's righteousness, this means that Sanders ignores the righteousness found in the gospel for salvation through faith. In doing so, inclusivists fail to explain how anyone can obtain salvation apart from the gospel. It is not enough to claim that creation gives sufficient knowledge for salvation when even that knowledge fails to impart the understanding that God is its source. Coupled with humanity's natural tendency to suppress the truth (Romans 1:18), its futile thinking reduces the knowledge of God to idolatry. Understanding of God becomes elusive as idolaters substitute things of creation for God without any thoughts toward recognizing or seeking out the true God. This truth escapes the notice of the proponents of inclusivism.

Paul declares that no salvation exists apart from the righteousness of God (Romans 3:21-26). That righteousness is found in Christ alone (Romans 3:26-28; 2 Corinthians 5:21). God alone must reveal this knowledge and understanding without which no one can know Him and place faith in Him for salvation. Given that such knowledge and understanding comes from God, no other option remains available for being saved.

IGNORING DISTINCTIONS IN REVELATION

The revelation from the created order (general revelation) and that through Christ (special revelation) are distinct in purpose and kind. Creation reveals God's divine power and nature (Romans 1:20). The incarnate Christ through the gospel reveals God's righteousness (Romans 1:16-17). Inclusivists fail to acknowledge these distinctions between the two revelations regarding salvation. In this failure, one of the great truths of which the Scriptures testify escapes them. Only the divine can reveal divine redemption (See chapter four on **Uniqueness of Christ's Truth Claims**). Christ in His incarnation, death on the cross, and resurrection stands as the example of ultimate revealed divine redemption (special revelation). If the created order could reveal God's righteousness, there would be no need for Christ and the gospel. God chose His Son to reveal Himself in the glory of salvation. Christ alone was the only begotten of the Father full of grace and truth (John 1:14).

Sanders attempts to explain how faith in God without the benefit of Christ provides an avenue for salvation for those who have not heard of Christ. He does this by using the Apostle Paul's argument in Romans 4 to compare Abraham's faith to that of faith in Christ. In the use of this text, Sanders attempts to show that Paul had two ways to salvation in mind. He concludes that Abraham did not have the same content of faith as post-Christ believers. However, according to him, Abraham and post-Christ believers shared the same object of faith: God.

In making such a comparison, Sanders commits numerous interpretive errors. His whole point is that Abraham and post-Christ believers are saved through faith in God. Those in the Old Testament period trusted the same God without the benefit of Christ as those after Christ who had the benefit of

CENTER OF THE GOSPEL: GOD'S RIGHTEOUSNESS

Christ. While the Scriptures affirm faith in God, they also affirm what Sanders denies: faith in Christ is necessary for salvation for all, because He is God. Paul affirms continuously that Christ is the object of faith (Romans 3:21-26; Galatians 2:16; 3:26; Philippians 3:9; Colossians 2:5-6). To deny explicit faith in Christ for salvation is to deny the gospel as the only message for salvation.

Confusion arises for Sanders and inclusivists at this point. They insist on two ways for salvation: one for those who have not heard the gospel and one for those who have heard the gospel. They hold that those who have not heard the gospel can receive salvation through the knowledge they received from general revelation or, as Sanders states it, *"God's providential workings in human history."*[7]

The second category is the gospel or special revelation. They classify those in the Old Testament under the first category, that is, those who have not heard the gospel of Christ. Those whom the gospel has not reached after Christ's incarnation also are classed in this category. All those who have heard the gospel are in the second category, that is, they place explicit faith in Christ for salvation.

One problem with these classifications is that they do not recognize special revelation in the Old Testament, especially when God spoke directly to Noah and Abraham. Additionally, they ignore clear Scriptural statements concerning faith in Christ. Rather than recognizing such special revelation, inclusivists as Sanders and Pinnock must continue to revise the theology of revelation, salvation, and knowledge of God through speculation to accommodate their positions. Some to whom God directly revealed Himself they refer to as "pagan saints" because they had faith in God without the recognition of Christ. As such, the content of knowledge is unimportant. It varies according to circumstances. Sanders states,

> *"But the specific occasions for and content of the trust of the Old Testament believers varied. Abraham trusted God to give him a son in old age. Gideon trusted that God would be with him in*

> *battle, and Samson trusted that God would help him destroy a temple. The specific content of faith varied from one person to the next throughout the Old Testament, but the common threads were trust in the objects of their faith – God."*[8]

In other words, content is relative for salvation for Sanders. For Pinnock, content has little if any bearing in salvation in one sense while in another sense it matters altogether. While Pinnock discounts the *"content of theology,"*[9] he highlights God's judgment on them based on *"the light they have received and how they have responded to that light."*[10] It appears that Pinnock wants his readers to believe that received light is void of content and that using it to place faith in God is not theological. If such light lacks both content and theology (that is, knowledge of God), then faith in it resorts to a leap of faith into the dark and unknown. No one viewing this light could ascertain the true God sufficiently to distinguish Him from gods of one's imagination as the object of faith. Such light has no content for making distinctions.

REVELATION, RIGHTEOUSNESS, AND ABRAHAM

Inclusivists face a serious problem in terms of God's righteousness and salvation. According to Paul, God's righteousness is the necessary content of the gospel for salvation (Romans 1:17). If good news for those not hearing the gospel does not include Christ, it also does not include the revelation of the righteousness of God. Unless one believes the gospel, there is no justification by faith. Justification is God's righteousness displayed toward those who by faith believe Christ for salvation. When Paul takes up Abraham as an example of faith that justifies, he does so based on what God promised to Abraham (Galatians 3:16). Paul gives stunning insight into this promise. He writes,

CENTER OF THE GOSPEL: GOD'S RIGHTEOUSNESS

"Now to Abraham and to his Seed were the promises made. He does not say, 'And to seeds,' as of many, but as of one, 'And to you Seed,' who is Christ" (Galatians 3:16).

Paul announces that God made promises to two people: Abraham and to his Seed. Paul said the Seed to whom God made the promise with Abraham is Christ. In this letter to the Galatians, Paul speaks about an inheritance and its source. He names two possible sources: the law and the promise. From the two, Paul declares that the inheritance came by promise.

Inclusivists miss Paul's theological statement about the Seed of Abraham, the content of Abraham's faith. According to Paul, Abraham's faith was not based on a son but on a legacy (offspring). Jesus fulfilled that legacy as Messiah. Therefore, the content of Abraham's faith was the Messiah, who would save His people from their sins (Matthew 1:21).

By overlooking the context for Paul's argument in Romans 4 and Galatians 3, inclusivists, particularly Sanders, miss Paul's message. In missing Paul's message, Sanders makes the object of faith of greater importance than content. However, he overlooks Paul's argument. For both those in the Old and New Testament, the object of faith, God, is the content of faith. While the Scriptures indeed place emphasis on the object of faith, that object has its roots in the promise – that is, God's word, which arises from Him who keeps it and its promises.

Paul refers to the promise four times in Romans 4 and six times in Galatians 3. In each case, the substance of the promise is Christ. The importance of his emphasis cannot escape us. God's promise to Abraham is extremely clear from what we learn from Paul. Jesus is the Seed and recipient of God's promise. That is, through Him all the nations will be blessed. Christ is the Head of all recipients of the promise in Him.[11] Furthermore, through His promise arise the children of God.

Following Paul's argument in Galatians 3 leads to this conclusion. After establishing that God gave His promise to two recipients (Galatians 3:16), he then develops this argument through this chapter. In doing so, we learn about the nature of the promise as well as the content of Abraham's faith.

First, Paul's argument that the promise came before the giving of the Law to Moses places the promise as preeminent (3:17). The Law does not guarantee any inheritance, such as passing down a family's property through the generations.

Second, God's promise makes such a guarantee because of God's faithfulness (3:17). His faithfulness finds its source in God's righteousness and not in or through the Law (3:21-22). The Law simply exposed sin (3:19) and acted as a guardian until Christ came for fulfilling the promise (3:24-25).

Third, the promise held true for Abraham just as it holds true for us today. Christ opened up the promise for all without distinction: Jew and Greek, slave and free, and male and female (3:26-28). Christ stands as the center of God's promise, because He is that Seed to whom God promised the inheritance. In Galatians 3:39, the crescendo of Paul's argument reaches its highest point. It provides a clear melodious note concerning the nature of the promise and the content of Abraham's faith,

"And if you are Christ's, then you are Abraham's offspring, heirs according to promise" (3:29).

This verse concludes Paul's argument beginning at Galatians 3:15. Paul brings Christ and Abraham together, the two recipients of the promise. For Abraham, the promise resulted in heirs. For Christ, the recipients resulted in children of God. Both are the same, because all those who by promise were offspring of Abraham belong to Christ as children of God, heirs according to promise. That is, all who trust Christ as Savior and rely on God's promise are both the offspring of Abraham and the children of God.

Inclusivists miss the lofty truth and true meaning of justification by faith by not focusing on that which Paul emphasized: the promise of God in Christ. While they rightly focus on the object of faith as God, they divorce God's promise in His word from Him as the bedrock for His righteous acts.

CENTER OF THE GOSPEL: GOD'S RIGHTEOUSNESS

Consequently, Sanders and other inclusivists go in another direction and seek justification by another way through the light of the knowledge given them than through Christ. They minimize Christ and God's righteousness.

By overlooking Paul's emphasis on God's promise, they ignore God's faithfulness through His promise. They then attempt to divorce justification from God's faithfulness rather than centering it in God's nature of righteousness expressed through Christ. God's faithfulness, as revealed in His righteousness, acts as the guarantee and comfort of faith, for it finds both in Christ alone. Both His guarantee and comfort arise from His intent and realization that He acts to procure salvation rather than passively hoping that individuals will place faith in Christ. That is, He will accomplish what He promises. Paul declares to the Thessalonians,

> *"He who calls you is faithful, who also will do it"* (1 Thessalonians 5:24).

Inclusivists must minimize justification by faith and God's righteousness for two reasons. The first reason is to open up another way for salvation for the presumption of those who have not heard the gospel. The second reason is to attempt to support their claim that God cannot know the future due to the actions resulting from individual free will. Inclusivists such as Sanders and Pinnock refer to God's inability to know the future of individual free choices as open theism. Consequently, if God cannot know the future because of free will, then He cannot really make His promise certain.

Paul negates the argument of inclusivists concerning free will in Galatians 3. Paul states that transgressions held everyone captive and left them without life (3:19-21). He also said that the *"Scripture imprisoned everything under sin"* (3:22) and that *"we were held captive under the law, imprisoned until the coming faith would be revealed"* (3:23). The promise of God brings freedom and redemption. Nothing else can bring such freedom or salvation, especially from the created order. God's power, promise, and righteousness in the gospel stand opposite the captivity of humanity to sin. These attributes of God bring to fruition what those caught in captivity to sin cannot. They also mute the argument of inclusivists for another gospel of trust in the created order for those who have not heard the gospel.

IGNORING CONTENT AND THE CONTEXT OF PROMISE IN THE GOSPEL

Inclusivists ignore context and the author's intent. Even a casual review of the biblical text leads the reader to come away with a very different meaning than Sanders. Paul never had in mind to split the content from the object of faith. Nothing in Romans or in any of Paul's letters even suggested that content was unimportant. To raise the issue of the unimportance of content, as do Sanders and Pinnock,[12] is simply a distraction and anti-biblical, because the gospel and the Scriptures as a whole consist of content. Furthermore, all knowledge is content-based regardless of its source. The knowledge of the created order or general revelation as well as the knowledge of the gospel both consists of content. To attempt to make a distinction between general revelation and special revelation based on content is a false distinction. In fact, to Paul, the gospel was all about content.

We also find no reference to any other way of salvation. Throughout his letters, particularly Romans, the gospel took center stage and for a reason. Only through the gospel could anyone come to know the living God. Christ alone came as the only Mediator between God and humanity. He alone reveals the righteousness of God; for only through the gospel of Christ does God reveal His righteousness. Consequently, inclusivists must ignore the righteousness of God for placing Christ out of sight of the "unevangelized."

To minimize content relative to salvation is also ignoring God's promise beginning with Abraham and culminating with Christ. To point to any other object of faith than the promises of God to Abraham and his Seed is to nullify and dismiss God's

CENTER OF THE GOSPEL: GOD'S RIGHTEOUSNESS

promise of salvation through Christ. It raises a false gospel and removes hope.

AUTHOR INTENT VERSUS SPECULATION

Sanders engages in speculation concerning his assumptions about the "unevangelized" while clinging to his own "control belief." Sanders needs to substantiate his "control belief" according to the following,

> "God is pleased whenever and however a person manifests trust in Him. The specific occasions for and content of the trust of the Old Testament believers varied."[13]

He imposes his own meaning on the text rather than accepting Paul's intent and meaning. Speculation allows him to ignore the author's intent and impose his own. In this manner, Sanders can get away with skirting around God's righteousness, and he ends up defining salvation on his own terms rather than God's terms. These terms are through the mediation of general revelation of the created order.

The issue according to Paul is not only content and trust but also grace and debt (Romans 4:4). Paul used Abraham as an illustration to support justification by faith as opposed to works and not as an example of the differences between the content and occasion for faith as Sanders notes about Old Testament believers. The entire context surrounding the faithfulness and promise of God show Him as righteous. His righteousness is the fundamental basis of the gospel Paul preached. In Romans, Paul made clear that God revealed His righteousness through the gospel of Christ (Romans 1:16).

From that point forward, he went about to prove how God's righteousness prevails in salvation. God is not pleased when individuals set the terms for salvation as Sanders proposes, that is *"whenever and however a person manifests trust in Him."* Paul argues just the opposite. Sanders ignores the direction Paul takes in the letter to the Romans. Paul concludes his argument in Romans 4 by pointing to Christ, who is the promised Seed of Abraham (4:23-5:2). Although Sanders also highlights Jesus, he turns Paul's argument away from Jesus and His resurrection by stating,

> *"Many commentators interpret Romans 4:24 as specifying that we must believe in the resurrection of Jesus in order to be saved, but, as Godet correctly pointed out, Paul did not say "when we believe in the resurrection of Jesus" but 'when we believe in God who raised Jesus.' Paul definitely says we must believe in the same God as Abraham, but he does not say that we must know about the resurrection."* [14]

His conclusion nullifies the cross of Christ. His argument from absence, that is that Paul *"does not say we must know about the resurrection"* defeats Paul's argument altogether. He rests his argument on what Paul did not say. If we accepted his argument, then Paul would need to argue that proclaiming the gospel would be unnecessary whether in the past, now, or the future and that the knowledge from the light of creation preempts the gospel. Additionally, Paul would not be able to make His conclusion in Romans 4:23-5:2 if he drew the same conclusion as Sanders. Paul's conclusion includes the content of the promises of God in Christ, the resurrection of Christ, justification by faith, access to God's grace, and peace with God. Misplaced faith in the knowledge arising from the created order ignores all of these benefits and leads away from peace with God through Christ.

    Sanders removes Jesus from the argument in such a way as to exclude Him and His resurrection as having any importance for salvation. He marginalizes the preeminence of Christ for the sake of giving a stake in salvation for those who allegedly have not heard of Him whether in the Old Testament or in the Church era. By attempting to place a division between God and Jesus, Sanders ignores the mediation of Christ Paul brings out in this

CENTER OF THE GOSPEL: GOD'S RIGHTEOUSNESS

passage. Sanders does this so he could reduce the need for content and dismiss the gospel in favor of another way for those who have not heard the gospel. He also favors this position so he could exclude Christ as the object of faith while keeping Him as Savior, which contradicts the Scriptures.

For Paul, Christ's atonement through His death and subsequent resurrection from the dead meant everything. Paul intentionally brings up Christ when he does for showing that one's faith must necessarily have Him in mind for justification. To exclude Christ from the biblical teaching of righteousness is to downplay God's righteousness altogether and to deny the primary thesis Paul sets out to prove in the letter to the Romans:

"For in it [the gospel] *the righteousness of God is revealed from faith to faith"* (Romans 1:17).

God's revelation of righteousness is the predominate theme in Romans and one Paul sets out to show how central it is to the gospel of salvation. Christ is central to God's righteousness.

Sanders also must divorce Christ from the Trinity and place Him in a secondary role for salvation. Inclusivism fails to address this unique component of the gospel. According to Sanders and inclusivists, people discover God in creation and from that discovery place their faith in Him without knowing about Christ. If such people can place their faith in God apart from Christ, Christ necessarily must be separate from God in both His person and purpose. Furthermore, such action also renders Christ unimportant for the decision of faith for salvation and eternal life.

The Bible informs us that God and Christ are inseparable. Christ is God the second person of the Trinity. To believe in God is to believe in Christ. To believe in God without knowing Christ is to believe in another god. Christ cannot be someone hidden away or behind the scenes as Savior of the world and not known to the world. To separate Christ from God also separates God's justice and mercy from His righteousness. However, the truth of God's righteousness must necessarily take top priority when addressing the lost. In it, we discover not only God's faithfulness but also His mercy and unrelenting love. Paul joins God's righteousness, love, and mercy when he writes,

> *"For when we were still without strength, in due time Christ died for the ungodly. For scarcely for a righteous man will one die. But God demonstrates His own love toward us, in that while we were still sinners, Christ died for us. Much more then, having now been justified by His blood, we shall be saved from wrath through Him"* (Romans 5:8).

Christ's death on the cross fulfilled the righteousness and love of God in providing for salvation and punishing sin. Such an act is the highest demonstration of both righteousness and love. Unless recognized, embraced, and confessed through faith one cannot be saved. Such a requirement invalidates salvation by any other way, especially through the knowledge from the light of creation.

STARTING POINT FOR THE GOSPEL

In declaring the gospel, Paul begins with the righteousness of God. God's righteousness is the beginning point for redemption of the lost and central to His character. Any question concerning the unevangelized must necessarily encounter and take up God's righteousness. What does the preceding statement mean? Righteousness, just, and justice derive from the same word and describe the nature and act of God as He stands independent from creation and interacts with it.

Frequently, when the question arises concerning those who have never heard the gospel, God's fairness becomes the hot issue, and His righteousness receives little if any notice.

CENTER OF THE GOSPEL: GOD'S RIGHTEOUSNESS

Clark Pinnock quotes sympathetically from Elton Trueblood concerning the fairness of God related to the unevangelized:

> *"What kind of God is it who consigns men and women and children to eternal torment in spite of the fact that they have not had even a remote chance of knowing the saving truth? What sort of God would create men and women in love, only to irrationally punish the vast majority of them? A God who would thus play favorites with His children, condemning some to eternal separation from himself while admitting others, and distinguishing between them wholly or chiefly on the basis of the accidents of history or geography, over which they had no control, would be more devil than God."*[15]

The reason some people contest God's decisions and commandments is that they find them not to their liking. Often when such people are uncomfortable with biblical answers about salvation, they engage in an emotional appeal much like Elton Trueblood's statement. D. A. Carson is helpful in gaining insight in and responding to such an emotional appeal. He refers to such an appeal as the logical fallacy of *"Purely Emotive Appeals."* He states,

> *"There is nothing intrinsically wrong with emotion, or course. Indeed, it is scarcely proper to preach and teach about heaven and hell, justification and condemnation, and the forgiveness and retention of sins without expressing any emotion whatsoever. But emotive appeals sometimes mask issues or hide the defectiveness of the underlying rational argument. An emotional appeal based on truth reflects sincerity and conviction; and emotional appeal used as a substitute for truth is worthless (although unfortunately often successful in*

winning the gullible). The fallacy lies in thinking that emotion can substitute for reason, or that it has logical force."[16]

Such an emotional appeal can also hide deception by masking it with what appears to be truth. In the case of what Trueblood writes, it hides judgment of God in the matter of the lost and attempts to substitute another teaching concerning salvation and God other than what the Scriptures reveal. It is also a veiled attack on those who do not agree with the stated emotional appeal. It implies that an emotional appeal is equal to a rational one and such an appeal, presumably to what seems true, cannot be countered. Implicit in an emotional appeal is the question, "How can one invalidate personal emotion?"

Fallen humanity rapidly forgets that God is wiser than our finite reasoning and logic can express. We also forget that our sinful nature prevents us from recognizing and fully embracing God and His righteousness and love. Through our sinful nature, we tend to turn God's righteousness and justice into tyranny and His love into animosity. Tyranny arises in our minds about God with the issue of His fairness. If God presumably is not fair in His dealings with the unevangelized, then He must be a tyrant, dealing arbitrarily with individuals.

If He is a fair God, then He must be fair to all whether they hear the gospel or not. If the gospel does not come to them during their lifetime, then must God provide another way for them apart from the gospel? Those who hold to inclusivism begin with this logic, which is no more than a false dichotomy. That is, such thinking excludes other alternatives, especially explicit faith in Christ for all for salvation.

Questioning God's fairness is an attempt to cast Him down from His throne and to place ourselves there. However, all that results is bitterness toward our Creator and Redeemer and invites a wall between Him and us. We tend to reply with faulty logic to substitute our judgment for His. All such logic simply decimates faith and trust in Him to exercise righteousness and love in the world. What then do we conclude about those who have never heard the gospel before they meet

CENTER OF THE GOSPEL: GOD'S RIGHTEOUSNESS

their eternal destiny? The Apostle Paul suggests that we leave that to the righteous Creator of heaven and earth for making that determination. He saves.

David Linden highlights a similar argument concerning judging God for being unfair toward those who have never heard the gospel. Central to Linden's argument is God's righteousness in imputing righteousness to the sinner. If God is righteous, how can He send a vast majority of people to eternal damnation according to Pinnock and Trueblood? Linden writes,

> *"He is righteous in His kindness and righteous in His wrath, which is one reason the exercise of vengeance is withheld from us. God is not, and cannot be, embarrassed at any action, word or decision He has ever made. If we say man is without shame, we mean he is so evil as to be beyond feeling. When we say God is without shame, we mean that He is so righteous as to be beyond any evil. One of the favorite sins of sinners is to ascribe to God unrighteousness, when men with sin disagree with God's decisions and commandments."*[17]

As a central attribute of God, righteousness is the controlling factor in all of God's judgments. Our sinful nature separates us from such righteousness. It distorts all our judgments and decisions so that we commit error in both because sin clouds our thinking and reasoning. When we attempt to reason our way to God, we do so from the perspective of personal pride in vaunting ourselves higher than we should. John Calvin writes,

> *"For we always seem to ourselves righteous and upright and wise and holy – this pride is innate in all of us – unless by clear proofs we stand convinced of our own unrighteousness, foulness, folly, and impurity. Moreover, we are*

not thus convinced if we look merely to ourselves and not also to the Lord."[18]

It is easy to brush this statement aside by announcing that this is old school thinking of the sixteenth century. Calvinism is a pejorative to those whose focus is inclusivity regarding salvation. However, when we compare it to the pronouncement of Scripture, do we not walk away with the same conclusion? All are sinners (Romans 3:23). All take their lead from Adam as the one through whom sin and death entered the world and caused all to be sinners (5:17-19). The Apostle Paul provided a long list of what resides in each of us left to ourselves (Romans 1:28-32). We might say, "That is not me." However, no sooner that those words come from our mouths that pride fills our hearts into believing we are beyond such activities. How then can we make judgments of God concerning His actions with humanity if we cannot even think or act in a manner pleasing to Him?

INDEPENDENT EXERCISE OF GOD'S RIGHTEOUSNESS

We cannot convince anyone to place faith in Christ. The change of heart must come from God. In John's gospel, we learn about those who receive the new birth:

"The wind blows where it wishes, and you hear the sound of it, but cannot tell where it comes from or where it goes. So is everyone who is born of the Spirit" (John 3:8).

Jesus compares the wind with the Spirit. No one commands the wind or can even direct its course. Modern technology may be able to harness it and use it for energy, but the wind itself does not take direction from us. Just as the wind exercises power external to us, the new birth depends on a force outside of us.

CENTER OF THE GOSPEL: GOD'S RIGHTEOUSNESS

John says that the Spirit is that force who acts to give new birth. He comes upon a person and gives life.

It is little wonder that Nicodemus failed to understand spiritual birth. He thought in terms of the material world: earth, wind, fire, and other elements within creation. Jesus informed him that he could not think in those terms for coming to grips with the saving knowledge of God. The same is true in our understanding of God and the unevangelized. It is easy to be caught up in the world of the finite and to lose sight of the realm of the infinite where God dwells. Since we cannot fathom the infinite, how are we to answer questions where the answer lies beyond the finite? Jesus said much the same thing to Nicodemus.

Are we then to give up inquiry into the things of God? No! We inquire and God discloses and enlightens our minds and hearts through His Spirit. However, we can inquire only so far into the infinite mind and wisdom of God. Our inquiries should stop short of judgments of Him or glossing over or dismissing the Scriptures when we confront truths inconvenient with our "control beliefs."[19b] Even Paul thought as much about God's wisdom and knowledge when he exclaimed,

> *"Oh, the depth of the riches both of the wisdom and knowledge of God! How unsearchable are His judgments and His ways past finding out! For who has known the mind of the Lord? Or who has become His counselor? Or who has first given to Him and it shall be repaid?"* (Romans 11:33-35)

A tension will always exist with those who question God's fairness and judgment on one side and humanity's limitations to perceive God's wisdom and justice on the other

---

[b] Clark Pinnock holds to a "control belief." He defines it as a large-scale conviction that affects many smaller issues. He distinguishes it from a "pessimistic control belief," (p. 19) that is, "God is planning to send most of those outside the church to hell. This paradigm controls how those who take this viewpoint assess all the "smaller issues" that arise."

side. The finite mind blinded by darkness finds it much easier to suppress its own acknowledgement of sinfulness and fault finding. To the inquisitive mind living in the darkness of sin, speculation takes a greater importance than God's word and wisdom. Therefore, questioning God in our limited and finite thinking only goes to hurt us and to create a divide between God and us. We understand several truths from Paul's development of the gospel message in Romans:

1. It is the power of God for salvation to everyone who believes (1:16)
2. It reveals God righteousness (1:17)
3. Righteousness is an issue of faith (1:17)

Several implications arise from the above three truths Paul develops from the powerful statement he makes in this passage. He implies that by salvation, humanity is in the position of needing it because of its sinful state. This sinful state stands apart from and opposite God's righteousness. Faith is a core principle for coming to grips with this righteous God. Paul develops each of these premises in his continued argument concerning the gospel. One of the major arguments Paul proposes in his defense of the gospel is God's righteousness.

William Newall brings out that Paul addresses three dimensions of God's righteousness:[20]

1. From that of God Himself
2. From that of Christ
3. From that of the justified sinner

The salvation of the lost pivots on the righteousness of God, and that righteousness finds its centrality in the gospel. Any question that addresses the lost or those separated from God must find its answer in the righteousness of God. The third dimension that Newell cites raises the question, *"How can one be right with God?"* The answer, of course, is that God justifies the sinner, making him or her in the right. This question pertains primarily to unbelievers, because those who have already placed their faith in Him recognize such a standing of being right with God.

CENTER OF THE GOSPEL: GOD'S RIGHTEOUSNESS

All those separated from God need Him to forgive their sins. This forgiveness comes through justification by faith. By jumping ahead to Paul's argument concerning how a person is right before God, we discover that God is *"just and the justifier of the one who has faith in Jesus"* (Romans 3:26). Therefore, when a believer in Christ poses the question "How can one be right with God?" the answer quickly arises from his Bible: through faith in Christ the Righteous One (Acts 7:52; 22:14) who reconciled sinners to God through His death on the cross.

Although through doubt, the question about being right before God may from time to time arise in the believer's mind, that person finds assurance from faith, the witness of the Holy Spirit, and His testimony of right standing as God's child (Romans 8:16-17). Therefore, the question of right standing before God goes to the core of salvation to the lost. A person can never get to a truly biblical answer about those who have never heard by focusing on humanity first. The answer comes through the righteousness of God and focusing on God and His provision first.

The problem with the question concerning those who have never heard the gospel is that it places humanity front and center thereby blocking the sight of God as the starting point. The question concerns individuals. When speaking about those who have never heard the gospel, we must begin first with God and then work our way to humanity. That is how the Apostle Paul started. The three dimensions of righteousness that Newell addressed centers first on God, then on Christ, and afterwards on the sinner.

The question concerning those who have never heard reverses the order by focusing first on the sinner and indirectly on God Himself and Christ. To answer the question from those questioning God fairness or justice, the believer must bring the subject back to where the Apostle Paul starts – with God and His righteousness.

PIVOTING ON GOD'S RIGHTEOUSNESS

Paul opens his letter to the Romans with the dominate theme of righteousness and raises it first with God Himself (1:16-17). That is, in the gospel God reveals His righteousness. The validity of any question concerning the lost for arriving at a truly biblical answer must pivot on God's righteousness. More than likely, an unbeliever may deal with himself because of his concern with his own welfare and anxiety over his destiny or the welfare of those close to him. In responding to such a person, we must attempt a refocus from oneself to God.

By focusing on God, we are able to present a more clear reply that goes to the heart of the question about those without God and knowledge of Him. In fact, a true knowledge of ourselves and of God and our relationship with Him begins by focusing first on God and not on ourselves. John Calvin writes,

> *"In the first place, no one can look upon himself without immediately turning his thoughts to the contemplation of God in whom he "lives and moves" [Acts 17:28].*[21]

Calvin later continues,

> *"Again, it is certain that a man never achieves a clear knowledge of himself unless he first looked upon God's face and then descends from contemplating him to scrutinize himself."*[22]

The question concerning those who have never heard of Christ requires by implication a proper understanding of God. When asking the question "What about those who have never heard the gospel?" the person asking implies that God is in the picture. The question seeks to integrate knowledge of one's destiny with how one reaches God as the object of that destiny. However, the person in focus is the one who has never heard. Consequently, the question redirects focus from God to man.

CENTER OF THE GOSPEL: GOD'S RIGHTEOUSNESS

By approaching the question simply by focusing on oneself, it places God in a secondary position by not addressing Him first. This secondary role for God is not a proper understanding of Him. He, and not humanity, must receive first priority with any reply concerning salvation of the lost. By not considering God toward salvation first, this leaves a person free to speculate about God's fairness, justice, or anything else about Him. Such speculation opens the door for creating a god in the image of humanity.

Paul continues development of the three premises about God's righteousness and their implications by focusing on God's wrath. Paul makes clear that God reveals two complementary but almost starkly opposite characteristics of Him: righteousness and wrath. They complement one another in that a righteous God invariably must be a just God and must judge unrighteousness. That is, He judges rightly in all things. God's righteousness stands opposite the *"unrighteousness of men, who suppress the truth in unrighteousness"* (1:18).

The sinful condition of all peoples isolates them such a distance from God that no amount of activity on their part could bring them remotely close to Him. They would not even entertain taking such steps in His direction (Romans 3:10). Even the thinking of unbelievers is such that they would not even recognize the true God, even consider God worthy of their thoughts, or want to be near Him. Any step in the direction toward religious activity or affection leads to idolatry for them (Romans 1:21-23). To say this in another way, humanity's tendency is always toward idolatry.

Evert Osburn's speculation about the Yoruba tribesmen does not align with Paul description of sinful humanity. He points to Yoruba tribe as one that sought after God the Creator (Olodumare) and assigns salvation to them. He speculates,

> *"It is my contention that there is a possibility of salvation for the hidden peoples who, by the way of grace through faith, recognize their need and repent before God, seeking his forgiveness."* [23]

Osburn ignores Christ in his assessment of their salvation. The problem with his contention is that in such a condition as Paul describes all humanity as separated from God, no one can recognize one's true "need" from God's perspective without God revealing it. The Yoruba tribesman may recognize some deficiency or defect within himself. However, a vast difference exists between deficiency or defect and one who stands in rebellion against God, separated from Him, and in an unrighteous condition before God's judgment. The former arises from the mind of individuals while the latter has its source in divine revelation.

If a person refuses to entertain the knowledge of God and exchanges God for idols, one cannot and would not entertain a truly sinful condition. That person would simply acknowledge some angst or deficiency from a comparison to others or to an image of his imagination but not from God's truth and righteousness. That is, without entertaining the true knowledge of God, a person simply compares himself to others for determining shortcomings or defects. The gap must close between humanity's sinfulness and God's righteousness. That gap closing occurs from God's side and not humanity's side.

God's disclosure of His righteousness reveals to all people that their state of sinfulness and separation from Him requires a complete renovation that no one but God could accomplish. Only God's revelation of His righteousness could bring people to the awareness of their state of sinfulness. God does this through the gospel - the revelation of His righteousness on the cross of Christ. Consequently, such awareness cannot come from the imaginations of the heart or speculation out of which a false gospel arises.

CENTER OF THE GOSPEL: GOD'S RIGHTEOUSNESS
NOTES

[1] Newman, Carey C., "Righteousness" in *Dictionary of the Later New Testament and its Development* (Downers Grove: InterVarsity Press, 1997), Ed. Martin, Ralph P., and Peter H. Davids, 1053-1054.

[2] Onesti, Karen L., and Manfred T., Brauch, "Righteousness, Righteousness of God" in *Dictionary of Paul and His Letters*, Ed. Hawthorne, Gerald F., Ralph P. Martin and Daniel G., Reid (Downers Grove: InterVarsity Press, 1993), 836.

[3] Ware, *Father, Son, and Holy Spirit: Relationships, Roles, and Relevance*, Kindle location 2174.

[4] Newman, 1057.

[5] Fackre, Kindle location 429.

[6] Ibid, Kindle location 492.

[7] Sanders, *No Other Name*, 215.

[8] Ibid. 226.

[9] Pinnock, 157.

[10] Ibid, 158

[11] Pyne, Robert A., "The 'Seed,' the Spirit, and the Blessing of Abraham," *Bibliotheca Sacra*, Volume 152:606 (April 1995): 215, 222.

[12] Ibid, 157-158.

[13] Sanders, 226.

[14] Ibid, 227.

[15] Pinnock, 150.

[16] Carson, D. A., *Exegetical Fallacies* (Grand Rapids: Baker Academic, 1996), 106-107.

[17] Linden, David H., "A Study on Justification," *Reformation and Revival Journal*, Volume 8:01 (Winter 1999), 178-179.

[18] Calvin, John, *Institutes of the Christian Religion* (Philadelphia: The Westminster Press, 1960), 37.

[19] Pinnock, 18.

[20] Newell, William R., *Romans Verse-by-Verse* (Christian Classic Ethereal Library, June 11, 2009), Kindle Edition, location 2020.

[21] Calvin, 35.

[22] Ibid. 37.

[23] Osburn, Evert, "Those Who Have Never Heard: Have They No Hope," *Journal of the Evangelical Theological Society*, Volume 32:3 (September 1989), 368.

6 Centrality of Christ

The way of salvation must be through Jesus Christ. No other option exists. However, inclusivists such as Clark Pinnock and John Sanders want to affirm and simultaneously deny this proposition. Pinnock affirms that Jesus is the Savior and Mediator while looking to the light of creation as another mediator for the "unevangelized." He would probably deny creation as a mediator. However, as this book presented in chapter one, general revelation becomes mediator for the "unevangelized" by de facto.

This chapter will explore why Jesus Christ must have central place in salvation through the proclaimed gospel. Additionally, nothing else or no other person can act as a substitute in any form or manner for all people. This chapter will also show how inclusivism deprives Christ of this role and His glory by giving creation an equal standing with Christ concerning salvation.

In sharing with His disciples about His imminent departure to be with His Father and to prepare a place for them, Jesus told them, *"I am the way, the truth, and the life. No one comes to the Father except through Me"* (John 14:6). In making this statement, Jesus declared His mediation. That is, He alone had the central place in redemption.

Those words went right past them and failed to gain as much traction as His disclosure about His departure. His departure raised their anxiety level, because they had been together for three years. Jesus brought up this multiple disclosure of Himself in reply to Thomas' concern about Jesus leaving. He spoke of them about the way of eternal life, for they would be with the eternal God when they joined Him.

CENTRALITY OF CHRIST

The truth about Christ being the only way to God offends many. It offends those within the religions around the world or in our postmodern culture, which affirms many ways to God. It is a particularly troubling teaching with people who raise the question concerning those who have never heard the gospel. If the gospel proclaims Jesus is the only way to God, how could God pronounce people who never heard of Christ or the gospel condemned?

That is, the prospect of such narrowness would appear to exclude a vast majority of people according to the inclusive view of salvation. The outlook of narrowness surfaces the challenges that:

    a) God is unjust and unfair
    b) The gospel is not everything we think it should be
    c) We must seek another way for addressing the destiny of those who have never heard about Jesus Christ.

Pinnock cites Elton Trueblood's offensiveness to such a narrow view of salvation,

> *"...it is morally shocking and consequently not a live option of belief for truly thoughtful and sensitive persons of any faith. What kind of God is it who consigns man and women and children to eternal torment in spite of the fact that they have not had even a remote chance of knowing the saving truth? What sort of God would create men and women in love only to irrationally punish the vast majority of them?"* [1]

Notice that Trueblood and Pinnock with him in his agreement positions God's judgment on sinners against His love. They refer to the biblical proposition of God as *"irrational"* for punishing a *"vast majority of them."* That is, God's irrational judgment of sinners cancels out His love. This conundrum occurs because Pinnock makes God's righteousness derivative of His love and mercy rather than equally expressed from His nature.[2]

However, such derivation must necessarily cause a division between righteousness and love at the cross rather than finding both equally expressed through Christ. This is a division without merit in the Scriptures, for both exist together when stated concerning Christ's sacrifice. D. A. Carson shows how this is the case when he states,

> *"The Father, full of righteous wrath against sin and sinners, nevertheless loved us so much that He sent His Son... Thus God is necessarily both the subject and the object of propitiation. He provides the propitiating sacrifice* [He is the subject], *and He Himself is propitiated* [He is the object]. *That is the glory of the Cross."*[3]

To make righteousness derivative of God's love unnecessarily separates the provider (the Father) and the provision (Christ's sacrifice). It also makes wrath derivative of love, for God responds with wrath toward the unrighteous. This reasoning makes God confusing. Such derivative righteousness portrays God in this manner rather than seeing both righteousness and love co-existing in God's nature.

Earlier Carson shows how both righteousness and love are not only co-existent but also co-expressive. He states,

> *"The reality is that the Old Testament displays the grace and love of God in experience and types, and these realities become all the clearer in the New Testament. Similarly, the Old Testament displays the righteous wrath of God in experience and types, and these realities become all the clearer in the New Testament. In other words, both God's love and God's wrath are ratcheted up in the move from the Old Testament to the New. These themes barrel along through redemptive history, unresolved, until they come to a resounding climax in the Cross. Do you wish to*

CENTRALITY OF CHRIST

see God's love? Look at the Cross. Do you wish to see God's wrath? Look at the Cross."[4]

The cross brings together God's righteousness and love in the person who died on it. Although seemingly contradictory to us, both are necessary in dealing with our sin and disobedience. By not bringing the cross into clear view with the "unevangelized," God's righteousness and love are not seen in balance in God. Emphasizing love over righteousness marginalizes sin and makes it less than God's divine love. Emphasizing righteousness over love, presents God as rigid and ready to punish all without exception.

Righteousness alone offers no recourse other than perfect faithfulness or punishment, making righteousness less than God's righteousness. Love alone offers no recourse, because it leaves everyone buried beneath the unjudged debt of sin and fails to call to repentance. In both cases, righteousness and love cease to be what they are. Either perception could lead to a creation of a god from superstition: one to be appeased and the other as an appeasing and compliant god giving into the whims of humanity. The cross destroys both perceptions and presents the true triune God from the Scriptures: one who is truly righteous and loving.

An arbitrary and punitive God, if true of Him, is problematic not only for God but for us who trust Him to redeem us from eternal separation from Him. It is a problem for God because of the issue of justice and His fairness. The consequent challenge for us is faith resting on an unfair and arbitrary God. If He were unfair in dealing with those who have not heard the gospel, He would also be unfair in all His dealings. Accordingly, He could not be fair in one instance and not in all instances. The following discussion shows that these challenges are false and do not hold up to Scripture.

THE CENTRALITY OF CHRIST AND THE CHALLENGES OF INJUSTICE

When contending with God's justice, we must necessarily address the cross of Christ and Him as central to salvation. When we exclude Christ, justice has a sense of arbitrariness. Often, those who insist on salvation apart from the hearing of the gospel consider fairness in a narrow manner and fail to reflect on all its dimensions. They ask, "Is it fair to punish those who have never had the opportunity to hear the gospel?" The issue becomes all about opportunity and not about the gospel.

Posing the question about fairness implies a standard for judgment. When arising from humanity, arbitrariness surfaces from individual judgment. Standards for judgments multiply for the number of people who exist. In the absence of divine authority for establishing righteous judgment, justice is arbitrary according to an individual, societal, or cultural judgment. One needs only to observe the courts of the many nations to witness the conflicting judgments of judges, many times on the same issue.

Human punishment also becomes arbitrary, because it is punishment without regard for the true righteousness shown by the cross of Christ. Who makes the gospel available for them to hear? Who breaks through time and space to reveal the source of redemption? God does. By whose power does salvation come? Consequently, is God arbitrary in His selection of who hears the gospel? Again, a judgment of arbitrariness presupposes an implied standard by the one asking the question.

There is a supposed fairness issue rooted in the gospel itself. Those who bring up the challenge of fairness fail to consider this issue. They surface fairness in a contradictory manner. They recognize humanity's sinfulness and lack of innocence. In the same breath, they appear to question if God is fair in punishing those who have not heard the gospel although those who have not heard are not innocent. However, they do not consider fairness in terms of God punishing an innocent person for all sin of which all are partakers – Jesus Christ.

Another Look at Fairness

To consider fairness with one (Jesus) and not the other (the "unevangelized") is an inconsistent charge. Those holding to inclusivism accept God's penalty on an innocent person (Jesus) as an inescapable given. They see no unfairness in this action, because they simply accept it as the *"just for the unjust"* (1 Peter 3:18) for the penalty of sin. In this, they consider God fair. They accept Christ as substitute and do not question how God could be unfair in Christ dying for humanity. However, when it comes to sinners having to pay the penalty for their own sins with eternal separation from God, they consider God unjust if they have not heard the gospel. The inconsistency is glaring.

Many years ago, a work associate brought up that God is punitive and therefore could not be trusted. He saw the death of Jesus Christ as a punitive measure by punishing an innocent man and God's own Son in the most tragic and horrifying manner. His point was that if God was just and fair, He would not punish an innocent man like Jesus who did nothing wrong to command the punishment He incurred. This same argument is one that critics take up against God's wrath toward sinful people who have never heard the gospel. How can He be just with those who have not heard the gospel? These same people are willing to defend God against being punitive in relation to Christ. However, they are not as willing to acquit God of unfairness for supposedly allowing Him to condemn guilty people who have not heard the gospel.

Fairness and the Innocent for the Guilty

This inconsistency arises because of the failure to come to terms with the centrality of Christ in the gospel, not as a mere man but as God Himself bridging the gap between a sinful humanity and His Father. Those who blame God as unjust fail to connect sinners, Christ as Savior in the gospel, and the righteousness of God. The righteousness of God is the controlling force in the gospel concerning sinful humanity and Christ. When people raise the issue concerning the fairness or justice of God, none dare accuse Him of unrighteousness for sending His Son as an innocent man to die for sinners. Rather, the issue is all about justice and fairness as expressions of God rather than righteousness as the nature of God.

The truth of righteousness cuts two ways. First, God is right to punish sin. Second, He has the right to set the terms for relating with Him or salvation. Those who rebel against God are in no position to set the terms of redemption. Additionally, those in creation, finite as they are, do not possess the capacity to identify the means and message for salvation. However, sin and finiteness does not stop people from judging God.

Pinnock takes offense with such a God as arbitrary in condemning unbelievers to everlasting death when they have not heard the gospel. What appears arbitrary from humanity's perspective has meaning and purpose for God. To him, his perceived arbitrariness rips the love and mercy of God from the Bible. He writes,

> *"Does God take pleasure and actually get glory from the damnation of sinners as some traditions maintain, or is God appalled or saddened by this prospect? My reading of the gospel of Jesus Christ and my control belief causes me to celebrate a wideness of God's mercy and a boundlessness of generosity toward humanity as a whole."*[5]

Pinnock overlooks any other option. He views God as taking pleasure in punishing sinners as one option. His other option is God whose mercy and generosity short-circuits any pleasure He takes in punishing sinners. Even the way he frames the question demonstrates his bias. He applies pejoratives in his description of God in one instance (a punitive one) as opposed to God as merciful and generous in another instance. Such a

CENTRALITY OF CHRIST

comparison is known as a false dichotomy. That is, an argument omits any other option but presents the stated options against one another.

Inclusivism claims that God could not be both just and penalizing toward the "unevangelized." Rather he assumes that a God who punishes those who have not heard the gospel is unjust, making Him unrighteous. At this point, inclusivism introduces God's love and mercy as the way of dealing with the unevangelized. To be penalizing toward those who have not heard the gospel would disparage His love and generosity of His mercy.

To answer this claim, we must consider God's righteousness as it relates to His nature. If His righteousness pivots on the unfairness of punishing the "unevangelized," then righteousness itself depends on the actions of the finite and sinful humanity. Righteousness would no longer have its basis in the nature of the eternal God who exists above and independent of creation.

Additionally, Pinnock appears to ignore God's apparent punitive action with Christ the Righteous who died for the unrighteous. Might we ask the same question he asks concerning God taking pleasure and obtaining glory for sending His own innocent Son to die on the cross? How could God take pleasure in punishing innocence from Pinnock's perspective? It seems that Pinnock misrepresents God's glory and with what He takes pleasure.

Fairness Versus God's Righteousness

Pleasure and glory depend on purpose. If God's sole purpose were to punish in light of withholding the gospel, He would be arbitrary and brutal, exhibiting a dark character in seeking pleasure and glory in arbitrary punishment. This portrayal of God is foreign to the Scriptures and excludes or ignores God's righteousness. Righteousness excludes arbitrariness. Punishment would magnify brutality if directed toward those presumed innocent. How then do we assess those

NOTHING BUT THE GOSPEL

guilty of rebellion and rejection of God? A vast number hear the gospel and still reject it. Those who have not heard the gospel exercise the same rebellion and unbelief as those who have heard it and reject God.

The common denominator with those who hear the gospel or do not hear it is the rebellious heart toward God. God's righteousness stands opposed to sin and rebellion. He takes no pleasure and receives no glory in arbitrary punishment. Pinnock's rhetorical question takes a wrong turn with those who hold to the explicit proclamation of the gospel for salvation. He assumes that they believe God takes pleasure in punishing people who never hear the gospel. He fails to consider rebellion and guilt in his equation. The penalty for sin is death. God takes no pleasure in sin or death.

The key to the change of heart is not justifying God's way to man[6a] but God regenerating and justifying the sinner to change rebellion to a new creation (2 Corinthians 5:17). Rebellion is from humanity. The new person and transformation of life is from a righteous God who initiates the change rather than from humanity, which resists change of life. Righteousness embraces the salvation of sinners found in Christ's death and resurrection for sin to redeem sinners from eternal death. God takes pleasure with Christ and His death for sinners. Through His act on the cross, Christ claimed many sons and daughters for glory (Hebrews 2:10). This act glorifies God.

---

[a] In putting forth his thesis in his grand argument of *Paradise Lost*, John Milton wrote, "That to the highth of this grand argument I may assert eternal Providence, and justify the ways of God to man." While Milton seeks to show that God cannot be seen as unjust in His dealings with humanity, Pinnock, Sanders, and other inclusivists attempt to make the true biblical God as unjust for withholding the gospel from the unevangelized. By using this phrase in this book, I seek to show that inclusivists are ironically wrong in their indictment of the God of the Bible. Milton seeks to show the opposite of inclusivist in beginning with God in His initiative of coming to sinful humanity. Inclusivists begin with humanity and argue for their portrayal of God from the position of humanity. Consequently, inclusivist shift authority from God to humanity. Herein is the irony inclusivists fail to recognize in their erroneous assessment of a righteous God and sinful humanity.

CENTRALITY OF CHRIST

By ignoring the righteousness of God, Pinnock and other inclusivists bypass the eternal purpose of God before the foundation of the world (John 17:24; Ephesians 1:4). Just before Jesus went to the cross to die for sins, He prayed His deeply touching intercessory prayer. In it, He brings up the truth of Christ's shared glory with the Father. That is, Jesus glorified the Father in His ministry on earth and prayed,

> *"And now, O Father, glorify Me together with Yourself, with the glory which I had with You before the world was"* (John 17:4-5).

His prayer is within the context of salvation, making this glory the finished work of Christ not only while with His disciples but also when He went to the cross. He later spoke of being glorified in them (17:10), of His resurrection, ascension, and return to claim the redeemed (17:11), and of His disciples eternal security (17:12). It is with this salvation with which the Father takes supreme pleasure and glory.

In writing of God taking pleasure and glory in sending the unevangelized to hell, inclusivists subtly shift their focus to humanity from God's righteousness expressed on what Christ accomplished on the cross. They diminish God's eternal purpose and righteousness in redemption in favor of a presumed innocence of those who live their lives in rebellion against God. In doing so, inclusivists attempt to blame God for not being fair with those living in rebellion as though they did not deserve condemnation.

Pinnock and other inclusivists misunderstand the gospel, especially the righteousness and love of God, which highlights the depth of sin and necessity of Christ's death on the cross for it. Because of their misunderstanding of the gospel, they must substitute another message for it. This message consists of salvation through faith in the light they received from creation for those who have never heard the gospel. They dismiss the biblical gospel for everyone for a false one.

The Bible informs us that all humanity stands before God as sinners. Does the condemnation of those who do not believe in His Son dilute His love since the Bible states that God loved the world that He gave His only Son? To answer this question, we return to the distinction between the Creator and creation. As God, the second person of the Trinity, Jesus stands above all the created order as the total expression of God's love when He died on the cross for the sins of the world (Romans 5:8). He fulfilled the Father's righteousness and love. Is then God's love compatible with His righteousness that expresses His justice in judging unbelievers in His Son? The next section replies to this question.

PROBLEMATIC CHALLENGES TO THE CENTRALITY OF CHRIST IN THE GOSPEL

Another way to salvation calls into question whether our faith rests on a trustworthy foundation. Another way removes Christ from the central place in salvation. The direct proclamation of the gospel versus a gospel resting on the light of nature, reason, or other religions leaves us in a tension regarding the witness of Christian faith and missions. Do we share that individuals have an option message? Options open a door to many other ways and eventually include individuals creating their own ways for salvation.

Furthermore, consider the competing theologies and the repercussions between the proclaimed gospel of Christ and faith in the light of creation or some other source apart from Christ. What would the theology of faith in the light of creation look like? How would this theology stand up to the salvation theology of the imputed righteousness of Christ, justification by faith, sanctification, and glorification of which Paul writes (Romans 4:1-18; 8:29-30)? The theology of the knowledge from the light of creation would indeed be devoid of content. Consequently, it would require a leap of faith into a void.

CENTRALITY OF CHRIST

Challenge of Shifting Theology

The adherents of the inclusive view of salvation may argue that nothing really changes in terms of these truths. They allege that Paul's theology of salvation remains applicable. According to inclusivists like Pinnock, people simply do not need to know the whole realm of salvation for saving knowledge.[7] To him the content of theology is not an issue but rather faith in God. By dismissing the importance of the content of biblical theology concerning those who have not heard the gospel, Pinnock can substitute it with the theology of general revelation. Consequently, he makes Christ simply a silent partner as Savior of the world of which creation stands as an equal. Accordingly, one does not have to acknowledge Him as Savior for salvation. That would be in fact His theological statement of Christ.

According to inclusivism, insisting that He is Savior and granting Him the status of "high Christology" makes it so. He becomes Savior in theory but not through knowing Him in practice. That is, He serves as Savior whether people know it or not. Such a view of Christ leaves the Christian faith based on a shifting and dissolving foundation and not the content of the cross. This view also contradicts Jesus' own words concerning the meaning of salvation: knowing Jesus is knowing God (John 17:3). One cannot know God without knowing Jesus Christ.

Pinnock shifts Jesus as the acknowledged Savior for those who heard the gospel and a silent Savior for those who have not heard the gospel. Such a shifting theology requires a confused theology of Christ: one whom God declares as Savior and Mediator but one who remains behind the scenes and silent. This silent Savior permits the alternate of creation to arise.

When Christ no longer has the central role in the message for salvation or Christ is silent, everything changes. If hearers have not heard the gospel, but they apply faith in what they know from the light given them, how could they realize saving knowledge? The message becomes one of the mediation of the knowledge of general revelation. How would they understand the very heart of faith – Christ? How could they recognize this

Savior and Mediator? He could not be either, since He would be unknown to those not hearing the gospel.

Challenge of Reconciling God's Love and Righteousness

The above discussion serves to lead to a resolution for the tension between God's love and His righteousness (justice or supposed fairness). Both find their source in the cross if we are to accept Paul's argument in Romans 5. Paul in this chapter brings together love and righteousness in one person, Jesus Christ, particularly when he claims,

> "God shows His love for us in that while we were yet sinners, Christ died for us" (Romans 5:8).

Explicitness stands out in the the word *"show."* God's expressed love and righteousness are inseparable, because they dwell together as qualities of God's nature. He expresses both of these qualities together on the cross, one toward those whom He loves and the other toward the sin He hates. In Christ, God *"condemned sin in the flesh that the righteous requirement of the law might be fulfilled in us who do not walk according to the flesh but according to the Spirit"* (Romans 8:3-4).

This condemnation of sin means that He shifted His judgment from those whom He justified to sin so that by the Holy Spirit we might be set *'free in Christ Jesus from the law of sin and death"* (8:2). The shifting of His judgment of condemnation had its basis in both His righteousness and love in that He is a righteous God and showed His enduring love toward believing sinners in His perfect righteousness. Through His righteousness and love, He places the sinner in right relationship with Him through Christ.[8] This right relation occurs only by grace through faith in Christ.

From the view of inclusivism, Pinnock makes righteousness and other qualities of God derivative of God's

CENTRALITY OF CHRIST

love rather than all His character traits as full expressions of His nature.[9] This portrayal of God is inclusivism's understanding of Him and one it claims to be more faithful to the Bible. However, a derivative righteousness in God is foreign to the Bible. Such a derivative means provides for and leads to an open theistic concept of God and away from what inclusivism calls the traditional view.

This openness, in the view of inclusivism, allows God to respond to the complete freedom of individuals in a *"give-and-take"* interactivity with God. That is, there is a certain compliancy with God. It also allows individuals to disregard or minimize their sinful nature as Paul describes it (Romans 3:10-23) and respond to God apart from the benefit of Christ. Such a provision on God's part (the general revelation of creation) shows His flexibility in catering to individual free will. That is, according to inclusivism,

> *"We respond to God's gracious initiatives and God responds to our responses...and on it goes. God takes risks in this give-and-take relationship, yet he is endlessly resourceful and competent in working toward his ultimate goals. Sometimes God alone decides how to accomplish these goals. On other occasions, God works with human decisions, adapting his own plans to fit the changing situation. God does not control everything that happens. Rather, he is open to receiving input from his creatures. In loving dialogue, God invites us to participate with him to bring the future into being."*[10]

Open theism reduces God's righteousness to a subordinate role and rejects the biblical understanding of humanity's sinfulness and its destructive effects. John Macarthur states that open theism and corresponding inclusivism desires to eliminate any negative form of God's actions so as not to confront and struggle with difficult biblical truths such as God's wrath and righteousness.[11] By marginalizing, ignoring, or redefining God's wrath and righteousness, inclusivists can place greater emphasis on human cooperative freedom.

Consequently, humanity is not wholly constrained by and a slave to sin. This assessment of God's wrath and righteousness also permits inroads of an alternative way to God through general revelation. Once God's wrath and righteousness receive secondary roles, it leaves God open to responsiveness to Him through nature or other religions. The problem with a natural theology or religiosity, both in reality and by the authority of Scriptures, is that they cannot express God's righteous love. Even humanity, as part of the created order, cannot love as God loves.

A "FAITH PRINCIPLE" OR FAITH IN CHRIST

Clark Pinnock advocates a "faith principle."[12] He substitutes a principle for the person of Jesus Christ. That is, faith is a response to the light one receives from the created order. For inclusivists as Pinnock, it does not depend on theological content but on some impersonal light received from finite creation. If salvation through a "faith principle" toward God (excluding Christ) does not rest on theological content as Pinnock argues, on what does it rest? No definite object of faith exists for him. It could be different for everyone. John Sanders centers the "faith principle" in Hebrews 11. He states,

> *"If I were asked to summarize the overall teaching of the Bible on faith, I would say that faith involves three elements: truth, trust, and effective action. Genuine faith in God contains some truth about God whether that truth comes from the Bible or from God's work in creation."*[13]

Scripture affirms faith but rejects Sanders' account of it. He misses the true object of faith – the centrality of Jesus Christ.

CENTRALITY OF CHRIST

His reading of Hebrews 11:6 neglects the context and primary theme of the book. Faith centers on Jesus. He is *"the author and finisher of our faith"* (Hebrews 12:2). Omitting Christ ignores the author and object of faith.

Inclusivism divorces faith from the gospel and centers it on creation. It also divorces faith from content.[14] By stating, *"According to the Bible, people are saved by faith, not by the content of their theology,"*[15] Pinnock's statement is a contradiction. By pointing to the Bible, he relies on its content to brush aside content for faith, thus voiding his argument. Pinnock creates a division between faith and theological content. He refers to theology as *"certain minimum information,"*[16] and in doing so marginalizes any basis or foundation for faith. Rather, faith becomes rooted in nothing except perhaps some sort of nebulous "light" as its object.[17] Furthermore, the "faith principle" is impersonal as is the medium through which inclusivism claims one comes to God – creation.

A faith rooted in light displaces God's redemptive qualities of righteousness and love. This displacement not only fails to reveal the true God, but it also does not provide means by which one comes to know the personal Creator and Redeemer. The light from the knowledge of creation is far too generalized to act as any kind of means for knowing God redemptively. Such knowledge comes only through Jesus Christ who perfectly discloses His Father's love and righteousness. Faith is not a principle but rather arises from the personal God drawing the sinner to Himself through His Beloved Son. God's righteousness expresses His enduring faithfulness, a faithfulness that reveals His outstretched arms in loving redemption. Nothing can replace the Father's outstretched hand or the love He shows through His Son.

NOTES

[1] Pinnock, *A Wideness of God's Mercy*, 150.

[2] Pinnock, Clark, Richard Rice, John Sanders, William Hasker, and David Basinger, *The Openness of God: A Biblical Challenge to the Traditional Understanding of God* (Downers Grove: InterVarsity Press, 1994), Amazon Edition, Kindle location 191.

[3] Carson, D. A., "God's Love and God's Wrath," *Bibliotheca Sacra*, 156:624 (October 1999): 392.

[4] Ibid, 391.

[5] Pinnock, *A Wideness in God's Mercy*, 18.

[6] Milton, John, *Paradise Lost* (New York: D. Appleton & Co., 1851), 116.

[7] Pinnock, 157-158.

[8] Toon, Peter, "Righteousness" in *Evangelical Dictionary of Biblical Theology* (Grand Rapids: Baker Books, 1996), Ed. Walter A. Elwell, 688-689.

[9] Pinnock, Clark, Richard Rice, John Sanders, William Hasker, and David Basinger, *The Openness of God: A Biblical Challenge to the Traditional Understanding of God* (Downers Grove: InterVarsity Press, 1994), Amazon Edition, Kindle location 191.

[10] Pinnock, et al, *The Openness of God*, Kindle location 16.

[11] Macarthur, John, "Open Theism's Attack on the Atonement," *Master's Seminary Journal*, Volume 12:1 (Spring 2001): 5.

[12] Pinnock, 157-158.

[13] Fackre, Nash, Sanders, Kindle location 345.

[14] Ibid.

[15] Ibid.

[16] Ibid, 158.

[17] Ibid.

7 Christ in the Scope of Salvation

The scope of salvation the Bible teaches in the gospel encompasses life for time and eternity. This salvation involves deliverance from the penalty of sin (justification), from the power of sin (sanctification), and from the presence of sin (glorification). In each of these areas of salvation, believers trust God and the provision He made in Christ for deliverance.

When initially placing faith in the sacrifice of Christ, one may not understand the full implications and scope of salvation. Lack of understanding does not diminish or discount theological content or the expression of saving faith from the righteousness of God. Rather we embrace what we learn for giving assurance that we stand before God as righteous and as a member of His family forever (Romans 3:21-26). As we grow in the knowledge of the Scriptures, we also grow in faith in God. This process increases our faith toward a life of holiness. All other messages and means leading to understanding of or embracing salvation are wholly inadequate.

INADEQUACY OF INCLUSIVISM'S "FAITH PRINCIPLE"

What does the "faith principle" provide for those who have never heard of Christ but according to inclusivism must rely on the light of nature? Inclusivism assumes content as unimportant for faith. If theological content were not that important for salvation, by what would a person know and understand their salvation? A faith without content is a faith substituted by speculation and guided by superstition, human

CHRIST IN THE SCOPE OF SALVATION

reason, or ignorance. The "faith principle" relies on the theology of the light of creation or some other means acknowledged for salvation no matter how crude or rudimentary this theology may be. It caters to speculation.

Without content, a "faith principle" does not know what kind of God really exists. Without true knowledge of God, idolatry and superstition arises, leaving salvation without foundation or direction until individuals give it a foundation or direction of their own. Therefore, a message without the foundational content of Christ is a message without which God Himself vested it. It is empty, hollow, and void.

What do we communicate concerning missions or sharing our faith with others if we subscribe to a "faith principle?" When we bring the message of the gospel to other groups or tribes, do we attempt to blend God with theirs and their theology with ours? As noted in chapter four, Evert Osburn cites the Yoruba tribe of Nigeria as an example of people who appeared to worship the same God of the Bible whom they called Olodumare. Osburn listed the traits of this god and concluded that they had obtained the knowledge of God because their god possessed the same attributes as the God of the Bible.[1] From this conclusion, he extrapolated (or speculated) the possibility for those who never heard of Christ. Additionally, he states,

> *"This, the atonement of Christ, though it occurred in a particular time in history, extended to all time in its effectiveness. If the eternal God, who does not necessarily view time sequentially, has applied Christ's blood to people of faith in the OT who has no knowledge of Jesus, why can He not do likewise for the unreached person today who has no explicit knowledge of Christ but may believe in the One who raised Jesus from the dead?"*[2]

It is a stretch to conclude that similarities between religious beliefs give rise to the same source for faith. We also have to question his speculation that such people groups would actually recognize the God *"who raised Jesus from the dead."* Any faith comparing God to other gods is a false faith and insults God. Any faith taking its cue from the comparison of God to other so-called gods is faith in the created order and not in the unseen God.

INADEQUACY OF SPECULATION

From Sanders' perspective, speculation has greater importance than the Scriptures themselves. Much like Clark Pinnock's argument, he also emphasizes personal judgment that takes precedence over Scriptures. From speculation, he branches out into conclusions reached apart from the text of Scripture. He assumes that God will work salvation apart from His word, an assumption foreign to Scripture. Divorcing God from His own word permits speculation to go into any direction a person sees fit.

Sanders also gives an example of the missionary Don Richardson who claimed to have *"documented numerous cases where God was at work redemptively with people groups prior to Christian missionaries."*[3] By redemptive work, Richardson refers to worship of the true God. This assessment is nothing more than projecting on others that their god is the same God the Scriptures teach and then assuming they worship the biblical God.

Speculation stands opposed to biblical authority. It begins with individuals rather than with God. It leads to the autonomy of humanity from the Creator and permits individuals to derive thinking about God according to the imagination. Speculation's ultimate path is the suppression of truth and the acceptance of a lie through twisting the truth to agree with human philosophy.

Unless any argument for salvation has its basis in the Scriptures, it is conjecture or speculation and cannot stand up to the test of truth. Faith in any other message arising from the light of creation or other religions is faith in an inadequate source. It is not genuine faith but a counterfeit. Such faith renders commitment to something other than God and the medium He chose through Jesus Christ. Faith taking its cue from speculation dilutes and misdirects it toward human-centeredness, thus making it an inadequate approach to and application of truth.

INADEQUACY OF EXPERIENCE

According to inclusivism, experience and not the Scriptures becomes the primary mechanism for determining truth. Sanders concluded that an Indian tribal people called Santal "speak of the 'genuine God,' Thakur Jui" and that the missionaries "concluded that Thakur Jui and the God of the Bible were the same." Consequently, they began to inform the people of what this God had done through His Son to reconcile them."[4] We encounter a similar situation with Richardson's experience that we do with Sanders. Reliance on experience also plays a role in faith in the knowledge of the light of creation.

While there may be a number of parallels in cultures and our discoveries from the Scriptures, we stand on shaky ground in making experience equivalent to or above Scriptures and relying on that experience to guide Christian practice and missions. Attempting to apply experience in finding parallels to Christian faith in other religions or the knowledge of the light of creation preempts the message and authority of Scripture. Those who rely on such experience shift authority for faith from the Scriptures to human experience. This shift also stands the risk of entering into syncretism (or blending) in attempting to align the God of the Bible with the gods of other cultures.

While God encounters us in our experiences, experience is not the authority by which we live our lives. Since we exist as finite beings within time and space, we have difficulty separating experience from faith. Life encompasses our experiences, and faith involves experience as we engage our mind and body in spiritual activity. While we engage God through experience, finite experience severely limits us in coming to know Him. For this reason, we depend on the greater authority of the revealed Word of God in the disclosure of God.

Sean Lucas highlights the authority of the Scriptures over experience in describing J. Gresham Machen's defense against those who desire to reverse such authority. He writes,

> *"Machen carefully clarified the relationship between doctrine and experience – for example, Machen argued that doctrine came logically prior to experience, though perhaps not temporally prior to experience, and that right doctrine produced holy experience."*[5]

That is, if experience takes priority over Scripture, it rules as the authoritative role in our lives. Whatever experience we have can preempt Scripture. In the case of a missionary observing (experience) people groups worshipping other gods, that missionary can draw a parallel between their gods and the God of Christian faith. Their personal experience can lead to the erroneous conclusion of a parallel. Machen shows the fatal trap of this conclusion. He notes that relinquishing Scriptural authority to experience can lead to the acceptance of another message for those who have not heard the gospel.[6]

When Scripture no longer becomes binding as the authoritative message of salvation, experience drives us to another way and message. That is, reasoning from observations (experience) drives Scripture to a secondary authority. Finite reasoning, experience, and speculation rationalize away the authority of the gospel for all and open the door for another message.

Faith raises us above experience to a greater authority – God Himself and His spoken word to us. When we rely on experience as authority, authority shifts to our encounter of the temporal things of the world and our own whims. As finite beings, we tend to rely on experience since it is difficult to separate ourselves from our experiences. Genuine biblical faith resists reliance on experience for authority and practice of the truth. Truth transcends personal experience, since it rests in God alone. Truth renders experience inadequate for dictating the terms of salvation or living by faith. Since God reigns as the source of truth, it comes to us through His spoken word disclosed in the gospel found in the Scriptures.

Furthermore, when we rely on experience, we tend to shift our focus from God to ourselves and from an eternal focus to a temporal one. Reliance on the experiences we have gravitates us toward that which we see rather than toward the unseen reality. Our faith follows that direction. The Apostle Paul warned the Corinthian church not to follow their impulses toward seen reality but to keep their spiritual eyes on the unseen. He writes,

> *"For our light affliction, which is for a moment, is working for us a far more exceeding and eternal weight of glory, while we do not look at the things which are seen but at the things which are not seen. For the things which are seen are temporary, but the things which are not seen are eternal"* (2 Corinthians 4:17-18).

In the next chapter of his letter, Paul once again surfaces this core truth about faith when he writes, *"For we walk by faith, not by sight"* (5:7).

The reason for his warning is that it is easy to set our eyes on the temporal things of the created order and to trust in that which appeals to our senses, especially in trials (4:8-9), hardships, and desire for spiritual connection (5:2-4). That is the reason Paul stresses that hope depends on the unseen promises of God (4:13-14). Trusting in sight redirects our faith from God to the things of the world. Not only does inclusivism redirect faith in this manner by reliance on the created order, but so also do the occult, cultic practices, Eastern religions, and secular philosophies. The tragic consequence of these redirections, as inclusivism has shown, is trust in another message for salvation – the knowledge of the light of creation.

The knowledge from the light of creation depends on personal perceptions leading to the logical conclusion of my truth may not be your truth. Personal perception is highly subjective, easily translating what one observes in the temporal world as divine rather than from God. A multitude of religious experiences within the occult, animism, pantheism, and the resulting New Age movement[7] illustrate such subjective application. The Apostle Paul also informs us that the tendency of humanity without God is to engage in futile thinking and to exchange God for idols designed from temporal creation (Romans 1:21-23).

Gordon Lewis refers to trust in that which one sees as the "new spirituality." He cites J. Gordon Melton's assessment of this new spirituality as *"built much more around vision and experience than doctrines and a belief system."*[8] Those who subscribe to this new spirituality are not satisfied with faith in the unseen reality of God's promises and the disclosure of Himself in the Scriptures. They seek other authorities among not only mystics and those who hold to special or secret knowledge but also within themselves. Lewis names a host of sources from secular philosophy and eastern religions.[9d] These alone inform of the dangers of seeking to live by sight rather than by faith as inclusivism advocates. Biblical faith trusts in God's word and not in the senses, feeling, emotions, and the visible things of the temporal order. False faith relies on sight and the temporal things of the created order.

Don Cook expands on the false faith of sight in his analysis of Christian illuminati. He highlights the sight-oriented approach many Christians take. He identifies the reaction of many postmodern Christians to humanism by noting,

---

[d] Among those whom Lewis identifies are atheist psychologists Carl Jung, Abraham Maslow, and Carl Rogers; liberal theologian Paul Tillich; founder of American Buddhism Alan Watts; and Eastern religious guru Maharishi Mahesh Yogi. For the new spiritual consciousness sources, Lewis also cites Zen Buddhism, Islamist Sufism and Baha'i, Scientology and Silva Mind Control.

CHRIST IN THE SCOPE OF SALVATION

"What have Christians done in the face of such an approach to life [humanism]*? They have tried to reduce revelation to a personal experience. Spiritual life is real because it can generate genuine emotions which I personally experience. Miracles are real because I can experience them first hand. Revelation is possible because I can have personal revelation or be in direct contact with those who do. Christians have accepted the presumption of the age and are trying to limit spiritual life and its expression to the confines of a severe materialism."*[10]

Living the Christian life by sight takes its cue from the temporal created order, especially from human experience. Professor Fruchtenbaum notes that the Book of Acts centered on the authority of the Scriptures and not experience. While the Book of Acts contains a wealth of narratives about the experiences of the early church and Paul and his companions, Fruchtenbaum highlights,

"The thing you find Scripture emphasizing is that the final authority must be the Scriptures, the written Word of God, and not anyone's experience. Certainly, the Apostles could have related many of their experiences with Jesus in trying to defend their preaching about Jesus. One thing the Book of Acts keeps re-emphasizing is that Paul, Silas and the others always made their final authority the Word of God and not their own experiences, as incredible as those experiences were by God's grace."[11]

Later in his article, he analyzes the reliance on experience from the Toronto Vineyard church movement. He points out,

"The Scriptures are sufficient to make one thoroughly complete. There is no need to try to

receive some supernatural "zapping" from some spirit world. There is no need to spend money to travel to Toronto for someone to lay hands on you until you either fall into uncontrollable, unstoppable laughter or make animal sounds. The written Scriptures are able thoroughly to complete you and furnish you for every work that you need to do. You can become spiritual and mature in the faith through the Scriptures alone."[12]

What inclusivism, Cook's explanation of "Christian illuminati," Lewis's assessment of "new spirituality," and Fruchtenbaum's assessment of the Toronto ecstaticism have in common is the challenge of reliance on sight. Sight focuses on one self rather than reliance on the unseen and the authority of Scripture. Inclusivism's emphasis on creation demonstrates its sight-oriented approach to salvation. It ends up relinquishing the knowledge and theology of Scripture for living by faith. It fails to point to the unseen reality of God's righteousness and promises. Consequently, it opens the door for a sight-oriented message, one catering to content unique for everyone, the content of experience.

Lewis, Cook, and Fruchtenbaum illustrate that Christians are also not immune to the temptation to rely on experiences and corresponding seen reality. It is often easier to place faith in hidden knowledge,[13e] mystical experience,[14] dreams, visions,

---

[e] Books on Amazon.com illustrate that many people lay claim to secret or hidden knowledge they have received through dreams, visions, and revelations (http://amzn.to/Vd4Efy). Such secret knowledge comprises a subtle segment of inclusivism in that the mediating factors for faith is different for everyone and does not depend on a specific amount of knowledge or information (See John Sanders, *No Other Name*, p. 233 and Clark Pinnock, *A Wideness in God's Mercy*, 158). These differences establish a uniqueness for each recipient of the knowledge from the light of creation. This knowledge depends on personal perception seen through cultural and geographical lenses. Frequently, those within a given society possess a single person or group mediating this knowledge for the rest as the keeper of such knowledge. Gurus, witch doctors, and the shaman are

direct contact with the spirit world, and revelations rather than in God's promises and His authority found in the Scriptures. Christians throughout the centuries have veered off into these various directions. They have taken a large number with them in seeking to satisfy their longing for spiritual fulfillment through sight and not through faith in the unseen promises of God and Scriptural authority.[15]

The above-mentioned philosophical ideologies, like inclusivism and New Age spirituality, are an assault on the faith of which the Epistle of Hebrews speaks of trust in *"the evidence not seen"* (Hebrews 11:1). These ideologies form the theology for one's "control beliefs"[16] for the reading of Scripture (or reading into Scriptures) and discovery of truth leading to the overthrow of true biblical faith. Furthermore, experience, as the basis for living by sight, sets up a human standard instead of God's standard for judging and applying truth.

INADEQUACY OF CULTURAL RELIGION

Those in other cultures may hear that the God of the Bible is the same one they have worshipped. However, in their minds, they may still be thinking in terms of their god and simply incorporating the God of the Bible into the ones they worship. Therefore, the God of the Bible may become one of many gods. To associate God with gods makes Him less than He is. It places Him on equal standing with idols of humanity regardless if viewed on a higher level. The Athenians' unknown god illustrates a society elevating one god above others. They incorporated their unknown god with a pantheon of others (Acts 17:16-21). The Scriptures warn against such comparison,

> *"Therefore, know this day, and consider it in your heart, that the LORD Himself is God in*

---

examples of the holders and mediators of secret knowledge. They also have access to the supernatural through séances, visions, and dreams as they interpret them through the visible world.

heaven above and on the earth beneath; there is no other" (Deuteronomy 4:39).

In his blessing over Israel, King Solomon announced,

> *"And may these words of mine, with which I have made supplication before the LORD, be near the LORD our God day and night, that He may maintain the cause of His servant and the cause of His people Israel, as each day may require, that all the peoples of the earth may know that the LORD is God; there is no other."*
> (1 Kings 8:59-60).

Isaiah declared numerous times that there was no other god besides Him (Isaiah 44:6; 45:14, 18, 21-22). Associating God with any other created gods constitutes not only a breach of the Creator-creation distinction but also makes a comparison of God the LORD with idols. This comparison insults God and destroys the only message able to save humanity from the curse of sin. It also opens the gates to idolatry.

Unless Jesus is central to the message of salvation to all, the gospel becomes diluted to something other than the message of redemption. God ordained the gospel to draw people to faith and repentance (Mark 14:9; 16:15; Acts 15:7-8; 16:10; Romans 1:15-16). It is the only message calling people to obedience of faith (Romans 10:16). If it is veiled (unheard), it is veiled to the lost (2 Corinthians 4:3).

Any other message has its source in human-centered religion. Only through the proclaimed gospel can one know the forgiveness of sins (Acts 13:38). The gospel is the explicit and revealed knowledge of Jesus Christ apart from whom no one receives salvation. That knowledge arrives through proclamation. Other religions are human-centered and draw one away from true worship of God through Jesus Christ.

CHRIST IN THE SCOPE OF SALVATION

REPLYING TO CHARGES AGAINST THE PREEMINENCE OF CHRIST

Embracing any so-called faith than the faith the Bible teaches holds to presumption, speculation, and even superstition. It places trust in something other than Christ of the gospel. We must be prepared to give an answer as Peter encouraged us (1 Peter 3:15) concerning any charges of unfairness against the God who insists on faith in His Son for salvation. Our proactive defense is of utmost importance because it addresses our hope. The strength of the gospel is the strength of our hope. Just as the gospel provides hope to the lost without Christ, so also does it provide the answer for our hope in Christ. In terms of the hope of the gospel, Paul wrote to the Corinthian church,

> *"For if the ministry of condemnation had glory, the ministry of righteousness exceeds much more in glory... Therefore, since we have such hope, we use great boldness of speech"*
> (2 Corinthians 3:9, 12).

Paul makes clear that the basis of Christian hope is the *"ministry of righteousness."* The ministry of righteousness glorifies God because, as stated before, it elevates God's judgment on sin, makes Christ central to the proclaimed gospel, and enables believers to stand just before God resulting from Christ's imputed righteousness to us.

Notice that Paul declares, *"...we use great boldness of speech"* (3:12), emphasizing the proclamation of the gospel. Proclamation does not point to *"the value of God's revelation in creation."*[17] The gospel, not creation, reflects God's righteousness, because that righteousness finds its source in the death and resurrection of Christ.

NOTHING BUT THE GOSPEL

Christ's Preeminence in the Gospel Message

How then does the ministry of righteousness reply to those who may not have ever heard the gospel? Only the power of the gospel saves and imparts new life. The answer begins with this truth. Power resides in the gospel and not in the created order. The power of God revealed through creation cannot save or even impart the knowledge of salvation. The knowledge and rejection of the created order does not hold people accountable for their eternal destiny. Rather, faith in or unbelief of the Son of God holds them accountable (John 3:18). That is not to say that people are not held accountable for rejecting the knowledge of God through creation. They are. However, God's righteousness and power in the gospel press on people greater accountability in relationship with God. Furthermore, the gospel has the power to draw people to the living God. The elements of creation possess no such power.

The key issue is the gospel and its acceptance or rejection. How then can a person be held accountable for rejecting Christ if they have not heard of Him? Jesus said that people are held accountable for their evil deeds. The gospel passes judgment on sin and provides a remedy for the sinner. Because of evil deeds, people reject the light that has come into the world (John 3:18-21). That light is not from the created order but from God through Christ the center of the gospel. The key issue remains the same,

> *"And this is the condemnation, that light has come into the world, and men loved darkness rather than light, because their deeds were evil. For everyone practicing evil hates the light and does not come to the light, lest their deeds should be exposed..."* (John 3:19-20).

The issue of salvation is not about choice but about the heart driving choice. Since the hearts of all humanity are evil, God must change the heart for one to come to the light found in

CHRIST IN THE SCOPE OF SALVATION

Jesus for salvation. Neither Sanders, Pinnock, nor other inclusivists hold this position in its entirety. Pinnock writes,

> *"In my judgment, the faith principle is the basis of universal accessibility. According to the Bible, **people are saved by faith, not by the content of their theology**. Since God has not left anyone without witness, people are judged on the basis of the light they have received and how they have responded to that light."*[18]

Christ's Preeminence as Faith's Object and Content

Several problems exist with what Pinnock states. First, he presents false opposites by presenting salvation by faith against salvation by the content of theology. These are not true opposites, because faith, contrary to Pinnock, relies on content and theology. To pose them as opposites cancels his argument. Faith without content is a leap into the dark. Christ Himself is theological content for faith. Furthermore, by raising the knowledge of the light of creation as the focus of faith, Pinnock must also regard creation as content. To deny this is to redefine content and to confuse readers.

Once again, such faith is a leap into the dark and invalidates the "faith principle." The Scriptures provide the true meaning of faith by centering it on the historical Jesus, the divine Son of God and His death and resurrection. This faith is not one devoid of content. Rather it is one focused on content, and that content is the gospel of Jesus Christ. It alone serves as our only authority apart from which no one receives salvation.

Accepting Biblical Authority Alone

Second, Pinnock places his judgment above God's word. This reply may seem a minor point, but judgment runs the risk of reading into Scripture something that does not exist. It also replaces God's authority with his own. Such a statement does not preclude human judgment but subjects judgment to the Scriptures. However, when that judgment seeks to override Scripture with opinion, it trumps God's word.

Unless we subscribe to the Bible as final authority for all of life, we run the risk of substituting it with authorities of our choice. Christian faith has one authority – the word of God. It reigns supreme in our lives without which we select the authority of other sources and eventually raise these sources up as the object of worship. Among such sources is human judgment and speculation. Behind these sources resides human reason, feeling, or personal senses. When joined with Scriptures, they tend to subject them to the teachings of men and make men the authority over God. This move provides an environment in which we do what is right in our own eyes and opens salvation through other avenues as inclusivism has done.

Exposing God as a Debtor in Inclusivism's Theology

Third, Pinnock links his *"faith principle"* to some sort of *"universal accessibility."* This *"faith principle"* places an obligation on God and compels Him to be indebted to humanity or be unfair. If individuals exercise faith in a god they recognize as being the true God regardless of how they frame this god, it remains faith in something other than the biblical God. It does not matter how much their sinful state distorts the divine as long as they exercise faith.

Accordingly, God is obligated to grant them access to salvation because He recognizes the sincerity of faith. This reasoning steps out onto the dangerous cliff of idolatry by not having the content of God's word as final authority for it. Rather it relies on the content of the created order as its basis for its placement in God. By redefining faith, Christ becomes subject to humanity's assessment of Him and makes Him secondary.

Fourth, Pinnock's argument from a *"universal accessibility"* has some faulty logic issues. Prior to making his statement about *"universal accessibility,"* he writes,

CHRIST IN THE SCOPE OF SALVATION

> *"If God really loved the whole world and desires everyone to be saved, it follows logically that everyone must have access to salvation."*[19]

Pinnock again makes God's love one of indebtedness inasmuch as a spouse's love would be indebtedness to his or her marriage partner in response to the following statement,

> *"If you really love me and desire for me to be happy, it would follow logically that you would buy me a $100,000 diamond ring or a $2 million house."*

This is not love but dependency and obligation. It bases action on presumption, turns love into servitude, and surrenders power to the recipient over the giver. It also defines love from the perspective of humanity and not from truth in God disclosed in the cross of Christ.

The "Faith Principle" as a Presumptuous Faith

Fifth, to cite faith without theology is a presumptuous faith lacking content or an object. God, Jesus, and salvation are all about theology. Trevin Wax also notes,

> *"The inclusivist downplaying of doctrine and theology virtually empties "faith" of all its objective content. What is important is trust in whatever god or whatever light has been given, not a correct understanding of God revealed in Jesus Christ."*[20]

Wax also affirms that Pinnock removes the exclusivity of Christ in the gospel by making Him irrelevant to those who have never heard of Him. By making access to salvation universal, he allows mediation to extend beyond the Mediator to creation. As noted earlier, Pinnock claims content unimportant so that the "faith principle" can center on God without Christ and still open salvation to anyone who exercises this principle while taking a leap of faith into a void. It allegedly widens the mercy of God and the gates of heaven to anyone with a faith empty of theological content. Consequently, the Christ of Pinnock's high Christology becomes marginalized rather than exalted.

Many years ago, a missionary gave an address to a group before going to the mission field in another nation. He said that the team was not concerned about theology but in sharing the gospel and making disciples. What he did was divorce the gospel from theology. The theology of God is not as important as sharing the gospel, which includes numerous theological truths. His statement also created a division between theology and the gospel. If this division existed, what kind of gospel would we share with the lost?

This statement echoes what Pinnock claims. Minimizing theology is marginalizing biblical content. Marginalizing the Bible's content is discounting the gospel. To refer to the Bible as claiming that people are saved by faith and then marginalizing theology is to empty the Bible of its content and the gospel of its message. Without a clear message, Christ has no value for salvation.

The "Faith Principle" as Misdirected Faith

Sixth, Pinnock misdirects faith. It is not "the basis" of some sort of "universal accessibility." No such teaching exists in the Bible. Citing the Bible as the source for this kind of "faith principle" is a misreading of it. Rather, the Bible declares, *"Jesus is the author and finisher of our faith"* (Hebrews 12:2) on whom we set the eyes of our heart. All of Hebrews 11 points toward this crescendo at the beginning of Hebrews 12. Since Jesus is the beginning and end of our faith, it leaves no room for faith as the "basis of universal accessibility." Faith narrows to Jesus and access through Him alone. Faith is the basis for access to the Father through Jesus Christ.

If by *"universal accessibility,"* Pinnock refers to *"whoever believes in Him should not perish"* (John 3:16), or

CHRIST IN THE SCOPE OF SALVATION

"whoever calls on the name of the Lord shall be saved" (Romans 10:13), faith still narrows to Christ. If by *"universal accessibility"* Pinnock refers to the light of nature, this way falls short as a means of salvation. God chose to reveal His righteousness and power through the gospel and not through the light of nature. According to Paul, righteousness and power in the message of the gospel stand as foundational to salvation (Romans 1:16).

Deterrent from Biblical Faith: Love of Darkness Rather than Light

Seventh, Pinnock combines two disparate and unrelated concepts. He joins people not being left *"without witness"* with the basis of God's judgment of them contingent *"on the light they have received and how they have responded to it."* Concerning creation as a witness, Pinnock strikes an accurate chord. Creation does indeed give witness to the eternal God. However, such a witness acts to judge people for rejecting God not for giving or leading to salvation (Romans 1:20-32).

Jesus said much the same thing to Nicodemus. People reject the light because their deeds are evil, and this rejection calls for condemnation (John 3:18-21). Given that people's love for darkness leads to evil deeds, they reject the light and do not come to it. Therefore, those who love darkness will never respond favorably to the light. Their only response always will be to reject the truth from whatever source.

Seeing the condition of people's hearts, that they will never respond favorably to the light because of their love of darkness, God's judgment is righteous. Those who love darkness reject faithfulness to God. Rather they remain faithful to darkness. When critics of the more pessimistic "fewness doctrine," as Pinnock puts it,[21] view society and see all the evils that exists and then look at themselves, they cannot help but conclude that unrighteousness exists.

They may call this unrighteousness by a different name, such as defects, evil, immorality, corruption, moral debt, or some other related term, but it remains unrighteousness. Evil is not simply something external in the world. It is intrinsic to human nature and drives humanity to be inclined to it. Christ is the only remedy for the sinful state of humanity and toward whom every person must look for salvation (John 3:14-15).

A Return to the Proclamation of the Gospel

Where then do these conclusions leave us in terms of those who have not heard the gospel? We land at the same place as Paul when he declares,

> *"...for it is the power of God for salvation for everyone who believes... For in it the righteousness of God is revealed from faith the faith; as it is written, 'The just shall live by faith'"* (Romans 1:16-17).

This passage brings us full circle to the two pillars found in the gospel: God's righteousness and power. If God is righteous, then He will make the right decisions concerning the destiny of all. His righteousness also guarantees He will be faithful in carrying out His purpose. People can accuse Him of injustice or unfairness, but such accusations arise by sidestepping God's righteousness and failing to deal with it. Such sidestepping dons on blinders that eclipses what the eyes cannot see on either side of them. It fails to see that *"...everyone practicing evil hates the light and does not come to the light, lest his deeds should be exposed"* (John 3:20).

Whether the light of creation or Jesus comes to them, the fact remains the same. The hatred of the light and the love of the darkness turn them away from the light of creation or Jesus. Again, the issue is not about choice but about the condition of the heart driving choice.

On the other side of the blinders is God's righteousness. Without the ability to see and comprehend God's righteousness, the question of God's fairness and justice cannot be understood.

CHRIST IN THE SCOPE OF SALVATION

To relieve the tension concerning God's fairness or justice toward those who never hear the gospel, Pinnock and Sanders offer the "wider hope" or the "wideness of God's mercy" by opening up to the light of creation. However, these cases do not address God's righteousness and the condition of the heart. Rather the "wider hope" assumption directs people away from righteousness and sin and toward hopelessness by not recognizing the only hopes of their salvation – believing the gospel and turning to God.

CONSEQUENCES OF LEAVING CHRIST OUT OF THE MESSAGE

To support their approach of the "wideness of God's mercy," Pinnock and Sanders make a subtle shift with Christ in the gospel. Pinnock writes,

> *"This means that universality (salvation for the world) is reached by way of particularity (salvation through Jesus) in Christianity. Our proclamation is that God is healing the nations through the mediation of His Son, rather than in some other way. In His wisdom, God is reconciling the world to Himself, not through religious experience, not through natural revelation, not through prophets alone, not through all the religions of the world, but through Jesus Christ."*[22]

The subtle shift Pinnock makes is both how he expresses the work of God in the world through Christ and in his application of terms. It is with his definition and application of terms that he takes the step toward his outlook of universality and particularity. This universality is not so much that God will save everyone but that the gospel must be accessible to all people. His statements are appealing because they sound biblical. Who would disagree that *"God is healing the nations"* or that *"God is reconciling the world to Himself?"*

This shift causes him and inclusivists to claim that Christ is Savior of the world (functionally) while not everyone needs to hear of Him in the gospel (ontologically or actual knowledge of Christ). His statement rest on these two fundamentals, and this is the subtlety of His approach to salvation. This subtle but dangerous shift pushes aside Christ as necessary for salvation through the hearing of the gospel while making Him Savior of the world without His notice in the gospel.

The danger in this shift is using extra-biblical terms as universality and particularity so that Christ is not central to the message. Pinnock attempts to make Christ central to salvation without referring to Him in any message to the unevangelized. These two positions are at odds with one another and contrary to Scriptural authority. He does this by referring to Him as *"...the decisive manifestation and ground of God's grace toward sinners."*[23] However, the problem with this description is that if the message does not disclose Christ to the unevangelized, He cannot be *"the decisive manifestation."* Manifestation means to reveal or to appear. A hidden or behind the scenes Savior is not a manifested Savior or Savior at all.

Inclusivists shift the focus from Christ to a generic theocentric position. This shift is especially noticeable in Pinnock and Sanders' interpretation of Hebrews 11. This shift allows them to ignore the entire emphasis of Christ in the Book of Hebrews, specifically related to faith in chapters 11-12.[24]

The author of the Book of Hebrews takes the reader through chapter eleven to arrive at Christ as the object of faith in chapter twelve (Hebrews 12:1-3). The author's whole intent throughout Hebrews is to show the superiority of Christ in all things so that He might be the sole object of Christian faith for salvation. Inclusivism ignores this context and thereby misses this glorious truth to its detriment. By ignoring it, they take the liberty of creating another gospel and mediator. Consequently, inclusivism robs Christ of His rightful place as the only Mediator (Hebrews 8:6; 9:15; 12:24) by substituting one in His place – that of the created order.[25]

CHRIST IN THE SCOPE OF SALVATION

This is not a high Christology, as Pinnock claims, but a false Christology. While he attempts to elevate Christ in terms of inclusivism's wider hope to a greater number of people, he minimizes Him in the message of the gospel and creates no hope for all because his message is not Christ centered. A numbers game has greater importance than the message. According to inclusivism, the success and effectiveness of the object of faith rests on numbers, that is, the number of people reaching heaven. As opposed to this view, the gospel rests on the power and righteousness of God whose purpose is redemption and not quantity. Essential to God's righteousness and power to execute salvation is the centrality of Christ in the message. The failure to recognize the difference between these two perspectives is the difference between assurance of salvation and hopelessness.

PROCLAIMING CHRIST'S PREEMINENCE

When addressing the unsaved, the message they receive is of utmost importance. The Scriptures make Jesus Christ preeminent for salvation both as Mediator and proclaimed Savior. As those who express faith in God for redemption, He must be the center of the Father's redemptive proclamation. Any Christology must not only point to Christ as Savior but must also make Him the center of the message. The Scriptures make clear that He cannot be behind the scenes or incognito. To separate His position as Savior from the message to the lost defeats the purpose of God's redemptive plan. In other words, God would be saying, *"I have salvation, but I am not going to tell the lost about it."*

No faith is truly biblical faith unless it looks to Jesus as its author and finisher (Hebrews 12:1-3). Faith in what we know from the created order is faith in creation or something we create from creation to represent a god we want to worship. It is a god or mediator infinitely less than God's appointed means.

The tendency of the heart is toward idolatry (Romans 1:22-23). Any religion or faith beginning with the created order is a false religion and false faith. Faith cannot discover salvation in the knowledge of any light from nature or in reference to anything from the created order. Faith leading to salvation must be in the One who stands apart and distinct from creation: the eternal Son of God.

While Jesus Christ was God incarnate, He dwelled among those in the created order. However, as God, He existed and exists distinct from creation. For that reason, He alone deserves to be central to the proclamation extended to all peoples for faith unto salvation. There is no "faith principle" as inclusivists define it but biblical faith centered on Christ. Pinnock's "faith principle" is his own definition of faith and not one that the Bible proclaims.

Christ procured our salvation from beginning to end. He paid the penalty for our sins and freed us from that penalty – God's judgment of eternity without Him and all the Bible states that encompasses. We are in Christ Jesus *"who became for us wisdom from God – and righteousness and sanctification and redemption"* (1 Corinthians 1:30). These characteristics exist for us because Christ is our advocate before the Father. The power of sin no longer reigns over us because He alone broke its power and grants us the power to live sanctified lives (1 Corinthians 1:24). Christ will also come to take us to His glory where He prepared a place for us (John 14:1-2).

If then the entire scope of salvation centers on Christ, it must be the message to the lost when or where they may be. Otherwise, when Christ comes to claim those who belong to Him, He will be an unfamiliar face if all they knew was the light they gleaned from creation and followed it. They would be following some sort of nebulous light and not Christ. Consequently, they would miss the gospel and be without hope.

Furthermore, when those who did not place their faith in Him as the Light of the world see Him face to face, they will be speechless. The guilt of their sins from enjoying the life of darkness will prevent them from blaming God for being unfair or unjust. They will have no excuse for intentionally suppressing the truth, engaging in futile worship, and knowingly living a lie (Romans 1:18-25).

CHRIST IN THE SCOPE OF SALVATION

NOTES

[1] Osburn, 368.
[2] Ibid.
[3] Fackre, Nash, Sanders, Kindle location 427-447.
[4] Ibid, 436.
[5] Lucas, Sean Michael, "Christianity at the Crossroads: E. Y. Mullins, J. Gresham Machen, and the Challenge of Modernism," *Southern Baptist Journal of Theology*, Volume 3:4 (Winter 1999): 61.
[6] Machen, J., Gresham, *Christianity and Liberalism* (Grand Rapids: Wm. B. Eerdmans Publishing Company, 1923, Reprinted 2001, Kindle Edition, location 1287-1297.
[7] Johnson, Phil, "What's New with the New Age? Why Christians Need to Remain on Guard Against the Threat of New Age Spirituality," *Southern Baptist Journal of Theology*, Volume 10:4 (Winter 2006): 77-79
[8] Lewis, Gordon R., "The Church and the New Spirituality," *Journal of the Evangelical Theological Society*, Volume 36:4 (December 1993): 434.
[9] Ibid, 435.
[10] Cook, Don, "Christian Illuminati," *Reformation and Revival*, Volume 3:4 (Fall 1994): 124-125.
[11] Fruchtenbaum, Arnold G., "The Toronto Phenomenon (Part 2 of 2)," *Chafer Theological Seminary Journal*, Volume 2:2 (Fall 1996): 10
[12] Ibid, 12.
[13] Tunnicliffe, Patty, "Everything Old is New Again: Oprah Winfrey, Her Guests, and Their Spiritual Worldview: Developing Spiritual Discernment in an Undiscerning Age," *Christian Apologetics Journal*, Volume 8:2 (Fall 2009): 34-53.
[14] Collmer, Robert G., "The Limitations of Mysticism," *Bibliotheca Sacra*, Volume 116:462 (April 1959): 128-135. See also
[15] Carson, D. A., Mark Coppenger, Joel R. Beeke, and Pierre Constant, "The SBJT Forum: Thinking about True Spirituality," Southern Baptist Journal of Theology, Volume 10:4 (Winter 2006): 87, 89, 91-92)
[16] Pinnock, 18-19, 37
[17] Fackre, Nash, and Sanders, Kindle location 135.
[18] Pinnock, 157-158.
[19] Pinnock, 157.
[20] Wax, Trevin, "Inclusivism: What is "Faith" Anyway?" *The Gospel Coalition: Kingdom People, Living on Earth as Citizens of Heaven*, http://thegospelcoalition.org/blogs/trevinwax/2007/11/page/2/, 2. Accessed July 26, 2013.
[21] Pinnock, 154-156.
[22] Pinnock, 49.
[23] Pinnock, 49.

[24] Morgan, Christopher W. and Robert A. Peterson, Ed., *Faith Comes by Hearing: A Response to Inclusivism* (Downers Grove: InterVarsity Press, 2008, Kindle Edition, location 2473-2482.

[25] Sanders, 215.

8   Case for Explicit Faith in Christ

The Scriptures call for faith to receive salvation. Many so-called "faiths" exist in the world. All except biblical faith are false and leave one without hope. Inclusivism also calls for faith, a faith based on speculation and not biblical authority. Clark Pinnock uses the term "faith principle" to refer to a faith applied by those who have never heard the gospel and rely on knowledge from the light of creation. It is separate and distinct from the faith of those who hear the gospel for biblical salvation. Therefore, given the supposed two classes of people, inclusivism raises two types of faith. Do we discover these two faiths in the Bible? How do we identify true biblical faith? When discussing faith, we must identify its object, the basis for it, and the kind of faith that leads to salvation.

BIBLICAL VIEW OF FAITH

As we review the Scriptures, we must determine the true nature and object of faith for salvation. It is important to make the distinction between biblical faith and other false faiths. When speaking of faith, the Bible notes several truths about it. First, biblical faith focuses on the unseen. Second, faith has an object. Third, faith must be applicable to all and be active.

As opposed to biblical faith, inclusivists redefine it. Pinnock claims that the seen elements of general revelation mediate faith through the "faith principle."[1] Sanders takes the position that all revelation is saving revelation regardless if it comes from the general revelation or through Christ (special revelation).[2] This faith principle proposes trust on what one

CASE FOR EXPLICIT FAITH IN CHRIST

sees. Inclusivism cites Hebrews 11 as proof text for its support of faith in God through the light of creation. A closer look at how inclusivists interpret Hebrews 11 reveals a redefinition of faith altogether. Scripture rejects the light received from nature as a mechanism through which salvation comes from God because it relies on what one sees: creation.

Faith in the Unseen

Biblical faith by its very nature focuses on the unseen for substance and evidence as opposed to what one sees (Hebrews 11:1). Otherwise, it would not be faith. This aspect of faith stands as one of the more important truths about it compared to other views, particularly inclusivism. The Book of Hebrews highlights several examples illustrating this quality of faith. When speaking of creation, Hebrews points to the unseen Creator as its origin (11:3). The author stresses that the invisible resided behind the visible. That is, the visible did not create the visible. Rather, God's word brought about the visible creation. Faith has its trust in this unseen as the One who oversees and commands through His word creation (Colossians 1:17).

For each person Hebrews mentions as placing faith in God, the elements of the unseen stands out. Enoch pleased the unseen God (11:5). Noah showed fear toward God word and obeyed Him (11:7). Abraham and Sarah believed God's unseen promise and showed their faith through obeying God (11:8-12). Hebrews gives so many more examples of faith in the unseen, and they are similar to the ones mentioned. Not only is God the unseen object of faith, but the promises in His word serve as unseen realities. This latter truth will be explored more fully later in the chapter.

"Looking to Jesus..."

Faith has an object, and that object is the unseen God who is not from the created order. The Scriptures attest throughout that the true object of faith is God. However, this God is like no other. He is the triune God of the Father, Son, and Holy Spirit. Expressing faith in God without acknowledging the triune God the Scriptures reveal is trust in another god, a god arising out of creation. Faith in the triune God alone is the only genuine faith. All other so-called gods are unbiblical and fail to provide entrance to salvation.

One of the earliest confessions of the Christian Church, the Nicene Creed (325 A.D.), stresses such faith in the triune God through which one comes to know God.[3] By beginning with, *"I believe,"* those who gathered at the Council of Nicaea established as wholly biblical and true that God consisted of the three persons of Father, Son, and Holy Spirit. Apart from the Trinity, there is no God. To suggest faith in God who is not the Trinity is to claim a false faith. To proclaim faith in any other God is faith in a false god. To consider a god unknown as Father, Son, and Holy Spirit is to look to or for a false god and false faith.

The 18th century German theologian Friedrich Schleiermacher once stated,

> *"Our faith in Christ and our living fellowship with him would be the same even if we had no knowledge of any such transcendent fact [as the Holy Trinity] and even if the fact itself were different."*[4]

This assessment of the Christian faith goes counter to genuine biblical faith. It establishes faith in a god unknown to the biblical authors and denies the core distinctiveness of the God the Scriptures uphold. Schleiermacher undercuts the historical, source, word, and foundation of faith by dismissing God and history and making faith a leap into a vacuum – no object and no connection with reality (history).

Genuine faith declares, *"I believe..."* It announces a personal commitment that includes not only acknowledgment that God exists, speaks, and acts in and exercises providence over history. That faith trusts His promises. The path of faith uses Hebrews 11 as a launching pad into the opening of the next chapter that confesses with those listed in chapter eleven,

> *"...looking unto Jesus, the author and finisher of our faith, who for the joy that was set before Him endured the cross, despising the shame, and has sat down at the right hand of the throne of God. For consider Him who has endured such hostility from sinners against Himself, lest you become weary and discouraged in your souls"* (Hebrews 12:2-3).

Just as the launching pad for a space shuttle is the means for reaching the shuttle's goal, so also does explicit faith in its object, Jesus Christ, lead us to recognize the salvation He procured for us.

Bruce Ware asks,

> *"...would God have chosen to reveal Himself to us as the one God who is Father, Son, and Holy Spirit, unless He knew that this would be important to our understanding of Him and to our faith? Must it not be the case that God cares greatly that we 'get it,' that we see Him for who He is? And must it not matter to our own lives whether or not we understand Him as the triune God that He is?"*[5]

Of course, the answer to these rhetorical questions is yes. Ware's questions lead to the core of Christian faith. God desires for us to understand Him. For that to happen, we must be on the right path, the path on which explicit faith in Christ takes us. God had an intentional goal for us to know Him. He did not leave it to our imaginations to make our own spiritual choice. God considered His way much more important than any way we choose. He recognized that our way leads to death and His to life. He also knew that any spiritual search we designed would lead down an uncertain path toward a more uncertain object, an object from the imagination. For these reasons, He chose the specific revelation that leads to salvation. He not only chose it, but He also placed Himself clearly with the cross of Christ. The act of Christ on the cross revealed the triune God, and through it showed us the Father, Son, and Holy Spirit.

Just as the object of faith is divine so also must its mediation be divine. The Trinity makes such mediation certain. The Son of God, Jesus Christ, became the Mediator between God and humanity because of His divinity. Nothing from the created order could mediate or interface between God and humanity. Nothing satisfies God the Father as much as His only Son. He stands perfect before the Father – a perfect sacrifice for sin (Hebrews 10:1-12), a perfect life lived before humanity and His Father (2 Corinthians 5:21; Hebrews 4:15; 1 Peter 2:22; 1 John 3:5), and a perfect priest who offered up Himself as sacrifice for sin (Hebrews 5:5-6; 7:11-16; 8:1-2).

The Application of Faith

Faith is more than simply acknowledgment of God. To have that acknowledgment requires revelation from God, revelation that transpires into His written word. This statement asserts two important truths that counter the "faith principle" of inclusivism. The first truth is the acknowledgment part. Acknowledgment is a tip of the hat that says, "I recognize you." While faith is recognizing God, it is more than a tip of the hat as though simply acknowledging the presence of someone or, for that matter, God.

Certainly, the Scriptures inform us that faith accepts God as the unseen reality. The Scriptures also inform us that this unseen reality, God, requires two components: revelation (His word) of Him and trust. Revelation precedes knowledge. Knowledge precedes trust. God initiates both. Carl Schultz is helpful concerning this point,

"Limits of human knowledge are recognized in the New Testament. It is not through wisdom that the world knows God, but

CASE FOR EXPLICIT FAITH IN CHRIST

rather through the divine initiative (Gal. 4:8-9). It is through the kerygma [proclamation, gospel] *that humans can know God (1 Cor. 1:20-25). Spiritual discernment is not the result of profane reasoning (1 Tim. 6:20). God's revelation in Christ has made knowledge of Him possible."*[6]

While we perceive the world and gather knowledge from it, God alone informs us of Himself and that this world comes from Him. The letter to the Hebrews confirms God's initiative when its writer states,

"By faith, we understand that the worlds were framed by the word of God so that the things which are seen were not made of the things which are visible" (Hebrews 11: 3).

Understanding of the divine requires faith. Perception, human wisdom, or reason cannot bridge the gap between that which we see and God. Perceiving unseen reality requires an act of God in the human mind and heart. Knowledge and discernment of the world and of spiritual realities need divine enlightenment or spiritual understanding.

Consider an illustration. Evolutionists would not draw the same conclusion as the writer of the Epistle of Hebrews. Atheistic evolutionists would disagree with the understanding that the *"worlds were framed by God."* They would reach a very different understanding. Rather than claiming faith in God gives understanding, evolutionists would claim science gives understanding. That is, a Big Bang occurred apart from any God and eventually produced the worlds in space. The evolutionist begins with what one sees and draws the conclusion about evolution and the origins of the universe. Such an understanding is devoid of faith in the God of the Bible. Rather, it is faith in seen reality. Faith in unseen reality gives understanding of the origins of creation – God.

Hebrews offers a stunning conclusion. Faith in the unseen helps us grasp and understand even what we see – the created order. Faith in the unseen reality enables us to understand seen reality and its order as from God. Evolutionists depend on seen reality. They cannot to come to grips with the material world as created. Their faith resides within the scope of the material world and cannot reach beyond it without the Creator giving the understanding that He created all things. This brings us back to the original premise concerning understanding seen reality: revelation precedes true knowledge. Knowledge precedes trust. Faith is trust in the unseen God.

Much like evolutionists, inclusivists begin with seen reality and then work their way back to God for those whom they perceive as not hearing the gospel. Consequently, they see faith arising from seen reality – knowledge of the created order, which is a contradiction of faith. Faith assumes the unseen. Faith in what one sees is the reverse of what Hebrews 11:1-3 teaches. This passage begins with God, or the unseen reality, for understanding seen reality. Faith in the unseen reality (the Creator) gives understanding about seen reality (the creation).

The "faith principle" of inclusivism does not and cannot have standing in Scripture. Additionally, inclusivists cannot arrive at their "faith principle" from Hebrews 11:1 since they approach faith from the wrong way – from seen reality rather than from unseen reality. They begin with creation and work their way toward God. The Scriptures begin with God and His declaration, *"In the beginning, God..."* (Genesis 1:1). Creation follows as that which derives from God.

FAITH AND DIVINE REVELATION

To press this point a step further, as does Schultz in his statement concerning Christ, human knowledge of salvation requires knowledge of that which saves. For this reason, the Bible distinguishes between general revelation (understanding the invisible God behind visible creation) and special revelation (understanding of redemption in Christ Jesus). The Scriptures reveal these two revelations as distinct and separate with their own purposes. Gordon Lewis and Bruce Demarest point out that general revelation contains no redemptive truths. Rather, God designated its purpose to reveal Him as a personal God, worthy of worship, and separate and distinct from the created order.[7] They bring us back to the pronouncement in the Epistle of Hebrews that the unseen gives humanity understanding of creation's source – God. This understanding shifts focus from atheism, polytheism, pantheism, and inclusivism all of which have their source in that which one sees or creation.

Nowhere in the Scriptures do we discover the connection between general revelation and saving knowledge. Consequently, saving faith does not arise from general revelation, or seen reality, but from special revelation, or Jesus Christ, the expression of the unseen reality by God's word and through history. In discussing this special revelation, Lewis and Demarest emphasize the essential importance of the Trinity.[8] The Trinity is one of the major distinctions between general and special revelation. Not only does the triune God create a divide between general and special revelation, but God also defines redemptive activity in a way general revelation does not make possible. The Father, Son, and Holy Spirit all participate in divine redemption.

Several examples in Hebrews 11 give a glimpse into this special revelation. God spoke directly to Abraham and gave him a promise of the coming Messiah. With that promise in mind, he focused on an unseen future city that would come from God (Hebrews 11:9, 14-16). God spoke with Moses and Moses identified with his own people and the coming Messiah rather than with the present idolatry of Egypt (Hebrews 11:24-26).

Therefore, the proverbial tip of the hat toward God (acknowledgment of Him as Creator and trusting Him as Redeemer) has its initiative in God. Faith requires both of them together. Faith takes trust in Him and reliance on Him for one's life. Millard Erickson is helpful in pointing out the twofold essentials of true biblical faith as *"...assenting to facts and trusting in a person."*[9]

He stresses faith in content. Content consists of substance and evidence (Hebrews 11:1). He also notes that these two components must never be separate. If one divorces or de-emphasizes facts, information, or content from trust it becomes an exercise in either intellectualism or blind allegiance. Content matters to faith as the writer of the Epistle of Hebrews strongly insists when highlighting *"substance"* and *"evidence"* (11:1).

The historical figures in Hebrews 11 show that faith orders life around commitment (trust) according to content (promises). An examination of each person illustrates that the content of God's unseen promise aroused faith in the recipient. Noah received warning (content of promise) that God would destroy the world and save his family. In fear (trust), he built the ark. By so doing, *"condemned the world and became heir of the righteousness which is according to faith"* (11:7). God promised (content) Abraham an heir. He obeyed (trust) in faith (11:8-10). Scriptures note that Abraham waited (trust) for *"the city which has foundations, whose builder and maker is God* (content)*"* (11:10). Faith in unseen promises guided Moses, Rahab, Joshua, Gideon, Barak, Samson, and David (11:32-34).

They knew God as faithful in spite of not realizing God's promises in their lifetime (11:39). God's unseen word (content) served as the mainstay for their faith (trust). From their testimony, we realize God has something better (11:40). The promise they received came through the incarnation of Christ, the Savior and Mediator of that something better. Faith in Him moves us to trust His promise that He will come again and bring us to the *"city that has foundations,"* or as Jesus promised to take us to His Father's house (John 14:2-3). General revelation serves to reveal God and His handiwork. Special revelation reveals the Savior, and the Holy Spirit draws us to trust Him for salvation. All three persons of the Trinity procure that salvation.

INCLUSIVISM AND REDEMPTIVE FAITH

Those who hold to inclusivism also claim the requirement of faith but fail to recognize the unified activity and purpose of the Trinity in redemption. In their use of Hebrews

CASE FOR EXPLICIT FAITH IN CHRIST

11, they claim it as a proof text to support their advocacy of the mediation of creation toward salvation. If they also insist on faith, we must ask how they mean it in terms of its expression for making a distinction between biblical faith and any other so-called expressions of faith.

Pinnock uses faith in the opposite way of the Scriptures. While he states, *"faith in God is what saves,"*[10] he divorces it from substance or content while citing Hebrews 11:6 to support his case. The passage, as explained previously, teaches just the opposite by referring to the unseen promises of God as both substance and evidence of the content faith embraces. He ignores the dominant theme of the unseen brought out at the outset of the chapter and the continuous references to the unseen throughout it. In doing so, he builds his case on that which a person sees for his "faith principle" and invalidating biblical faith. In the same place Pinnock states,

> *"...people are judged on the basis of the light they have received and how they have responded to that light."*[11]

As he and other inclusivists make clear, that light comes forth from creation or general revelation to those whom they say have not heard the gospel.[12] Therefore, he refers to that which a person sees for mediating a person to God. He leaves the unified work of the Trinity completely out of the picture of such alleged salvation. While he notes the Holy Spirit in a wider work in the world, the Spirit does not glorify Christ in this wider work (John 15:16). Rather, Christ remains behind the scenes as some sort of *"finality"* or *"derivatively."*[13] That is, he seems to divorce Jesus from God as a derivative in terms of His uniqueness and finality as Savior. Scripture does not portray Him in such a manner.

While he correctly claims faith in God saves, he fails to show how a person not hearing the gospel knows the true God as opposed to false gods. If content has no place in the decision-making, on what basis does such a person understand God versus gods? There is no way to make that distinction for him, because such understanding comes through special revelation. Creation cannot give insight for distinguishing between the eternal God of the Bible and any god created from individual imaginations. Even if minimal content serves for decision-making, what prevents this content from corrupting the picture of God in the mind of the person who does not know God? Inclusivists give no answers to these questions except to claim that the Holy Spirit guides through His wider work rather than by His dedication to the gospel of Christ and Christ's glory.[14]

RESTING IN THE TRIUNE GOD

Three challenges exist with inclusivists concerning the wider work of the Holy Spirit in the world in either working through general revelation or religions.

The Unified Work of the Trinity

First, we trust in the triune God who works in unity to procure salvation. The Scriptures do not support the notion that the Father, Son, and Holy Spirit operate separately. An overwhelming number of passages attest to God as the triune God of three persons always focused on a singular mission and purpose. That mission and purpose is the divine redemption of the lost. The Holy Spirit glorifies Christ as Redeemer and testifies of Him (John 15:26; 16:13-14). He helps the redeemed in trials (Luke 12:11-12; Acts 4:1-10; 7:54-60; Romans 5:3-5) and dwells in them to conform them to the image of Christ and to guide them into all truth (John 14:16-17).

An Essential Understanding of the Trinity

Second, the Holy Spirit always works to glorify Christ. How can inclusivism claim that the Holy Spirit performs a wider work in the world in performing God's redemptive work through

CASE FOR EXPLICIT FAITH IN CHRIST

creation apart from Christ when the Spirit glorifies Jesus Christ as His mission? How could the Holy Spirit glorify Christ when Christ remains unknown to those who place their faith in God without knowing Christ? Inclusivists offer no answer.

While skirting around these questions, inclusivists attempt to direct their argument for their position in other directions. One direction is toward the mediation of general revelation, that is,

> *"...that general revelation if salvific because its source is in the saving God...Since all revelation is from God, 'all revelation is saving revelation. The knowledge of God is always saving knowledge.'"*[15]

This argument ignores or discounts the Trinity. If the source of salvation is in God, this means that it is in Christ. If *"The knowledge of God is always saving knowledge,"* then saving knowledge must also be knowledge of Christ since Christ is God, the second person of the Trinity. If Christ is not included in such knowledge, then the knowledge of God without knowledge of Christ cannot be saving knowledge. Additionally, one would not know the real God if Christ is absent from that knowledge. Therefore, inclusivists cannot make the claim concerning the knowledge of God being saving knowledge if Christ is unknown. This claim attempts to divorce Christ from God. It creates a god apart from Christ with those without the knowledge of Christ who look to the mediation of general revelation.

Ignoring the Trinity relative to salvation discounts the knowledge of Christ while claiming the knowledge of God. Knowing God is knowing Christ. This truth is inescapably taught in Scripture (John 10:14; 14:7; 17:3, 21; Ephesians 1:17; Philippians 3:9-11; 1 John 5:20). In doing this, inclusivists must somehow split the knowledge of Christ from the knowledge of God in salvation so that Christ is unknown to those who have not heard the gospel. If Christ is unknown while God is known, how then can Christ truly be the second person of the Trinity?

Sanders will claim that inclusivists do embrace the Trinity. However, they do so in name only and not in practice. For in practice, salvation and the Holy Spirit always glorify Christ and do not split Him from God in a silent partner position among those who never hear of Him and yet, according to inclusivists, are able to gain salvation. Such speculation places inclusivists in a dilemma in attempting to justify their position of salvation apart from the gospel.

The Full Work of the Triune God in Salvation

Third, why would the Holy Spirit only go part way in extending salvation? In leaving Christ out of the message and knowledge of God, the Holy Spirit only takes partial steps with revelation. Why does God only take partial steps when He desires individuals to know Him? Such partial action would be self-defeating for God. That is, saving people through the mediation of creation and later revealing Christ to them in eternity seems to be a roundabout way for God saving people. The triune God is fully involved in salvation. The Father determined it. The Son procured it. The Holy Spirit executed and guaranteed it. Our faith rests with all three persons. The next section addresses how inclusivists raise and apply free will theism, faith, and general revelation toward salvation.

FREE-WILL THEISM AND FALSE FAITH

Many Christians almost unquestionably accept that the Bible teaches autonomous free will without delving into the meaning of the term or the Scriptural evidence for or against it. One of the dangers of not searching the Scriptures for evidence of a particular teaching is opening oneself to error. One such teaching aligned with inclusivism is that of the openness of God or free will theism. The openness of God and its corresponding free will of individuals redefine God. That is, God is not

CASE FOR EXPLICIT FAITH IN CHRIST

omniscient and is dependent on the free will choices of humanity for what inclusivists refer as making *"room for genuine divine responsiveness."*[16]

It is not the intent of this book to give a critique of the openness of God or free will because of space limitation. Freedom and free will has taken up volumes of publications over several millennia with much speculation and philosophy attempting to support or deny its existence. While the Scriptures appeal to the will they also show how sin through the fall of humanity has severely limited our capacity to know God and come to Him. Therefore, it is not the intent of this discussion to debate the various theological and philosophical views, for there are many, and it would take more than space allows.

However, the brief discussion that follows narrows to and shows how inclusivism and the openness of God relate and compromise the biblically expressed nature of God. This discussion also examines the impact of free will theism on God's work in salvation and His limits in redemptive activity. According to inclusivists, as Clark Pinnock, John Sanders, Richard Rice, and Gregory Boyd, God necessarily must be limited in His nature. Why is this? Inclusivists hold the notion that God does not force His divine love on the will of humanity and He makes Himself vulnerable to rejection.[17] From this perspective, no other portrait of God could express genuine love and interact with those He loves if God did not share in a give-and-take relationship and limit Himself in such an interaction with individuals.[18] Such self-limitation assumes God does not or cannot change the heart for people to love Him freely.

However, a number of theological problems exist with this view of God and salvation. Inclusivism's free will theism presents God as incapable of knowing the future because of the multitude of free acts of individuals. Furthermore, inclusivists place God's love and humanity's free will in tension. Because of inclusivism's description of God and humanity being in a give and take relationship, individuals can accept or reject God's love. Any rejection or acceptance can occur regardless of the amount of influence coming from God through His Spirit. That is, love is *"freely chosen."*[19] As freely chosen, God becomes limited and vulnerable for its sake. Consequently, this "freedom" on the part of individuals creates a great unknown of future events for God, even the unknown of Christ dying on the cross. Taken to its logical conclusion, the free will of all those in the line of Christ could circumvent the plan of redemption. If God is not omniscient or all knowing, He could not have known prior to their occurrence the free choices of millions of individuals throughout time for planning redemption through Christ.[20]

Bruce Ware notes that ignorance of the future with God necessarily cast trust in Him to the wayside.[21] He also asserts that open theism attacks God's wisdom, causes us confusion in praying to God, and creates despair for us in our Christian life.[22] In terms of God's wisdom, Ware states that open theism demotes God while elevating the glory of human qualities and attributes. It questions divine guidance and diminishes faith in His ability to provide for us in our limited and finite capacity. Why do we pray in the first place unless we seek His wisdom to guide us into the future and seek His help (James 1:5)?

If God cannot know the future with certainty, our trust in Him to answer prayer would waver and be like the lack of faith of which James warns (1:6). When Paul shared with the Corinthian church of his despair (2 Corinthians 1:8-10), he would have remained in it rather than testifying to his trust in God's deliverance. Paul declared that God delivered him and his companions and would continue to do so (1:10). He could not commend the Corinthians for their prayers for him if God did not know the future of Paul's troubles and prepared deliverance for them (1:11). Besides, their supposed free will would be an obstacle to God's deliverance.

Free will theism that open theism-inclusivism proposes in its speculative manner reduces God to the level of the created order rather than apart and distinct from it. It leaves salvation uncertain, for individuals in their free will could turn their back on God at any given time. This action not only would surprise God but also would leave Him disappointed and compelled to honor such a decision. Not only would free will theism leave salvation uncertain, but it would also allow individuals to gain it on their own terms rather than on God's terms.

This scenario returns us to the two categories of salvation previously discussed: one category based on explicit faith in Christ (special revelation) and the other based on knowledge from the light given to those who have not heard the gospel (general revelation). In the case of special revelation from the perspective of free-will theism, individuals could decide whether to respond to the gospel. God simply would be a persuader and obligated to honor a person's decision for or against Christ as Savior. Since He would not force His will on a person, because of a person's freedom to choose, all of God's persuasion could be of no avail. Inclusivists subscribing to this free-will theism find themselves in a dilemma of advocating a helpless and weak God.

According to those who hold to free-will theism, those who have not heard the gospel, would have salvation almost entirely on their terms and merits. The knowledge of the light of creation or through another religion makes salvation available to them. Regardless of the influence the Holy Spirit in presenting such light, individual free will trumps Him. Individuals could choose that influence and mingle it with other influences and variables for creating one's theology with its rituals and content. Accordingly, the Holy Spirit would not force His influence for overriding such a theology.

As long as one accepted even a minimal portion of the light from the created order, God would be obligated to save them. Explicit faith in Christ would be inconsequential. No such light from the created order reflects God perfectly. They simply need to respond to the knowledge they receive regardless of how distorted or imperfect it is.[23] Such a scenario smacks of syncretism and creates a foundation for idolatry, that is, viewing the created order and fashioning a god according to what one sees. Consequently, such action would not be from faith but from sight.

CONFRONTING FALSE FAITH

Those who open salvation through another way recast faith in a different manner. It is not that they do not adhere to faith as a means to salvation. They redefine it. Pinnock writes, *"Faith is what pleases God."*[24] That is certainly a true statement. However, he then expands on this statement with the following,

> *"The fact that different kinds of believers are accepted by God proves that the issue for God is not the content of theology but the reality of faith. As dispensational theologians have observed, theological content differs from age to age in the unfolding of redemption, but the faith principle remains in place."*[25]

On its face, this statement may appear undeniable. However, it has a number of false premises and unclear generalizations. Pinnock does not explain what he means by *"different kinds of believers."* However, he creates his argument based on to what he refers as "fact." He also relies on "dispensational theologians" to support his claim of his *"faith principle"* rather than the Scriptures. He ignores Scripture altogether as authority for formulating his theology. Rather, he positions *"theological content"* opposite faith, suggesting that theology is irrelevant for faith. According to the Scriptures, faith in Christ is the only belief leading to salvation. If, according to God, theological content was unimportant for faith, then He diminishes His own Son's death on the cross and His word would have no importance for salvation. His statement relies on speculation rather than the authority of Scripture.

He refers to *"holy pagans"* and cites Abraham, Job, and Cornelius as such pagans. He appears to associate *"holy pagans"* with *"different kinds of believers"* to support his case for faith in another gospel found in the knowledge of the light from creation. Pinnock is not the only person holding to inclusivism to cite these men to support their approach to salvation.

Inclusivists Dwight Carlson[26] and John Sanders[27] also use them as examples. One of the reason they use them is because they fall in the pre-Christian era and presumably could not have placed their faith in Christ as their Savior. However, this assumption is not only speculation but also contrary to Scripture itself. In the cases cited for *"holy pagans,"* God's choice of each person preceded faith. God revealed Himself to each one initially prior to any response from them.

Inclusivists may argue that Job is certainly an exception, but such an argument is weak due to the silence of Scripture concerning him. Rather, to refer to Job as some sort of *"holy pagan"* much like his contemporaries is reading into the Scriptures when they are silent concerning an explanation of any redeeming relationship that existed between Job and God. The book of Job is not about eternal redemption but the suffering of one man and God's dealings with him according to His sovereign will. It was never the intent of the author of Job to characterize him as a *"holy pagan."* Inclusivists create it from speculation.

The book of Job simply does not inform us of any redeeming faith similar to faith in Christ. Such a comparison would be reading New Testament theology backwards into Job's time and projecting on him a similar faith as those in the New Testament. Rather, LaSor gives insight into an approach to take with Job and the theology surrounding him,

> *"All biblical books must be studied as a whole, with their parts seen in relationship to the author's overall intent. This is particularly true of Job. Its full message cannot be discerned short of the final page. The tracing of the book's movement has been an exposition of its message.*
>
> *The story is the message. Its parts must not be snatched from the whole, nor its main emphasis hardened into rigid principles or fine-*

tuned into narrow propositions. To do this would violate what the book teaches about the mysteries of God's workings in human lives."[28]

Wisdom embraces this advice. To read into the character some sort of *"holy pagan"* violates the principle LaSor sets forth. Disregarding themes and contexts lead to interpretations foreign to Scripture and results in drawing unwarranted conclusions and applications. Such conclusions also tend to create biblical theology unrelated to the whole context of faith and salvation.

Additionally, error easily takes it course when using specific historical characters apart from the roles the authors of the text intended. LaSor raises the author's intent as a cautionary boundary beyond which we do well to pay attention so we do not meander beyond the author's message and its application. Lifting specific characters from their historical settings without regard for the author's treatment of them can distort biblical teaching and impose a theology foreign to the Bible.

The clear reading of Scripture concerning Job, Abram, and Cornelius, reveals that their circumstances bear little resemblance to Pinnock's *"holy pagan"* outlook. They were not *"different kinds of believers,"* but those who placed faith in the same God who revealed Himself to them. Inclusivists disregard the author's message and intent with these men. They extract them from their historical contexts and read into the Scriptures. Pinnock attributes his own meaning of faith, a "faith principle,"[29] not found in the Scriptures, and makes it an avenue of a faulty *"basis of universal accessibility"* for salvation with those who have not heard the gospel.

Chapter five discussed this "faith principle" in detail, and it asserts that faith divorced from the gospel is not a valid faith. No amount of speculation and misreading of Scripture can stand up to the clear teaching of Scripture concerning the explicit proclamation of the gospel for salvation. The Scriptures alone and giving attention to the intent of the author and context must counter this false view of faith.

INSISTENCE ON BIBLICAL FAITH

Why do the Scriptures insist on explicit faith in Jesus Christ as the only means for salvation? God informed the biblical authors of the message He intended for saving people. They wrote as the Holy Spirit moved them (2 Peter 1:21). There are two other related reasons for the insistence on explicit faith. First, no one can come to God unless He reveals Himself. Second, God is not part of creation but stands apart from it as the Creator. As Creator, He is also infinite and we are finite.

While creation testifies to God's attributes and power (Romans 1:20) and declares His glory (Psalm 19:1), it is extremely limited as a finite means of revealing an infinite God. Creation can only reveal God and even then in an extremely limited manner the way He designates it. It has no power in itself to express God's redemptive nature, especially His righteousness. It is also subject to bondage and will pass away (Romans 8:20). The fall of man subjected all creation to corruption (8:21), and waits for redemption.

That which dwells in corruption and passes away has no capability or capacity to serve as a mediator for the glory of salvation. That also includes humanity. Those who point to creation as that which reveals light for salvation must necessarily include humanity since creation also includes humanity. Can we as part of humanity then look to ourselves as part of the general revelation of creation and express faith unto salvation? Such thinking rings of idolatry, especially when we examine what happens when people actually scan creation that surrounds them.

Our tendency when considering creation, including humanity, is to worship it. The darkness of the heart immediately grips it and turns it toward created things as objects of worship rather than lifting our eyes to the Creator who made it all. Paul states,

*"Professing to be wise, they became fools,
and changed the glory of the incorruptible God*

into an image made like corruptible man – and birds and four-footed animals and creeping things" (Romans 1:22-23).

The "change and exchange" truth inevitably takes hold. People change the glory of God into an image made after the likeness of the created order. The next step is the "exchange." Paul continues,

"...who exchange the truth of God for the lie and worshiped and served the creature rather than the Creator, who is blessed forever. Amen" (1:25).

This natural tendency occurs because of corruption due to disobedience of our first parents who permitted sin to enter into the world. From that point forward, the tendency of people's hearts was a turning away from God toward evil. They worshipped not only objects in the created order but also themselves.

Ronald Nash suggests that although God gave humanity sufficient information about Himself in nature, individuals rejected it anyway.[30] General revelation is not redemptive. Nash points out that those adhering to the inclusiveness position, especially Clark Pinnock, use Hebrews 11:6 to support their argument that it satisfies the condition of faith, particularly the "faith principle" Pinnock espouses. Nash counters Pinnock's use of Hebrews 11:6 in this manner by suggesting that this passage does not exhaust the content of faith.

We also discover another powerful argument in the Hebrews' application in addition to the exhaustion of the content of faith. After identifying all those who walked by faith from Abel through the persecuted prophets and Old Testament saints, the passage encourages the reader to consider the faith of those mentioned in Hebrews 11. The author of Hebrews then focuses directly on Jesus. The passage declares,

CASE FOR EXPLICIT FAITH IN CHRIST

"...looking to Jesus, the author and finisher of our faith, who for the joy set before Him endured the cross, despising the shame, and is seated at the right hand of the throne of God" (Hebrews 12:2).

This application summarizes the entire meaning and object of faith from Hebrews 11. That is, faith's sole object is Jesus. Notice how Hebrews treats Moses' faith,

"He considered the reproach of Christ greater wealth than the riches of Egypt, for he was looking to the reward" (Hebrews 11:26).

Hebrews also cites Abraham as looking ahead to a city God would create. In both cases, the passage strongly suggests that those mentioned had their faith in the coming Messiah whom Jesus Christ would satisfy. He was the author and finisher of the faith of all those mentioned in Hebrews 11.

Genuine faith has Jesus as its ultimate object and rules out any other object regardless of its source. This message dominates not only the immediate context but also the letter to the Hebrews entirely. The message of the superiority of Christ and His redemptive ministry threads its way through this eloquent letter to its conclusion at which point the author subscribes to Him all glory (Hebrews 13:21). Creation utterly fails to stand up to the unmatched and incomparable object of the eternal Son of God, Jesus Christ.

Such an act of turning to creation as the light toward which one could direct faith in God is radically misdirected and is not faith at all. That which is corrupt and passing away gives a very unclear and unrecognizable light. While we recognize through faith that God does indeed exist and that He exists in glory and power, sin muddies our perceptions of the unseen God. Creation also stands as an insufficient mediator for faith. It is finite and temporal while God is infinite and eternal.

For this reason, only Jesus can reveal God and be the object of salvation. As the Son of God from all eternity, He entered the temporal created order, *"taking the form of a bondservant and coming in the likeness of men"* (Philippians 2:7). To create a doctrine of the "wideness of God's mercy" around general revelation overlooks the fact that creation includes fallen humanity. While God created man and woman in His image and *"crowned [them] with glory and honor"* (Psalm 8:5; Hebrews 2:7), sin tarnished this glory.

Even if such glory shined in full force, we find no evidence in Scripture of any redemptive character in creation. Creation remains finite and temporal, and for these reasons, it is insufficient for faith for salvation. Even if we viewed humanity as part of creation, would one perceive any mediating element? Can humanity point to God or to many gods? How can fallen humanity in looking at itself distinguish the true God from false gods? Would the unevangelized determine God like himself and worship other people or even himself? Unfortunately, such is the case in postmodern society as well as throughout history (Romans 1:20-25). For this reason, the Scriptures throughout insist on explicit faith in Christ alone. God appointed Him alone as the merciful High Priest of our confession (Hebrews 3:1).

TRUSTING CHRIST FOR SALVATION

Throughout the New Testament, the authors stress not only faith but also the object of faith as Jesus Christ. There was little doubt with the gospel writers that explicit faith in Christ stood as foundational to relating to God. At the outset of his gospel, Mark recorded Jesus declaring, *"Repent and believe in the gospel"* (Mark 1:15). Luke records Jesus rebuking two of His followers on the road to Emmaus for their unbelief in the testimony of the prophets concerning Him (Luke 24:13-27).

Throughout his gospel, the Apostle John places emphasis on faith in Jesus. He makes faith one of his major themes not only in his gospel but also in his letter of 1 John. He carried this theme of faith in the special revelation of God through His Son Jesus Christ from the beginning of his gospel (John 1:9-13) to

CASE FOR EXPLICIT FAITH IN CHRIST

his conclusion (20:31). Jesus is central to the gospel, and the gospel is the message that is central to salvation (John 3:16).

Jesus confronted specific individuals concerning their lack of faith in Him (John 3:12; 4:48; 5:44-47; 6:36, 64; 8:24, 45-46; 10:25-38). In his historical account of the birth and growth of the church, Luke places the highest priority on faith in Christ. The Church's birth and growth rested on faith in the gospel of Christ (2:14-41; 6:7; 11:24; 14:22-27; 16:5). Jesus not only must be the *"ultimate revelation of God,"*[31] the atonement for sin, and the complete expression of God's love,[32] but He also must be believed for salvation. Unless a person embraces explicit faith in the revelation of Christ and in His atonement for sin, there can be no salvation. The omission of faith in Jesus is a grave and fatal error.

Those who place faith in another source than Jesus reject the only means God appointed for salvation. To reject Christ as the object of faith because some people may not ever hear about Him excludes the only way to God. Allowing the issue of fairness to stand in the way of eternal life is the rejection of God Himself and with that life without Him forever. Seeking another source for faith makes light of the gospel's testimony of sinful humanity and brushes aside the reason for Christ's coming. Because of this sinfulness, those who reject God love darkness more than light because their deeds are evil (John 3:19-20).

The Bible teaches that a person not hearing the gospel and believe will not see God. If an explicit confession of faith for all is unnecessary, Christ is secondary or not at all relevant to salvation. Confession of Christ is the essence of faith (Romans 10:9-10). While faith alone is the undisputed biblical means for salvation, the practice of faith is a necessary ingredient. If explicit faith were unnecessary, where would such a faith lead regarding its practice? Explicit faith regards Christ as its direct object.[33] If faith excludes Christ, what would then be the object of obedience (John 14:21)? These questions beg for an adequate answer, and that answer finds its source in the Scriptures and its authority: *"Believe in the Lord Jesus Christ, and you will be saved"* (Acts 16:31).

NOTES

[1] Pinnock, 158.
[2] Sanders, 233.
[3] Schaff, Kindle Edition), Kindle location 1187-1193.
[4] Schleiermacher, Friedrich in Toon, Peter, "Ways of Describing the Holy Trinity," *Reformation and Revival*, Volume 10:3 (Summer 2001): 108.
[5] Ware, Bruce A., *Father, Son, and Holy Spirit: Relationships, Roles, and Relevance*, Kindle location 89.
[6] Schultz, Carl, "Know, Knowledge" in *Evangelical Dictionary of Biblical Theology* ed. Walter A. Elwell (Grand Rapids: Baker Books, 1996), 458.
[7] Lewis, Gordon R., and Bruce A. Demarest, 72.
[8] Ibid, 109.
[9] Erickson, *Christian Theology*, 953.
[10] Pinnock, 157.
[11] Ibid.
[12] Sanders, *No Other Name*, 233. See also Rhodes, Ron, *Heaven: the Undiscovered Country* (Eugene, OR: Harvest House Publishers, 1996), 133; Fackre, *What About Those Who Have Never Heard?"* Kindle location 343, 417.
[13] Pinnock, 53.
[14] Pinnock, 78.
[15] Sanders, *No Other Name,* 233 (The latter part of this quote is a citation from Alan Richardson, *Christian Apologetics*, 127.)
[16] Pinnock, Clark, et al, *The Openness of God: A Biblical Challenge to the Traditional Understanding of God*, Kindle location 1152.
[17] Ibid.
[18] Ibid, 18-19, 201, 1139.
[19] Pinnock, Clark H., "Open Theism: 'What is this? A New Teaching? – And with Authority?" (Mark 1:27), *Ashland Theological Journal,* Volume 34:0 (2002):44.
[20] Ibid, 45-46.
[21] Ware, Bruce A., *God's Lesser Glory: The Diminished God of Open Theism* (Wheaton: Crossways Books, 2000), Amazon Kindle edition, Kindle location 1902-1904. 1728-1901, 2360-2384.
[22] Ware, 1645-1714,
[23] Sanders, *No Other Name*, 233.
[24] Pinnock, 105.
[25] Ibid, 105-106.
[26] Carlson, Dwight, *Who'll Be in Heaven & Who Won't?* (Bloomington, IN: WestBow Press, 2012), Amazon Kindle Edition, Kindle location 229-348.
[27] Fackre, Amazon Kindle location, 379-399.

[28] LaSor, William Sanford, David Allen Hubbard, and Frederic Wm. Bush, *Old Testament Survey: The Message, Form, and Background of the Old Testament* (Grand Rapid: William B. Eerdmans, 1996), 493.
[29] Pinnock, 157.
[30] Fackre, Nash, Sanders, Kindle location 1160.
[31] Fackre, Kindle location 182.
[32] Ibid, Kindle location 182-192.
[33] Dennis L. Okholm and Timothy R. Phillips, eds., *More than One Way* (Grand Rapids: Zondervan, 1995), 24.

9   Fairness and God's Justice

Is God fair and just? This question often arises concerning those who have never heard the gospel. Will they suffer eternity separated from God although they have never heard the message of the gospel? Clark Pinnock writes,

> *"Is He the kind of God who would be capable of sitting by while large numbers perish...Does God take pleasure or actually get glory from the damnation of sinners as some traditions maintain...?*[1]

Those traditions to which Pinnock refers are evangelical exclusivists who believe in the biblical call of explicit proclamation of the gospel for salvation. That is, Pinnock takes issue that the proclamation of the gospel is the only way to salvation. The proponents of inclusivism, such as Pinnock and Sanders, began to question God's fairness and justice from the view of the proclamation of the gospel while ignoring the core of His character - righteousness. While the Bible frequently discusses justice, fairness is not a word normally applied to God, especially in the manner inclusivist use it.

Frank Thielman proposes a rare exception. He suggests that the word *"righteousness,"* as used in Romans 1:16-17 has the meaning of fairness with God. However, Thielman's presentation of God's fairness is substantially different from that of inclusivism. Inclusivism raises God's fairness from the perspective of whether God remained fair in allowing those who have not heard the gospel to perish.

Thielman takes a different approach. He relies on the third century theologian, Origen and context of the Greco-

FAIRNESS AND GOD'S JUSTICE

Roman world to ground his meaning of the word righteousness. Consequently, he comes to a very different conclusion than inclusivists. God's fairness according to Origen referred to *"the righteousness of God is the fairness of God in bringing salvation to all kinds of people regardless of their social standing or ethnic origins."*[2] That is, the cross of Christ demonstrated how God was *"fair, even-handed, and equitable in the way He distributed salvation."*[3]

Thielman's case is not one of whether God is fair at all but how He demonstrates His fairness. The inclusivist perspective passes judgment on God while Thielman explains God's fairness from His disclosure in His word. Inclusivists challenge God's fairness if He is as biblical exclusivism claims. Thielman defines how God is fair. That is, fairness pertains to Jew and Gentile, slave and free, male and female rather than to those who heard or fail to hear the gospel. The two approaches to fairness are categorically different.

Another major difference involves Thielman's reliance on Scripture as final authority. Inclusivists rely on speculation and their "control belief" as bases for biblical interpretation. As noted in chapter three, inclusivists define control beliefs as convictions they hold when reading the Scriptures. That is, they use their pre-formed convictions as interpretive measures rather than allowing the Scriptures to speak for themselves and drawing from them the truths God discloses to us. Such an approach shifts authority to the reader of Scriptures rather than in the Scriptural authors. A call for speculation in approaching Scripture is a call to render Scripture to a lessor authority.

When approaching the issue of fairness with God, inclusivists use it against those who oppose their position. It also becomes a means to defend their argument that God must provide another way other than the gospel for salvation or be unjust. Consequently, in defending their position, they raise the question, "Is God fair to condemn people to hell who have never heard the gospel?"

When the Bible discusses fairness, it does so on the human level (Deuteronomy 25:15; 2 Corinthians 8:13-14) and not between God and humanity except perhaps in the manner

Thielman proposes. Therefore, the basis for fairness with those favoring inclusivism places speculation above divine revelation. That is, inclusivists attempt to apply their reasoning and speculation to divine judgment and action rather than rely solely on the Scriptures as the disclosure of God's revealed will.

WHAT IS FAIR?

Fairness and justice refer to equal standing and often used interchangeably. All desire fair treatment from others, and often associate such fairness with the "golden rule" (Matthew 7:12). Treat others in like manner. Another word for fairness is equity. In the court of law, equity consists of a large portion of the law in civil matters. For this reason, the court of equity rose up under English common law for giving remedies for actions other than damages. People want fair treatment, and they often enter into contracts for seeking fair and equal treatment. This meaning aligns closely with the Scriptural testimony of fairness in terms of one's treatment of another. Equity pre-dates the court of equity and English common law, finding a large portion of its origins in Aristotle.[4]

Harold Cunningham refers to the Scriptures in discussing equity in relation to guidance in life,

> *"From the Hebrew we get the ideas 'to be straight' or 'even'; 'to make right'; 'to be acceptable'; 'to be straightforward or upright'; 'that which makes for concord and harmony'. In English law that which is equitable is that which is in accordance with natural justice, and when it is difficult to establish what is 'fair' it defers to a matter of conscience. Equity acts as a moderator by reforming the rigor and rough edges of the law."*[5]

FAIRNESS AND GOD'S JUSTICE

Aristotle saw differences between justice and equity because laws do not cover all circumstances. Such equity, fairness, or decency finds its place among finite beings whose finiteness and own failings as sinful people recognize the shortcomings of others. A sinful state impairs judgment and actions so that we commit personal or property trespasses with one another. When this happens, we want restoration, and we cry out for fairness.

However, what occurs between God and humanity? God is different from humanity, because He is of a different order and perfect in His being, nature, and ways. How then do imperfect and sinful individuals and a perfect God come to terms with justice, fairness, and equity? This question goes to the core of the issue inclusivists raise concerning those who have not heard the gospel. Is God just to send them to hell without even a hint of the saving message of the gospel? This question assumes that God is sending them to hell, an assumption that overlooks the sinful condition of humanity. People voluntarily take the path to condemnation through sinning against God and rejecting Him (John 3:18-20).

It is one matter to define fairness on the horizontal level among individuals of equal standing. However, when introducing God into the picture, one who is separate and distinct from the created order, an entirely different circumstance arises. Cunningham is helpful again with this matter when he states,

> *"Equity is an abiding principle. The various theologians describe it as 'a principle of eternal justice.' Like natural law, it is of an enduring substance. Calvin considers equity as belonging to the precepts of love, which are perpetual."*[6]

While Cunningham gives guidance on the horizontal level in our relationships with others concerning equity, he still stops short of applying fairness in relationship with God toward humanity. He brings out that equity is abiding and even universal in nature. Fairness and equity also, as Calvin subscribes, has relationship with love or that of doing right as the 'golden rule" implies (Matthew 7:12), making it a gift from God.

Different Bible versions render the words *"righteous"* and *"equity"* as translation of the same word. Is then *"fairness"* similar or the same as *"righteous?"* One distinction needs clarification before addressing the question of fairness related to those who have not heard the gospel. That distinction is that justice and fairness have their source in God. He gives people His gifts out of His mercy toward their fallen condition and as means of redemption. God's nature was righteous prior to the sin and fall of humanity. While the issue of equity or inequity is universal and enduring with others, it arises due to separation from our Creator. Equity or inequity comes into play from the perspective of the fall. Righteousness is eternal as existing in God's nature. We rightly honor God by extending His gifts to others as those called to the ministry of redemption.

At the same time, when we find God's display of His justice and righteousness not to our liking, many mistakenly call Him unfair or inequitable. God created humanity in His image and endowed individuals with numerous gifts. His intent with these gifts is for displaying His image toward others to draw all to worship Him. Fairness, equity, and righteousness are among those gifts. Because of humanity's fallen condition, the issue of unfairness arises and inhibits worship of Him.

W. Gary Phillips combines fairness with justice in God's economy. He writes,

> *"This* [justice] *is not simply an abstract problem in theodicy,*[f] *occupying the speculations of armchair theologians. The question of those in other religions – particularly of those who have*

---

[f] Theodicy derives from two Greek words: "theos" (God) and "dike" (justice). According to Patrick Sherry, it is an "explanation of why a perfectly good, almighty, and all-knowing God permits evil. The term literally means "justifying God" (Sherry, Patrick, Encyclopaedia Brittanica, n.d., http://www.britannica.com/EBchecked/topic/590596/theodicy. Accessed August 9, 2013.

FAIRNESS AND GOD'S JUSTICE

not heard the gospel – tugs deeply at one's emotions.

This challenge to theodicy is compounded when one reflects on the concept of absolute justice. People often (incorrectly) assume fairness may be approached inductively; surely it is a matter of common sense to examine all variables and then to state what is or is not "fair."[7]

When speaking of absolute justice, only one such justice exists and that is God's justice. To attempt to discover and make a judgment inductively from all finite variables, let alone variables existing beyond the realm of our knowledge, according to Phillips, is impossible. While we can use inductive reasoning to derive biblical teachings, one cannot exhaust the knowledge of God, and justice by way of His knowledge, inductively through finite reasoning. No being has the ability to exhaust the knowledge of God in one's thinking, and that limitation presents a problem for us in understanding and applying justice.

When we do not understand something, we tend to pass judgment on it or engage in speculation. Speculation goes beyond the Scriptures. On the other hand, God limits revelation to us, just as He limits spiritual illumination through the Holy Spirit. He does not reveal everything about Himself to us. Otherwise, we would be overwhelmed. He is infinite and we are finite and therefore unable to comprehend His infinite being and nature. Justice and righteousness are among those attributes of God we are unable to exhaust and fully comprehend about God. Consequently, our limitations and sinful state lend to speculations about God. Speculations can lead to judgments of Him if we do not find His justice and judgments to our liking.

Phillips also recognizes the elusiveness of fairness arises because *"other inequities besides ignorance vie for attention."*[8] He names such things as hearing the gospel from an abusive parent or from a pastor who committed adultery. These inequities exist among individuals and their interactions in societies. He concludes,

> *"All of these, through no fault of their own, would be negatively disposed toward the gospel."*[9]

However, God becomes the target of individual flexible, shifting, and subjective application of justice from a fairness standpoint. Rather than God being the judge, humanity judges Him by ever changing and speculative criteria dependent on culture, whim, individual preference, and one's own distorted idea of fairness. In conjecturing why such inequities occur, eyes rise heavenward, and people ask, "Why, God, did you not stop it or do something about it?" God receives the blame.

Those questioning God's fairness are like the grumbling laborers who questioned the vineyard owner's fairness in paying those who came later in the day compared to those who worked all day (Matthew 20:1-16). Jesus drew the conclusion that they questioned the vineyard owner's generosity and his ultimate decision as the proprietor, a position in which they possessed no right. They, like us, focused on themselves and not on God's generosity toward those who came later in the day. Fallen humanity turns God's generosity upside down and grumbles that God is unfair. A. B. Canady associates this parable to God giving eternal life (or kingdom life). God gives the gift of eternal life and access to His kingdom whether they received it early in life or much later. They all received the full gift just like the vineyard workers, some of whom came early in the day while others came much later.[10]

Regardless of the numerous counterarguments in defense of God's fairness, inclusivists still finds a way to charge God with unfairness. They in turn seek justification for another means to salvation apart from the proclaimed gospel of Jesus Christ. Counterarguments, then, are not enough to deflect charges of unfairness against God. Fairness stands as inclusivism's trump card in spite of counterarguments leveled against unfairness with God. Such charges amount to irrationalism, because they level charges against the truth. In turn, they turn people away from the gospel.

Those who question God's fairness fail to realize their tunnel vision or that they have on blinders like a horse. These blinders prevent them from seeing humanity's deeply sinful condition, on one side of the blinders. This blinder hinders the ability to comprehend one's own condition and flawed way of viewing truth. The blinder on the other side also prevents one from seeing God's righteous character. By displacing these two truths from one's sight, it becomes easy to overlook them when questioning God's fairness in light of those who never hear the gospel before they die.

UNLOCKING JUSTICE AND FAIRNESS

In chapter five, this book explored the key to understanding the gospel – the righteousness of God. The question concerning the destiny of those who have not heard the gospel must consider three major issues concerning the gospel: a) God, b) the message, and c) the recipients of the message. God's righteousness addresses each of these issues concerning the lost and salvation. It is the starting point for discussing not only the gospel but also concerning fairness. This discussion addresses the following questions regarding these three major points of the gospel:

1. Is God unfair or unjust toward the lost who do not hear the gospel?
2. Does a problem exist with the message of the gospel if another means and message is necessary?
3. Are people free and capable in themselves to respond to God for salvation apart from the revelation of Jesus Christ in the gospel?

NOTHING BUT THE GOSPEL

The Question of God's Fairness

The question of God's fairness and justice takes center stage with inclusivism. John Sanders, Clark Pinnock, and other inclusivists raise it and seek another way through their "wider hope" for satisfying God's fairness.[11]

Those subscribing to the "wider hope" pay little attention to the righteousness of God nor use it as the starting point for addressing the challenge of the unevangelized. While they raise the charges of injustice or unfairness with God with Evangelicals, they side step God's righteousness. They divide God's righteousness from His justice and consequently raise a false conclusion about His fairness.

The Bible treats justice and righteousness together. God's justice arises from His righteousness and finds its landing point with Christ's sacrificial death on the cross. Because He is righteous, God always does what is right in justice. The cross of Christ expresses God's full righteousness and justice. It judges sin and rescues the sinner. Creation does not even point to God's righteousness, for the gospel alone reveals it. How then could it mediate salvation?

Sanders rightly highlights the nature of God related to divine law and justice. However, he fails to pivot back to God's nature as righteous and His unswerving faithfulness arising from it related to the gospel and its message to the unsaved. He rightly states that the challenge of justice and fairness touches on other areas of theology. However, he seems to skip over the theology of God and the core of His character as righteous.[12]

In his argument for the incentive of missions, he creates two logical fallacies: a straw man argument[g] and a false

---

[g] A straw man argument is an attempt to attack a misrepresentation of an opponent's position. For example, John says George holds position A+B when in fact George's position is A+D. This does not stop John from attributing position A+B to George and then attacking it.

FAIRNESS AND GOD'S JUSTICE

dichotomy.[h] He uses both to bring divine justice into question. He states,

> *"If God wants all to be saved but none can be saved except those who hear about Christ, then God cannot save those He desires. Moreover, if salvation is entirely dependent on human preaching, then some people will suffer eternal damnation due to the failure and disobedience of Christians. Is this divine justice?"*

He assumes that those who believe the gospel proclamation to all the unsaved adhere to this line of reasoning (straw man argument). He also begins with two flawed premises and thereby reaches an erroneous conclusion from them.

First, Sanders positions God as wanting all to be saved (universalism) against those who eventually receive condemnation through rejecting God. He creates this false dichotomy and places God Himself in a trap. The trap is positioning God's desire against His righteous judgment toward those who reject His Son. Implied in this juxtaposition is that those who have no knowledge of the gospel cannot reject the Son. This, accordingly, is a conundrum for God and not for those who live in darkness. In his premise, Sanders ignores that a) God takes the initiative in sending the messenger, and b) that men love darkness rather than light (John 3:19) whether they heard the gospel or not. Love of darkness brings God's judgment on them. By ignoring these two truths, he presents a fallacious premise. Furthermore, Sanders himself does not believe that all will be saved, thereby catching him up in his own argument.

This argument also is another way of accusing God of injustice and unfairness. To turn the argument around, we can ask, "Can God have a desire He cannot will to execute?" This question is also similar to asking, "Can God create a stone He

---

[h] A false dichotomy assumes that there are only two options or positions and that no other positions exist. Consequently, the person using this argument assumes that an opponent must accept one or the other.

cannot lift?" That is, it places God against Himself by creating instances in which God would have to deny Himself by one way or another. One is creating something that would cause Him to deny His omnipotence. The other is denying Him the position of being above all He created. If God created a stone He could not lift, the stone would be greater than God, and God would then have to deny Himself, again. In both instances, it makes God false by denying His omnipotence and integrity. He would deny His integrity by subjecting Himself to human reasoning and its entrapments. On biblical grounds, God cannot deny Himself (2 Timothy 2:13), making the question a false and entrapping one based on finite human reasoning that attempts to ensnare God and to create Him in the image of the creature.

The Pharisees attempted to apply similar logic with Jesus. They showed Him a coin with Caesar's image on it and asked Him, "Is it lawful for us to pay taxes to Caesar or not" (Luke 20:22)? The reply Jesus gave uncovers their deception, "Why do you test me" (20:23)? They attempted to question His allegiance and integrity. We might ask that of Sanders and his reasoning. Sanders' conclusion about whether God truly is just, assuming His desire of salvation for all and His dependence on human preaching, is equally deceptive. It renders entrapment for God by pitting God against Himself, that is, God's alleged desire against His will and faithfulness. Furthermore, Sanders fails to connect "God's desire" with God's activity in the world in redemption and judgment. He is not passive. If God desires to save people, would He not take the action to insure it? Sanders fails to address this question.

His second argument of the salvation dependent on human preaching does not follow from his first argument of God's desire, making his argument disjointed. It also makes his conclusive rhetorical question about divine justice unrelated to his argument. He assumes the success of the gospel and salvation dependent entirely on human preaching rather than on God's initiative. However, he fails to show how such dependency on human action reflects God's desire and initiative to carry out His will in salvation and judgment on unbelief. It is also a false premise that salvation rests entirely on human preaching. Such a premise leaves out Christ's death on the cross and the work of the Holy Spirit. His arguments are simply set ups for accusations against God.

Sanders reduces the effectiveness of God's justice to the supposed failure of Christian obedience, making Him dependent on humanity. At best, he ends up blaming God for human failure in a similar manner that a person asks, "Why, God, did you not stop it or do something about it?" He fails to raise the most fundamental truth from which the Apostle Paul begins with the gospel: the righteousness of God for salvation.

A right understanding of the gospel is that salvation depends on God and not on human effort. While God uses human effort in the preaching of the gospel, He does the saving and insures salvation comes to the unsaved by sending the messenger. God's righteousness insures that He keeps His promises and faithfully executes His will in salvation. God not only makes salvation accessible by sending the messenger to the unsaved, but He also reaches out redemptively with a powerful hand to save according to His will.

Is the Gospel Message Inadequate and Unfair?

Inclusivism's reliance on the knowledge from the light of creation raises the question for this section. The lost requiring another avenue implies the inadequacy of the gospel message. That is, the gospel's content is not sufficient to save all. Rather, according to inclusivists, it requires a supplement for those who have not heard it. Furthermore, if some do not hear the gospel, this places a burden on God to prove that His gospel is fair for all. The gospel's adequacy does not so much rely on one hearing it but on God's righteousness and power to execute it. Inclusivists do not appear to have a clear grasp of this truth.

In sidestepping the righteousness of God, Sanders and other inclusivists ignore Paul's reason for the power of God found in the gospel. That power arises from His righteousness, showing His sovereign will in His message the gospel (Romans 1:17). God's righteousness also refutes any charge of unfairness

with God. God exercised His righteousness in Jesus on the cross in the three ways mentioned earlier:
1. The judgment on sin fell on Christ (2 Corinthians 5:21).
2. Christ became our righteousness (1 Corinthians 1:30), both as Mediator and Savior.
3. God's eternal power and righteousness reside in Him alone, and these two characteristics of God are what make the gospel. Without power, the gospel would be ineffective. Without righteousness, there would be no gospel.

By reducing God's justice and "fairness" to dependency on human obedience, Sanders and inclusivists dismantle the true biblical gospel and remove the two pillars on which it stands: God's power and righteousness, foundations of His faithfulness.

These two pillars in the gospel not only expose the weakness in Sanders argument, but they also give the reason for the hope that is in us. Hope stands on the power of God and the righteousness He exhibited through Christ. Christ rose from the dead through the power and promise of God. This same power gives us new life through the Holy Spirit. Therefore, the righteousness and power of God is the gospel in its fullest sense for all the unsaved, because they exhibit His enduring faithfulness upon which salvation rests. Therefore, is the gospel message inadequate or unfair? The answer is NO, because God is faithful.

Does Free Will Circumvent the Power of the Gospel?

Inclusivism places more power in individual free will than in the power of the gospel as God's declaration of salvation. That is, according to inclusivism and its corresponding free will theism,

"The all-powerful God delegates power to the creature, making himself vulnerable. In

FAIRNESS AND GOD'S JUSTICE

giving us dominion over the earth, God shares power with the creature...God allows the world to be affected by the power of the creature and takes risks accompanying any genuine relatedness."[13]

Accordingly, individuals apply the power of the will to pierce spiritual deadness to respond to God. Consequently, sin does not hinder or distort individual free will from recognizing and sufficiently responding to the true God through the knowledge from the light of creation for salvation without turning to idolatry.

This speculation runs contrary to Scripture. It also does injustice to God's righteousness. As the righteous God, He remains faithful in saving those He calls (1 Thessalonians 5:24). The Apostle Paul declared all without exception are slaves to sin and dead to God's righteousness. All are subjected to the power of Satan and darkness (Romans 6:16-19; Ephesians 2:1-3). Paul ties God's righteousness to His power (omnipotence) (Romans 1:16-17) and His capacity to know the future (omniscience) in His faithful care over those who trust Him for salvation (Romans 8:29).[i] The certainty of His oversight and faithful care is the essence of His righteousness. That is, God remains faithful to His promises to the very end.

Furthermore, His faithfulness requires nothing less than His all-powerful word and not one who delegates His power to the creature. Speculation cannot explain away the clear teaching

---

[i] Foreknowledge as Paul discusses it in this passage is rooted in a guarantee or certainty of purpose. The calling of God arises from His electing purpose, and His purpose is the overarching umbrella for the destiny of the elect as noted in the progression of Paul's thought process here: purpose, foreknew, predestined, conformation to Christ, justification, and glorification." If foreknowledge meant that God simply knew in advance that which would come about, then He would be at best a passive God with just knowledge of events. However, the next phrase expands on the meaning of "foreknew" – predestined. God assures this process of His will so that Paul can state without doubt, "What shall we say to these things? If God is for us, who can be against us" (Romans 8:31)? The answer to this rhetorical question is that no one can prevent God from guaranteeing His faithfulness to the elect. Without the capacity to be faithful, He would be unrighteous.

of the Scriptures concerning God's knowledge of the future and His power to carry it out.

God's righteousness and power trump the idea of a shifting notion of fairness arising from faulty reasoning. Rather, righteousness is the core nature of God[14] demonstrated in His judgment on sin He displayed through Christ on the cross.[15] In this demonstration, God's righteousness cuts two ways. First, it shows God's judgment on sin by issuing a penalty for it. Second, God placed the penalty for sin on Christ so that it did not rest on those who believed. In both His judgment on sin and His provision for it, God fulfilled His faithfulness in the promise He made to Abraham about the Messiah. This fulfillment was the pinnacle of His righteousness.

In doing so, God demonstrated His grace by reconciling rebellious sinners to Himself through faith in Christ (Romans 3:23-25). The entire teaching of justification by faith rests on and rises from the righteousness of God. Jesus Christ alone made justification a reality. In the righteous act He performed by giving His life *"the abundance of grace and of the gift of righteousness will reign in life through the One, Jesus Christ"* (Romans 5:17). This righteous gift is the proclaimed gospel unmatched by any other man created message.

Any challenge to God's fairness must confront the gospel, its disclosure of the state of humanity, and the truth that salvation begins with God (John 15:16; 17:6; Ephesians 1:4; Hebrews 2:13). He sets the terms for salvation and establishes the redemptive message. God fulfills them with those He calls and saves from among the lost. His faithfulness defines His mercy. No one has any say with its definition or application, because God is the source of mercy. He created men and women to worship Him and to accept His loving and righteous authority. If God is both righteous and infinitely loving, who among fallen and sinful humanity can rightly question the mercy and generosity that proceeds from His righteousness and love?

FAIRNESS AND GOD'S JUSTICE

NOTES

[1] Pinnock, 18.
[2] Thielman, Frank, "God's Righteousness as God's Fairness in Romans 1:17: An Ancient Perspective on a Significant Phrase," *Journal of the Evangelical Theological Society*, Volume 54:1 (March 2011): 48.
[3] Ibid, 36.
[4] Cunningham, Harold G., God's Law, "General Equity" and the Westminster Confession of Faith," *Tyndale Bulletin*, Volume 58:2 (2007): 306.
[5] Ibid, 312.
[6] Ibid, 312.
[7] Phillips, W. Gary, "Evangelical Pluralism: A Singular Problem," *Bibliotheca Sacra*, Volume 151:602 (April 1994): 141
[8] Ibid, 152.
[9] Ibid.
[10] Canady, A. B., "The Parable of the Generous Vineyard Owner (Matthew 20:1-16)," *Southern Baptist Journal of Theology*, Volume 13:3 (Fall 2009), 44.
[11] Fackre, et al, Kindle Edition, 180 (See also Pinnock, Clark, *A Wideness of God's Mercy: The Finality of Jesus Christ in a World of Religions*, 149-180).
[12] Fackre, Nash, and Sander, Kindle location 136.
[13] Pinnock, Clark, et al, *The Openness of God,* Kindle location 1367.
[14] Erickson, *Christian Theology*, 968.
[15] Ibid, 969-970.

10 Destiny of Those Not Knowing Jesus Christ

Where do we obtain our answers for addressing the destiny of the lost – those who do not know Jesus Christ? Since the question of the destiny of the lost focuses primarily on God, it is really from Him alone an adequate answer derives. The Scriptures are God's word through which He informs us of the way to eternal life with Him. To seek answers from our own speculations or other sources as final authority is to minimize or dismiss God's authority.

Inclusivism's claim of faith and salvation through what God reveals in creation diminishes the proclamation of the gospel for the destiny of the lost. The implication of this dismissal is that God cannot be fair and possess integrity if some do not hear the gospel.[1] How could the gospel be the saving message for everyone if, according to inclusivists, a vast number are shut out from it and only a few hear of it and receive it?

Inclusivism downplays that God initiated, defined, and revealed redemption, its meaning, and the message for it. Inclusivists also redefine sovereignty to diminish God's knowledge and power. Scriptures declare that God provides for salvation and promises to bring it to the lost (Ezekiel 36:36; Isaiah 45:1-8; 51:5-6; John 10:27-30). His integrity and character are at stake concerning their salvation. Given these truths, we can only conclude that He alone possesses the authority and power to carry out what He determines to do.

It does not follow that salvation only through the proclaimed gospel is an unfair proposition. If we use this logic, then we could also conclude that it is unfair of God not to use the Quran, Veda, the Analects, or Bhavagad Gita to draw people to salvation. These works arose from those where the gospel is scarce. Would then God be fair to use works of other religions for faith unto salvation? God's authority expresses itself through the medium He desires – His word as He communicates it through whom He chooses to reveal it. As His word, the Bible is our final authority for addressing theological and related issues, which also includes the proclamation of the gospel and God's saving activity.

God in His faithfulness reveals in the Scriptures all we need to live lives of saving faith and in relationship with Him. They are sufficient. God does not leave us without witness to His will. We can and must trust Him to understand it and to know Him. This brings us to the knotty challenge concerning how the Bible answers the question about the destiny of the lost and how salvation reaches the unsaved. Working our way through how the biblical authors address the issue allows us to arrive at a reply that fits the question.

LETTER OF ROMANS AND THE GOSPEL

The interpretive process gives a roadmap for discovering and understanding the message of a given biblical passage. God discloses His truths through the inspired biblical authors. We discover and seek to understand what God discloses. When we encounter difficulties in our spiritual walk or with understanding God, His ways, and how we relate to Him, our authority is God and His revelation. Inquiring about the unsaved is no different.

God saved us to become His ambassadors of reconciliation (2 Corinthians 5:18-20). We can be confident that the same God who called us also will be with us in reaching the lost. He remains faithful toward accomplishing His redemptive purpose (1 Thessalonians 5:24). Since He is sovereign, He anticipates the challenging struggles and questions we ask about His redemptive mission. His word to us replies to them.

Although the destiny of the lost troubles us, and it should, we can be confident that God has already addressed questions about those who have not heard the gospel for their salvation.

One place where we discover the question about those who have never heard the gospel is Romans 10. Paul also struggled with the same challenges as Clark Pinnock, John Sanders, and other inclusivists over the destiny of the unsaved. However, in his struggles, he did not speculate but relied on the Holy Spirit and Scriptures for disclosing truth and divinely revealed answers.

In Romans 10, Paul expresses his deep-felt love for and desires to reach his own people, the Jews. He also encountered the same issues inclusivists posed. His letter to the Romans suggests He received similar questions against the gospel inclusivists raised about God's fairness. If the gospel of Jesus Christ is the genuine message of salvation, why do so few Jews accept it? Pinnock also pointed to what he considered a "fewness doctrine" of Evangelicals. That is, since a vast number of people will enter eternity without hearing the gospel, the proclamation of the gospel means that only a few will enter heaven's kingdom.

Concerning the Jews, the questions continue. Were they not God's chosen people? Did God leave His chosen people for the Gentiles since the Gentiles appeared to outnumber the Jews in receiving salvation? If the gospel was indeed the message from God for salvation, did God renege on His promise He made to Abraham? Has God broken faithfulness to His people and laid claim to another group of people with the Gentiles? Paul provides methodical reasoning in his reply to these types of questions implied in Romans 10. He countered them by explaining how God remained faithful in fulfilling His promise by appealing to God's righteousness.

He anticipated these questions through his original premise in chapter one about the basis of the gospel – the righteousness of God (Romans 1:16-17). He claimed his fellow Jews failed to grasp the gospel because they suppressed the knowledge of God (10:2-3). The core element of that knowledge consisted of the righteousness of God. They failed to submit to God's righteousness because they ignored it, and in ignoring it, they trusted heritage. In chapters one (1:16-17) and ten (10:4-6), Paul connects the gospel, faith, and God's righteousness. The Jews rejected the way of faith and took their status as God's chosen people through Abraham as an unconditional given. In other words, their faith rested on legacy instead faith in God's righteousness.

Paul rebuked them for their misplaced faith by directing their attention to the true object of faith, the Lord Jesus Christ (10:8-9). Trusting in their heritage in Moses left them without hope because of the law's demands on them and their violation of those demands (10:5). Besides, as he wrote in his letter to the Galatians, the promise came 430 years before the law and trumped it (Galatians 3:17-18). The shortsightedness of the Jews hindered them from recognizing the 430-year gap in their thinking. It also prevented them from understanding that the promise to Abraham centered on Christ in whom they needed to place their trust. Therefore, Paul concluded,

> *"For 'whoever calls upon the name of the Lord shall be saved'"* (10:13).

At this point, Paul commences a series of questions among which one stands out central to the discussion about those who have not heard the gospel,

> *"How then shall they call upon Him in whom they have not believed? <u>And how shall they believe in Him of whom they have not heard?</u> And how shall they hear without a preacher? And how shall they preach unless they are sent?"* (10:14-15)

The context and the occasion differ from those who currently pose the question about the "unevangelized." However, it directly relates to the challenge about the destiny of those who have not heard the gospel. It is an appropriate beginning for a direct answer to similar questions people ask about the lost.

In his series of questions, Paul has a sequential logic in asking them. One question leads to another and that one to still another. From this series of questions, Paul carries the reader toward several conclusions that support one of the grand themes that runs through this letter. That theme is God's righteousness prevails and is the basis for the salvation of the lost anywhere, anytime, and in any culture. He expresses His righteousness in His faithfulness to His people – those whom He saves. The means through which God expresses His righteousness to and through His people is Jesus Christ.

The contexts of these questions are also extremely important for gaining an understanding of Paul's answers and conclusions. The various contexts drive the intent behind Paul asking these series of questions. To understand the four questions Paul asks in Romans 10:14-15, the entire context of Romans 9-11 must receive careful scrutiny. The context of Paul's argument that moves toward these four questions actually begins at Romans 9:1.

A cursory reading of the beginning of Romans 9 gives the impression that Paul launches into a very different subject than what he discussed in Romans 1-8. An appearance of a lack of transition from his concluding remarks in Romans 8:39 seem to indicate a pivot into another direction. Where is any transition statement? Many have taken the abrupt beginning of Romans 9 to suggest a parenthesis or sidebar discussion. Others see Romans 9-11 as a continuation from the first eight chapters. It is worth addressing these conflicting sides, because they could lead to very different reasons for Paul's four questions in Romans 10:14-15. A proper understanding of Paul's four questions in this passage depends on an accurate assessment of how he leads up to them from the beginning of Romans 9.

THE FRAMWORK OF ROMANS 9-11

Some interpreters claim that Romans 9-11 is a parenthesis or separate argument from the rest of the letter. They suggest that Paul takes the time to address another challenge concerning the Jews and their destiny in God's sovereign plan. These interpreters believe that he then returns at Romans 12 to where he left off at the end of Romans 8. William Newell states,

DESTINY OF THOSE NOT KNOWING JESUS CHRIST

"Paul turns aside from the glorious exposition of Grace, in the first eight chapters, to the explanation of God's present dealings with Israel."[2]

He calls these three chapters "a parenthesis"[3] or a departure from the argument of the first eight chapters. That is, Paul turns aside from God's redemptive plan outlined in the first eight chapters to deal with the question of Israel in God's continuing plan. Newell suggests that Paul needed to address several questions about Israel, especially with the blessings of salvation coming to the Gentiles. He writes,

"Where then is the Divine faithfulness? The question, therefore, is, how to reconcile the "no distinction between Jew and Greek" message that Paul is here preaching, with God's former manner of speech to Israel..."[4]

He appears to echo Paul's question – *"I say then, has God cast away His people"* (Romans 11:1)? Newell appropriately emphasizes mercy and grace as qualities of God in the redemption of His people. However, they alone do not fully capture the central source of these two expressions of God – His righteousness. Paul emphasizes God's righteousness from the beginning of his letter to his conclusion. The central part of the gospel he sets forth concerns God's righteousness (Romans 1:16-17). John Calvin affirms *"nowhere else does God reveal to us His righteousness."*[5] Douglas Moo expands on this further when he states,

"But what is this "righteousness of God"?...in asking this question, we get into a matter crucial to the interpretation of Romans, as the phrase occurs eight times in Romans...and only once elsewhere in Paul's writings."[6]

Moo also notes that this center of the gospel has also stirred up much controversy among scholars because of four interpretations of the phrase *"the righteousness of God."* These four interpretations are as follows:

1. the justice of God
2. the faithfulness of God
3. the status of righteousness given by God
4. the act of putting people in the right performed by God[7]

These four interpretations are an attempt to explain God's righteousness and His dealings with humanity. Given the difficulty in understanding the meaning of righteousness, the task of addressing Paul's four questions in Romans 10 becomes even more important. If we treat this letter to the Romans as a single argument concerning the gospel, its message becomes clear as we focus on God's righteousness. If we view Romans 1:16-17 as its starting point, it follows that a connection exists between that passage and Romans 9-11. Therefore, we must link them for understanding Paul's answer to the four questions he poses in chapter ten.

One of the places in which God's righteousness appears is in Romans 10:3 where it appears twice. Paul's use of this phrase here makes the connection between Romans 1:16-17 and his answers to the four questions in Romans 10 of greater importance. His answers also apply to the destiny of those not hearing the gospel. Therefore, since the phrase *"the righteousness of God"* appears in the beginning of Romans 10, it has a direct bearing in answering the critical question: *And how shall they believe in Him of whom they have not heard* (Romans 10:14)?

ROMANS: ONE MESSAGE THROUGHOUT

Other commentators of Romans consider no such parenthesis. Rather they view chapters 9-11 as a continuing argument from the preceding chapters and a logical conclusion from them.[8] How do we determine which approach best fits Paul's argument? Douglas Moo states,

DESTINY OF THOSE NOT KNOWING JESUS CHRIST

"Other interpreters have suggested that the chapters are a kind of personal excursus, as Paul the Jew expresses concern for his kinfolk. But when we remember the overall purpose of Romans, these chapters fit quite naturally into the argument of the letter. Paul is presenting his gospel. He especially wants to show how it embraces Gentiles without breaking continuity with the Old Testament. The relatively small number of Jews that have become Christians is a severe challenge to this continuity. God seems to have abandoned the people he chose and made promises to in the Old Testament in favor of a new people. If this were so, then the connection between Old Testament and New Testament would be broken, and God would be revealed as capricious and undependable.[9]

Working from a Core Premise

Moo's remarks address Paul's core premise in Romans 1:16-17 – the gospel finds its home in God's righteousness and its revelation through His promises and consequent faithfulness. God's righteousness acts as an umbrella over His purpose from the beginning of history when He revealed Messianic promises to Adam (Genesis 3:15), Abraham, and his descendants (Genesis 12:1-3) until Christ came through the incarnation. Consequently, Moo contends that Paul's presentation of the gospel runs through the entire letter without a parenthesis. Rather, Romans 9-11 makes up a central piece of that gospel. These chapters contend that God did not forget the Jews although they seemed to be few in number in responding to the gospel.

Because of this continuity in this letter, Paul can easily answer the question concerning the destiny of those who have not heard the gospel. The answer is similar to the one he supplied for the Jews, which he addresses in Romans 9-11. The rest of this chapter examines both issues and shows how the answer concerning the Jews and the destiny of those who have never heard the gospel dovetail.

What is Paul's intent of writing the letter to the Romans? What is the logical progression of his thinking and argument through it? What prompted the questions in chapter ten? These questions will enable us to understand Paul's intent in this chapter. To grasp Paul's answer to these questions, we must return to the main thesis he puts forth at the very beginning of this letter (Romans 1:16-17) and how his argument in chapters 9-11 progresses from it.

In chapter ten, we identified that Paul makes God's righteousness as one of the dominant themes of this letter. It is foundational to the gospel. Understanding the reason for Paul's questions in chapter ten relies on Paul's theology of God, especially His righteousness. Douglas Moo identifies God's righteousness as integrity. God's righteousness is his internal consistency and the expression of that consistency toward His creation in doing right with it and with humanity specifically. Doing right as Moo notes includes four areas: justice, faithfulness, status, and in the right. All of these find their source in the God who is righteous or the One who has total and complete integrity in all He is and in all He does.

This discussion of God's righteousness transitions naturally to Paul's explanation of the Jews in God's redemptive purpose. When He gave His promise to Abraham, it depended on His righteousness. Paul's discussion in Romans 9-11 illustrates how God remains righteous through the fulfillment of His promise to Abraham to the Jews and the Gentiles.

In Romans 9, Paul introduces His sorrow and grief over the Jews. He longs for their salvation (Romans 9:1-3). He recognizes God's generosity, benefits, and choice of them in history as His people (9:4). He takes us to the very first expression of God's righteousness in dealing with them – His promise (9:9). These benefits, choice, and promise conjure up Abraham, because he is central to God's Messianic focus. Paul's rhetorical question and his answer to it (9:14) punctuates that God remains faithful to His promise to those whom He

DESTINY OF THOSE NOT KNOWING JESUS CHRIST

chose from among all the nations of the earth. This question poses a negative challenge to God's righteousness Paul anticipates from his opponents: "Is God unrighteous?" Paul's reply is firm and to the point: *"Certainly not!"* (9:14)

A Return to God's Promise, Justice, and Fairness

Moo asserts that faithfulness is a key expression of God's righteousness,[10] and His promises rely on His faithfulness. He continues in His faithfulness and purpose in laying His claim on Abraham's children, that is, the children of the promise (9:8). It is because of God's faithfulness to His promises that Paul's reply is so forceful to his rhetorical question, *"Is there unrighteousness with God?"* Such a question is unthinkable.

To support the emphatic reply to his question, Paul takes the reader back to the Exodus and the example God made of Pharaoh to demonstrate that nothing or no one can stand in God's way of demonstrating His faithfulness to His chosen people (9:16-29). Four hundred years existed between God's pronouncement of deliverance and His actions to deliver the Jews from Egypt. The example of the Exodus sets the stage for God's mercy (9:16, 18), a mercy so hostile to humanity's way of thinking, especially the Jews, that Paul anticipates the question of God's unrighteousness and injustice.

Many bring up the fairness of God in a similar way concerning the question about the destiny of those who have never heard the gospel. In surfacing any thought of God as unjust, Paul turns the argument back to those who question God as fair if He leaves some without the gospel. He blunts the argument of injustice with God when he raises another question, *"But indeed, O man, who are you to reply against God"* (9:20).

Douglas Moo unpacks Paul's argument against injustice with God with the following,

> "In asking whether someone or something is "unjust," we presume a standard of "justness," or right, that we can use to judge that person or action. What standard do we apply when we ask

whether God is unjust? The minute we ask the question, the answer becomes obvious: we finite and sinful human beings can measure God only by the standards that he himself has revealed to us. Imposing our own standards of "right" on the God who created us and stands far above us would be the height of folly and presumption."[11]

Justice from blindness or the cover of sin's darkness places us at a handicap or disadvantage with such questions concerning God's justice. Sin is folly, but judging God raises that folly to a much higher level according to Moo. To judge the infinite God from a finite position is immensely presumptuousness. However, to add sinfulness to the mix of finiteness in judging God is complete arrogance and contempt for God's mercy.

The charge toward whether or not God is fair cuts to the core of His righteousness. If He is not fair, how can He be righteous? Righteousness and justice pivot on what or who defines it. Moo sufficiently addressed this in his previously cited remarks by referring to the measurements or standard used for determining righteousness. When asking who measures God and His integrity, the answer becomes clear. In citing humanity's finite and sinful state, Moo shows that no one is capable of judging God or His acts. For in doing so, that same judgment comes back to haunt those making it. Therefore, Moo refines the question, *"Has God acted according to His revealed will?"*[12]

If we accept God's measurement, we have hope that we can entrust our lives with the God of all creation. If we do not accept His measurement and judgment, no hope exists. Giving up and dying is better than facing an unrighteous and unjust God. However, God's revealed righteousness delivers us from such an assessment with a more sure foundation.

Consequently, a properly stated question renders a more accurate answer. Moo again informs us that the Apostle Paul transitions to the answers in Romans 9:15-18. God is not a tyrant but a merciful God. Humanity's resistance to His will inhibits us from understanding His mercy and turning to Him.

A Righteous Foundation for God's Faithfulness

Prior to answering the questions in Romans 10:14-15, Paul wants the church in Rome to realize that God's promise does not stop with Israel. To do this, he must spend time developing his argument concerning God's faithfulness to Israel as well as His call of the Gentiles. This development is germane to replying to those who question God's justice as well as to the questions in Romans 10:14-15. God's promise includes both ethnic groups: the Jews and the Gentiles.

Notice throughout Romans 9-11 Paul switches back and forth between the Jews and Gentiles, addressing the status of one and then the other. By basing salvation on promise (9:8) rather than physical lineage, Paul opens the door for salvation to those outside of physical Israel, that is, the Gentiles. In Romans 9:23-26, he makes this entrance to the Gentiles explicit by having God's promise rooted in the words of Hosea the prophet,

> *"I will call those who were not my people,*
> *'My people,' and I will call her who was unloved,*
> *'My beloved'"* (Hosea 2:23).

He quotes Hosea a second time to confirm that God unmistakably spoke of the Gentiles regarding God's redemptive promise,

> *"And in the very place where it was said to them, 'You are not my people,' there they will be called the sons of the living God"* (1:10).

By making this claim first, Paul is able to provide the basis for answers to his questions in Romans 10:14-15 concerning the proclamation of the gospel to the lost. He is also able to answer the rhetorical question haunting the Jews relative to the scant number who responded to the gospel and received salvation:

NOTHING BUT THE GOSPEL

"Did God fail in fulfilling His promise to Abraham that his offspring would inherit the promise?" (Romans 9:6)

Recall that Clark Pinnock surfaces to what he refers as the "fewness doctrine."[13] That is, Pinnock appears unknowingly to raise the same argument as the Jews concerning so few saved. Paul replies to the Jews and to anyone else raising the question of a few saved. He claims that the gospel proclamation is God's initiative according to His purpose and righteousness and not according to the dictates and judgments of any man, for Paul states,

> *"What shall we say then? Is there injustice with God? Absolutely not! For He says to Moses, "I will have mercy on whom I will have mercy, and I will have compassion on whom I will have compassion. So then, it does not depend on human desire or exertion, but on God who shows mercy"* (Romans 9:14-16).

In his statement, Paul joins God's justice, righteousness, and mercy. Those who question God's justice, as Moo wrote, also question God's love and mercy. Gabriel Fackre poses the question,

> *"How could God be fair to the countless millions before and since Christ who never heard the saving word?"*[14]

Clark Pinnock pens this thought in a similar manner,

> *"Is he the kind of God who would be capable of sitting by while large numbers perish, or the kind to seek them out patiently or tirelessly? Does God take pleasure and actually get glory from the damnation of sinners as some traditions maintain, or is God appalled and saddened by this prospect?"*[15]

DESTINY OF THOSE NOT KNOWING JESUS CHRIST

While these questions arise from the prospect of those who have not heard the gospel, they address the same issue to which Paul replies in a more compact form, *"Is there injustice with God?"*

Truth has a number of applications. The truth concerning God's character and actions replies to any number of questions related to the saving message of the gospel. Getting the truth about God's righteousness and corresponding faithfulness right will inevitably get the message of the gospel right as it bears on God's purpose in the redemption of the lost. It is for this reason that Paul spends so much time defending God's justice and righteousness.

The True Nature of Divine Mercy

Paul realized that when people questioned God's justice, they also questioned His mercy. Paul addresses both God's justice and mercy in the development of his argument throughout Romans 9-11. The word *mercy* appears more times in Romans 9-12 than the number of times prior to these chapters. Paul subsequently highlights the mercy of God as an application from these three chapters when he states,

> *"I beseech you therefore, brethren, by the mercies of God, that you present your bodies a living sacrifice, holy, acceptable to God, which is your reasonable service"* (Romans 12:1).

That is, since God showed mercy to us, He calls upon us to embrace it. Embracing it means casting aside any doubt of God's justice and being prepared to proclaim the gospel of mercy to the lost. This declaration from Paul is a direct application of God's mercy in the prior three chapters. God's mercy is not capricious. Rather it is rooted in His righteousness because it is the expression of His faithfulness. Being a righteous God moves Him to show mercy to the unrighteous, and He does so through the cross of Christ as Paul earlier explained,

> "...*whom* [Jesus Christ] *God set forth as a propitiation by His blood through faith to demonstrate His righteousness, because in His forbearance God had passed over the sins that were previously committed"* (Romans 3:25).

The New English Bible Translation has a more appropriate rendering for this passage especially regarding the word *"propitiation,"*

> *"God publicly displayed him at his death as the mercy seat* [propitiation] *accessible through faith. This was to demonstrate his righteousness, because God in his forbearance had passed over the sins previously committed"*[16] (NET)

The mercy seat is the place for atonement (propitiation). The word ἱλαστήριον (hilasterion) refers to that mercy seat or the golden slab that covered the Ark of the Covenant within the innermost room of the tabernacle. The word appears twice in the New Testament (Romans 3:25 and Hebrews 9:5). In the Epistle to the Hebrews, it literally refers to the gold slab whereas Paul applies it metaphorically to Jesus Christ who represents the mercy seat or in the redemptive sense the propitiation for sins.

The author of the Epistle to the Hebrews expands on its application by declaring that the literal mercy seat acted as a symbol (9:9) of what Christ accomplished (9:11-14). While Paul suggests in Romans that Christ was that mercy seat, the Epistle to the Hebrews pictures Christ as High Priest and sacrifice on the mercy seat. Therefore, when taken together, the entire picture of the mercy seat, the priest, and the sacrifice all center on Christ who metaphorically represent all of them in a stunning portrayal of redemption.

Daniel Bailey confirms Paul's allusion to the mercy seat in Romans 3:25,

DESTINY OF THOSE NOT KNOWING JESUS CHRIST

> *"By contrast, a more specialised allusion to the biblical 'mercy seat' (which is not a gift to the gods) does fit Paul's context, with plenty of support from lexicography (cf. LXX Pentateuch). Paul focuses on 'the law and the prophets' and then more particularly on the Song of Moses in Exodus 15. The combination of God's righteousness and redemption in Exodus 15:13 (ὡδηήγησας τῇ δικαιοσύνῃ σου τὸν λαόν σου τοῦτον, ὅν ἐλυτρώσω[a]) closely parallels Romans 3:24 (δικαιόω[b] and ἀπολύτρωσις[c]). Furthermore, Exodus 15:17 promises that the exodus would lead to a new, ideal sanctuary established by God himself. God's openly setting out of Jesus as the new ἱλαστήριον —the centre of the sanctuary and focus of both the revelation of God (Ex. 25:22; Lv. 16:2; Nu. 7:89) and atonement for sin (Leviticus 16)—fulfils this tradition."*[17]

Through his letter to the Romans, Paul weaves mercy, righteousness, and justice as expressions of God's redemptive purpose. Christ is central to this purpose expressed on the cross. God pronounced His judgment on sin through the cross. Christ satisfied the penalty for sin and secured redemption for Jew and Gentile. In Him God fulfilled His promise, power, and provision for salvation.

The only other place Paul uses mercy is in Romans 15 where he concludes his argument for the redemption of both Jew and Gentile. He declares,

> *"For I tell you that Christ became a servant to the circumcised to show God's*

---

[a] NKJV translation: *"You in your mercy have led forth the people whom You have redeemed; You have guided them in your strength to Your holy habitation."*

[b] *"being justified..."* [Transliteral: dikaioō] NKJV

[c] Signifies redemption or a price paid to redeem [Transliteral: apolytrōsis]. See also Romans 8:23; 1 Corinthians 1:30; Ephesians 1:7, 14.

truthfulness in order to confirm the promises given to the patriarchs and in order that the Gentiles might glorify God for His mercy" (Romans 15:8).

His statement illustrates the difference between divine mercy and human mercy. Human mercy has its limits. Human failure and frailty cut short truthfulness and the full capacity to keep promises. Human mercy wavers. Frustration, impatience, prejudice, and similar human traits tend to short circuit or exhaust mercy because of underlying prejudice for upsetting truthful and faithful living. The attitude of the Jews toward the Gentiles exhibited such short-circuited mercy. They were appalled that God showed mercy to the Gentiles. This pretentiousness led to their arrogance and rejection of God's righteousness, which encompassed both Jew and Gentile (Romans 10:2-3).

The startling truth the Jews overlooked is that God's love of the Gentiles existed even in the giving of the Law to the Jews (Exodus 22:21; 23:9; Leviticus 19:34; Deuteronomy 10:19). The Scriptures inform us of God's enduring mercy (1Chronicles 16: 34, 41; Psalms 118:1-4, 29; 136) and grace which extends beyond the bounds of race or nationality.

In bringing in the circumcised again in relation to the promises given to the patriarchs, Paul echoes the benefits of which he spoke in Romans 9:4-5 concerning the Jews: *"the adoption, the glory, the covenants, the giving of the law, the worship, and the promises."* Paul follows these benefits by citing the patriarchs,

"To them belong the patriarchs, and from their race, according to the flesh, is the Christ, who is God over all, blessed forever. Amen" (9:5).

The above passage speaks of God's bountiful mercy to the Jews. However, God did not intend that His mercy stop with the Jews. The Law and the prophets spoke loudly that mercy also included

DESTINY OF THOSE NOT KNOWING JESUS CHRIST

the Gentiles. God's mercy saturates Romans 9-11 for both Jew and Gentile.

The Gospel of Righteousness and Mercy

Paul connects his conclusion in Romans 15:8-9 to chapter nine through the citation of the patriarchs (9:5) and God's mercy (9:15-16, 18, 23). He also traces the line of the promise of redemption from the patriarchs (Abraham, Isaac, and Jacob) to the promise realized in Christ. This connection supports the cohesiveness and continuity of Paul's argument from the beginning of Romans to its conclusion. It also shows how the entire letter proclaims the gospel and the urgent need for its proclamation. The weaving of his themes of promise, the righteousness of God, and mercy, as well as his reference to the patriarchs, specifically to Abraham, further demonstrate the unified nature of his argument. Promise, righteousness, and mercy are threads weaving through Romans for showing the greatness and proclamation of God's salvation through Christ.

This cohesiveness and continuity seem to refute any notion of a parenthesis of Romans 9-11. Rather, these three chapters expand on Paul's argument in Romans 3 thereby discounting any view of a parenthesis. Mark Siefrid gives a more detailed explanation of Paul's expansion,

> *"In Romans 10, in the midst of his discussion of the faith of the Gentiles and failure of Israel, Paul provides a defense of his apostolic ministry in which he expands the highly condensed summaries of his Gospel that appear in 1:16-17 and 3:21-26. The passage provides a window to the way in which Paul's gospel came to expression in his proclamation, just as the earlier summaries display its deeper theological structure. Romans 10 therefore may be regarded as providing an interpretive key to his earlier characterizations of his gospel and as indicative of the message he proclaimed."*[18]

NOTHING BUT THE GOSPEL

By establishing faith as the key marker for righteousness, Siefrid shows how Paul brings his development of the righteousness of faith into his discussion in Romans 9-11. Siefrid regards Romans 10 as *"providing an interpretive key"* for the gospel. This chapter shows the foundational elements of the gospel – faith and justification.[19] Not only this, but Paul adds another dimension of the righteous acts of God, faithfulness, in the display of His mercy. God's faithfulness and mercy arise from His righteousness. Paul illustrates God's righteousness in a highly compact manner through His merciful acts toward both the Jews and the Gentiles (9:14-24).

This mercy arises from Christ becoming the mercy seat and providing access to God through faith (3:25). As justification signifies right standing before God, mercy is the means for that standing. The word mercy appears six times in nine verses in Romans 9 and four times in three verses in Romans 11. Such emphasis leads to his conclusion: mercy applies to both the Jews and the Gentiles (9:24; 11:31-32).

The conclusions in both places are breathtaking in the compact way he draws them. In Romans 9:14-24, Paul answers with the mercy of God in two instances. The first instance replies to an implied question: Did the inclusion of the Gentles show that God's promise to Abraham failed (9:6)? The second instance concerned whether God is unjust in His alleged decision of narrowness or fewness (9:14). In both instances, Paul affirms that God is both sovereign over and independent of His creation. His mercy and love do not depend on *"human will or exertion"* (9:16).

Inasmuch as we like to redefine mercy to depend on what we see in others or even showing pity for another, such a definition is not the way Paul describes how God expresses it. Rather, God's nature is mercy in that it expresses faithfulness to His promise as He proclaimed to Jeremiah,

> *"The LORD has appeared of old to me, saying: 'Yes, I have loved you with an everlasting love; therefore, with lovingkindness I have drawn you'"* (Jeremiah 31:3).

DESTINY OF THOSE NOT KNOWING JESUS CHRIST

The word for lovingkindness in the Hebrew can also express covenant love or steadfast loving commitment to His promise. When Moses met with God on Mount Sinai, he asked God to show His glory to Him. The Lord told Moses that no one could look upon His face and live. However, Moses insisted. The LORD then placed Moses in cleft of a rock and passed by him. The LORD commanded Moses to meet with Him the next day with two cut stones on which He would imprint the Ten Commandments once again.

When Moses came up to meet with the LORD, He descended in a cloud, passed before him, and declared,

"The LORD, the LORD God, merciful and gracious, longsuffering and abounding in goodness and truth, keeping mercy for thousands, forgiving iniquity and transgression and sin, by no means clearing the guilty, visiting the iniquity of the fathers upon the children and the children's children to the third and fourth generation" (Exodus 34:6-7).

The text uses the same term appearing in Jeremiah 31:3, expressing the same loyal love and faithfulness by which God draws people to Himself and remains faithful to them. This faithfulness is the essence of mercy and righteousness. It also encompasses forgiveness, goodness, truth, and patience. Often, we relegate mercy to the helpless in society such as in the work of the Sisters of Mercy. While such actions on the part of the Sisters of Mercy and similar organizations exemplify biblical mercy, they do not capture the full extent of God's mercy. The Apostle John writes of Jesus,

"The Word became flesh and dwelt among us, and we beheld His glory, the glory of the only begotten of the Father, full of grace and truth" (John 1:14).

In Jesus, humanity discovers the same glory God revealed to Moses, the same glory that expresses God's mercy and covenant faithfulness, a faithfulness that arises from grace and truth embodied in Jesus. Therefore, when we see Jesus, we not only realize God's faithful covenant but the same mercy God expressed to His people through Moses. They cannot be separated without separating the Father from the Son or the Son from God's revealed redemption. God's mercy depends on recognizing and placing faith in the Son, apart from whom no one can know it and the salvation it brings.

When Paul describes God's mercy, he cites the words of God to Moses when God revealed His mercy to him. When Moses asked God to show him His glory, God declared,

> "I will make all My goodness pass before you, and I will proclaim the name of the LORD before you. <u>I will be gracious to whom I will be gracious, and I will have compassion on whom I will have compassion</u>"
> (Exodus 33:19).

Paul quotes from this passage as a reply to the charge of unrighteousness with God in allegedly forsaking the Jews for the Gentiles (Romans 9:15, 18). It is mercy rooted in the character and covenant faithfulness of God and does not depend on individuals but rather on the exercise of His sovereign will and purpose. This seems inexplicable to sinful beings to the extent that we want to find fault with the way He expresses His mercy and love. It is baffling until we read Paul's quote from Isaiah 65:2,

> "All day long I have held out my hands to a disobedient and contrary people"
> (Romans 10:21).

This pronouncement of God stifles all argument that God is unjust or that He does not respond to humanity caught up in sin. Such independence does not mean that He does not respond to those needs and desires. Rather, Scripture is replete with instances when people have called out to Him, and He comes to

DESTINY OF THOSE NOT KNOWING JESUS CHRIST

their aid. He beckons individuals to call on His name (Jeremiah 29:12' 33:3; Joel 2:32; Acts 2:21; Romans 10:13). Additionally, consider God's response in light of human rebellion. His hands remain outstretched in an act of mercy.

By bringing in the Gentiles, Paul shows the infinite greatness of God's mercy, mercy beyond anything humanity can show. The Gentiles were not partakers of the enumerated benefits of the Jews (9:4-5). They knew nothing of the adoption, glory, covenants, the law, worship, and promises. They also lived in darkness and the Jews considered them as dogs. Through God's divine mercy, a mercy the Jews considered unthinkable and offensive, God called the Gentiles (9:24-26). Consequently, they attained righteousness through faith (9:30).

God works in and through the agency of man to fulfill His promise to Abraham. He is not subject to humanity's demands but to what He declares. He is the Creator and humanity is the creation. Humanity has no capability of demonstrating perfect righteousness and mercy as does God. Therefore, no one can judge God in these attributes without judging Him as God. He defines mercy; people do not.

The attempt to define God's mercy and to apply it is inclusivism's shortcoming. Pinnock, Sanders, and other inclusivists reach the conclusion about God's mercy from the view of the limitations and sinfulness of humanity. In doing so, they exclude God's righteousness and sovereignty. From the perspective of this exclusion, they launch the criticism of a "fewness doctrine" toward those who hold fast to the proclaimed gospel of salvation for all. Consequently, they raise another gospel, one that magnifies creation rather than the Lord and Savior Jesus Christ.

The only way for the lost to know God and the destiny of eternal life is through the gospel of Jesus Christ. Paul makes this clear when he claims that those calling upon the name of the Lord will be saved (Romans 10:13). Almost two thousand years before Pinnock and inclusivists raised the "fewness doctrine," Paul had already refuted it in addressing those who had not heard the gospel. He declared that God sends the messenger with the message and means – His power in the gospel. He also engaged the argument of fairness and justice. God insures that those whom He saves will hear the gospel. His faithfulness to His promises depends on this assurance. Because of the limitations of sin and its own created status within the scope of time and space, humanity cannot judge the Creator and Redeemer. As the righteous God, we can trust Him to fulfill His promise in redemption. God's righteousness prevails in the means and message of salvation.

DESTINY OF THOSE NOT KNOWING JESUS CHRIST

NOTES

[1] Fackre, Kindle location 615, 923, 1010.
[2] Ibid, Kindle Edition, 7788.
[3] Ibid, Kindle Edition, 7838.
[4] Ibid, Kindle Edition, 7803-7805.
[5] Calvin, John, *Commentary on Romans*, translated and edited by John Owen (Grand Rapids: Christian Classics Ethereal Library, n.d.), Kindle location 984.
[6] Moo, Douglas, *Encountering the Book of Romans* (Grand Rapids: Baker Academic, 2002), Amazon Kindle Edition, Kindle location 1163.
[7] Ibid.
[8] Utley, Bob, *The Gospel According to Paul: Romans* (Bible Lessons International, 2013),
[9] Moo, Kindle location 3502.
[10] Schreiner, Thomas R., "Paul's View of the Law in Romans 10:4-5," *Westminster Theological Journal*, Volume 55:1 (Spring1993): 117.
[11] Moo, Kindle location 3599-3611.
[12] Ibid, Kindle location 3613.
[13] Pinnock, 17, 30, 38, 42, 153-156.
[14] Fackre, Kindle location 923.
[15] Pinnock, 18.
[16] _____, Net Bible (New English Translation) (Bible Studies Press, LLC, 2001), 2121.
[17] Bailey, Daniel P., "Jesus as the Mercy Seat: The Semantics and Theology of Paul's Use of "Hilasterion" in Romans 3:25," *Tyndale Bulletin* (Volume 51:1, 2000): 158.
[18] Seifrid, Mark, "The Near Word of Christ and the Distant Vision of N.T. Wright," *Journal of the Evangelical Theological Society* (Volume 54:2, June 2011): 280.
[19] Ibid.

11   A Wider Mercy: A False Hope

In his book, *A Wideness of God's Mercy*, Clark Pinnock concludes it with a lengthy poem from Frederick W. Faber that points to the words that make up the title of Pinnock's book:

> *"There is a wideness in God's mercy*
> *Like the wideness of the sea..."*

It continues for several more lines, praising God's justice, grace, and love and showing how humanity sets limits on these and *"magnify his strictness with zeal he will not own."*[1] In addition to Pinnock, John Sanders, and other inclusivists advocate the position of salvation that espouses a wideness of God's mercy. While they speak bountifully of God's mercy and hope, they do not have a clear definition of His mercy with roots in the Scriptures. Pinnock writes around mercy, speaking of it relative to *"God's boundless generosity"*[2] and posing a number of emotionally laden questions concerning it as it relates to His acts toward the lost.[a]

---

[a] *A Wideness of God's Mercy*, 149. Pinnock asks the following questions: "Is there hope for the unevangelized, or (as it used to be phrased) what is the fate of the heathen? Will God extend an opportunity for salvation to them? If God has grace for all, how do people benefit from grace if they have not been told about it? Is the universal salvific will of God frustrated by accidents of birth? How can heaven be a delight for anyone who knows that there are large numbers of people suffering in hell that they had no possibility of avoiding?" These and many more he asks throughout his book include speculative assumptions and express a particular theological outlook: the theology of the Openness of God.

A WIDER MERCY: A FALSE HOPE

MISSING THE MARK WITH MERCY

When addressing God's mercy while citing the Bible, inclusivists offer little in the way of preciseness and definition toward true biblical application. A murky view of God's mercy could lead to a false hope. John Sanders also takes a similar approach as Pinnock. To support his interpretation of God's mercy, Sanders fails to offer a precise biblical meaning of mercy. He also tends to read into specific biblical passages to arrive at his view toward an application concerning the destiny of the unevangelized. In explaining how God's love differs from human love within the context of mercy, Sanders states the following about Pharaoh during the time of the exodus of the Israelites from Egypt,

"Some may seek to limit the divine affections to Israelite sinners alone, excluding Gentile sinners such as the pharaoh of the exodus. Yet an examination of the exodus narratives reveals that God's love and grace were shown even to the pharaoh who was brutally oppressing the people of Israel."[3]

He arrives at this conclusion from his interpretation of the word "know" used in Exodus 7:5, 17, and 8:10. He continues with his explanation of God's actions toward pharaoh,

"The Hebrew word for "know" here carries with it the idea of relational and redemptive knowledge. Yahweh, the God of Israel, wanted Pharaoh and the Egyptian people to experience his truth and life-giving grace. The plagues were designed to show the uselessness of the Egyptian deities. By demonstrating the impotence of the Egyptian gods, Yahweh sought to free Pharaoh and the Egyptians from this burden and grant them the opportunity to turn to him, the Creator and Redeemer. In other words,

God was trying to evangelize Pharaoh and the Egyptians!"[4]

Sanders assumes that the word translated "know" from the Hebrew carries the same meaning in the three Exodus passages he cites. In doing so, he commits the fallacy to which D.A. Carson refers as an "unwarranted restriction of the semantic field."[5] That is, the semantic or meaning range of a word is much wider than a single meaning. Words have primary and secondary meanings. Their use depends largely on context.

For example, the Hebrew word appearing in Exodus 7:17 and 8:10 occurs 29 times in the Old Testament. It could refer to the certainty of an event (Genesis 15:13; 1 Samuel 28:1; 1 Kings 2:37, 42), general knowledge (Deuteronomy 20:20), a disclosure (Exodus 9:29), expert knowledge (Proverbs 27:23), as well as God's disclosure of Himself (Exodus 7:17; 8:10). Such knowledge may or may not refer to redemptive knowledge of God or other gods (Hosea 13:4). Its meaning relies on context.

The Hebrew word for "know" in Exodus 7:5 is not even the same word used in the other two passages. It could also refer to God's self-disclosure as it does in this verse. However, it may refer to the knowledge of specific territory (Number 14:31), people groups (Isaiah 9:9), the understanding of truth (Isaiah 29:24), and God's vengeance (Ezekiel 25:14). The word itself does not signify or suggest redemption, but the context will bear out whether it has relationship with any redemptive theme.

For Sanders' claim that the words translated "know" in all three passages have the same meaning disregards context and the actual meaning of Hebrew words. Furthermore, to associate the word with redemption without considering context is presumptuous and erroneous.

Nowhere in the Exodus passage do we receive a sense that God tried to evangelize Pharaoh. Neither the use of the word *"know"* nor the context suggests that the redemption of Pharaoh or Egypt was in view. In fact, the narrative expresses a message that carries a meaning opposite that of Sanders. The passages Sanders cites carry no redemptive message from God toward Pharaoh. Rather God's message toward Pharaoh is that of wrath and retribution should he continue in his present stubbornness.

From the historical account in Exodus, we read that Pharaoh did indeed in the end experience God's wrath. Such wrath was not only because of the Pharaoh's refusal to repent but also because God beforehand determined His judgment and wrath would come upon him for His own glory. God had earlier informed Moses that He would harden Pharaoh's heart to the extent that he would reject the message He gave to Moses (Exodus 7:1-4). Pharaoh's rejection of God's message resulted in His judgment on him and all of Egypt. The only redemptive message from God is toward the Israelites.

Sanders commits the interpretive error numerous times. One other time is worth mentioning. He later addresses how God hardened Pharaoh's heart and asserts that such an act is quite different from what Sanders would want God to do. Sanders continues,

> *"But the God of Israel and the Father of our Lord Jesus is different: he patiently seeks Pharaoh's salvation.*
>
> *Moreover, the hardening of Pharaoh's heart does not overturn this view of things, since the hardening does not automatically determine what will happen. The Hebrew word for "hardening" means to strengthen, so hardening does not render a person unable to repent. This is easily seen by the fact that God hardens the hearts of Pharaoh's servants (Ex 10:1), yet they understand what God is doing and implore their master to release the Israelites" (10:7).*[6]

Again, Sanders commits the same interpretive fallacy by restricting the meaning of the word translated from the Hebrew to English as *harden*. While the meaning Sanders cites could apply to *strengthen* (Ezekiel 30:24), that is not the only biblical usage of the word.

Context provides an entirely different message. In several places, Exodus states that God hardened Pharaoh's heart. If the word meant *strengthen* as Sanders claims, then God would be working at cross-purposes to His intent in strengthening Pharaoh to repent. Such writing would be confusing and nonsensical for the audience reading of this event. Context reveals meaning opposite of what Sanders proposes.

In the cases where God hardened Pharaoh's heart, he became even more resistant. If Sanders' meaning were correct, we could conclude that the more God strengthened Pharaoh, the greater resistance to God he became. However, that is far from the context and makes no sense within the context. Paul's interpretation of this event contradicts Sanders when he writes,

> "For the Scripture says to Pharaoh, 'For this very purpose I have raised you up, that I may show my power to you, and that my name may be declared in all the earth.' Therefore, He has mercy on whom He wills, and whom He wills He hardens" (Romans 9:17-18).

Not only does Paul identify God's purpose with Pharaoh to reveal God's power and to declare His name, but Paul also contrasts God's mercy with the hardening of Pharaoh's heart.

The context of Paul's statement makes obvious that the focus of God's mercy was toward Israel and not toward Pharaoh. Paul's contrast of mercy and hardening does not reflect God's hardening of Pharaoh's heart as redemptive. Sanders simply applies his own meaning to Scripture to support his conclusions concerning God's mercy, a mercy foreign to what the Bible actually teaches.

GETTING GOD AND HIS MESSAGE WRONG

If we get God's mercy wrong, we can also come to misunderstand it and God and stand in judgment of Him for His

A WIDER MERCY: A FALSE HOPE

failure to show our understanding of it. Getting God's mercy wrong can come about from playing loose in interpreting biblical texts and reading into them one's own theories and views. Pinnock and Sanders' misunderstanding of God's mercy leads them to reject the clear teaching of Scripture concerning salvation through the proclamation of the gospel. They proceed to give their offering of alternatives. By posing other means for individuals to know salvation, they reject the knowledge of the gospel of Jesus Christ.

Because of their emphasis on the *"wideness of God's mercy"* and a *"wider hope,"*[7] they conclude that the direct proclamation of the gospel is insufficient for salvation for all. Rather, for inclusivists, God has other ways than the gospel for salvation of those who may not have heard the gospel. Their pivot on a misunderstanding of God's mercy leads them to substitute other means for the message of the gospel. Their misunderstanding also leads them down the path of presumption concerning God's mercy.

God's mercy undeniably is wide in its scope and breadth. Evidence throughout history in God's dealings with Israel in the Old Testament and in salvation to the Gentiles clearly illustrates the enduring nature of His mercy. However, its wideness as Pinnock and Sanders illustrate does not reflect the manner God expresses it. The authority of God's word gives us a much firmer foundation as well as greater assurance and comfort for the future. Relying on creation produces an unstable foundation.

The mercy on which inclusivism relies represents a false hope and lacks any assurance, for its strength resides in the openness of God and the free will theism. This openness informs us that God cannot know all of the future and thereby cannot guarantee an eternal future for anyone. Accordingly, He does not know the choices of the agents of free will. According to the theology of the openness of God,

> *"God gives room to creatures and invites them to be covenant partners, opening up the possibility of loving fellowship but also of some initiative being taken away from God and*

creatures coming into conflict with his plans. God gives us room to rebel against him, and when that happens patiently waits for the prodigal to return."[8]

In many respects, inclusivism's god is passive and helpless in bringing about His will. He surrenders His authority, initiative, and power to humanity. Since God does not totally control the universe or the individuals in it,[9] He cannot guarantee hope for anyone. Such hope rests on the free will of individuals, which is no hope at all. He simply desires individuals to respond to Him out of their free will. Without the capacity to guarantee their destiny, God cannot render faithfulness to His promise of redemption. Consequently, God cannot be providential and righteous within the scope of inclusivism's theology.

If He is not righteous, how can he be trusted to show genuine and faithful love and mercy toward those who believe in Him? How can He guide their lives and give them assurance that He holds the world in place and controls all events for working out all things according to His purpose (Romans 8:28; Ephesians 1:11; 2 Timothy 1:9)?

Bruce Ware aptly captures this line of reasoning about God when he states,

> *"While claiming to offer meaningfulness to Christian living, open theism strips the believer of the one thing needed most for a meaningful and vibrant life of faith: absolute confidence in God's character, wisdom, word, promise, and the sure fulfillment of his will. The strengthening and reassuring truth of Romans 8:28 ("God causes all things to work together for good ...")' is tragically ripped out of our Christian confession as it becomes an expression merely of God's resolve to try his hardest and to do the best he can."*[10]

A WIDER MERCY: A FALSE HOPE

God's righteousness and faithful love pivot on Him keeping His word. If He is uncertain about the future actions of individuals who exercise their free will, he cannot readily keep His word of all things working according to His purpose. If He has relinquished a certain amount of control to those He created, they can choose to accept or reject His will for them and in doing so suffer the consequences of such rejection. They can choose to place their faith in Him for salvation and later determine that God as the object of their faith is not to their liking. Nothing God does prevents them from later turning their backs on Him. He simply becomes a persuader who stands by patiently waiting for anyone to accept His offer for salvation.[11]

However, such a characterization is not according to the testimony of the Scriptures. Humanity can never inhibit or hinder the promises He makes. If Abraham could stifle His plan by calling into question God's word to him, how could Christ ever come as the promised Messiah? The risk for God would be insurmountable. In spite of the disobedience of the children of Israel and their turning away to idolatry in the wilderness, He brought them securely into the land of promise. He told Moses that He would make a covenant with the Israelites, and perform miracles and wonders (Exodus 34:10).

If God could not know the future of those making free choices, He could not have informed them of the certainty of whole cities falling before them (Joshua 8:8). They could have freely chosen not to engage in battle. His promise to which He spoke to Samuel concerning the future of Israel would not have come to fruition if the free choices of individuals could subvert that promise (1 Samuel 3:11). Finally, God could have never made the claim,

> "Remember the former things of old, for I am God, and there is no other; I am God, and there is none like Me, declaring the end from the beginning, and from ancient times things that are not yet done, saying, 'My counsel shall stand, and I will do all my pleasure, calling a bird of prey from the East, the man who executes my counsel,

from a far country. Indeed, I have spoken it; I will also bring it to pass. I have purposed it; I will also do it" (Isaiah 46:9-11).

These are only a few examples of so many of which the Scriptures testify concerning God's ability to know the future and to direct it according to His will and power. Consequently, He can be trusted to keep His word to all those who place their faith in Him. Just as God does not share His glory with any other, He also does not share or delegate His power and control with another as inclusivism proposes, *"making himself vulnerable"* to humanity.[12] This assertion does not mean that God does not endow individuals with power and authority as those whom He created.

However, power and authority does not constitute a sharing of what belongs to Him as the divine sovereign over the created order. Rather, the power and authority He endows humanity is within the limits of creation and does not span the divine. The divine and creation do not mix so that the creature becomes part of the divine and the divine part of the creature. Otherwise, God would be pantheistic or panentheistic.[b] Divine power and authority are His alone (Isaiah 42:8; 48:11).

Inclusivism weakens God and His independence from creation and makes Him more like humanity than the God portrayed in the Scriptures. It dilutes the sharp distinction between the divine and the created order and even makes Him in many respects dependent on the free choices of individuals. Inclusivism sits in judgment on God if He does not comply with

---

[b] Pantheism is a religious theology that holds that God is everything and everything God. Whereas, Panentheism holds that God is in everything. See the following cited articles in the *Stanford Encyclopedia of Philosophy* for a more detailed discussion of both theological philosophies. For Panentheism, see Culp, John, "Panentheism", *The Stanford Encyclopedia of Philosophy* (Spring 2013 Edition), Edward N. Zalta (ed.), http://plato.stanford.edu/archives/spr2013/entries/panentheism. For Pantheism, see Mander, William, "Pantheism", *The Stanford Encyclopedia of Philosophy* (Summer 2013 Edition), Edward N. Zalta (ed.), http://plato.stanford.edu/archives/sum2013.

the speculations of its proponents. It casts Him as unfair or unrighteous if He is not as inclusivism portrays Him. It offers no genuine Scriptural hope, because individual destiny ultimately depends on free choices and not divine sovereignty.

While some within inclusivism hold to divine sovereignty and that God ultimately will fulfill His purposes, the free choices of the multitude of humanity actually stand in His way of doing so. With God so limited in this manner, He cannot bring about His will with anyone. Although on the one hand inclusivist claim God is infinite in power,[13] on the other hand they limit Him through power delegation or relinquishment. Finally, the gospel message simply would be one of powerless persuasion rather than *"the power of God unto salvation to everyone who believed"* (Romans 1:16).

The biblical gospel gives hope. It finds its source in the righteousness of God that guarantees His faithfulness to His promises by His power through all generations to the end of time itself. Because God is righteous, the destiny of all who trust Him remains firmly in His grasp. Paul praises God's faithful love in his conclusion of Romans 11. After asserting God's mercy came to Jew and Gentile, Paul concludes on a high note that nothing else could be said but "Amen." He writes,

> *"Oh, the depth of the riches both of the wisdom and knowledge of God! How unsearchable are His judgments and His ways past finding out! "For who has known the mind of the Lord? Or who has become His counselor? Or who has first given to Him and it shall be repaid to him?" For of Him and through Him and to Him are all things, to whom be glory forever. Amen"* (Romans 11:33-36).

NOTES

[1] Pinnock, 183-184.
[2] Ibid, 153.
[3] Fackre, Kindle location 225.
[4] Ibid.
[5] Carson, D.A., Kindle location 787-849.
[6] Fackre, Kindle location 237-240.
[7] Fackre, Kindle location 180, 216, 333.
[8] Pinnock, et al, *The Openness of God*, Kindle location 1365.
[9] Ibid, 1393.
[10] Ware, Bruce A., *God's Lesser Glory*, Kindle location 152-155.
[11] Ibid, Kindle location 1519.
[12] Pinnock, et al, *The Openness of God*, Kindle location 1365-1367.
[13] Pinnock, et al, *The Openness of God*, Kindle location 63.

12 Implications for Missions and Evangelism

We have one source for coming to grips with those who have never heard the gospel – the Bible. God has not appointed angels or the realm of creation to proclaim the gospel. Not only does the gospel give us the message of salvation in the Scriptures, but it also informs us about how we understand it, take it personally, and apply it to ourselves and in missions to others. After His baptism and Satan's temptations of Him, Jesus immediately began preaching the gospel (Mark 1:9-14). When the Apostles received the Holy Spirit, they immediately gave witness to God's power of salvation in Christ's resurrection. Peter stood up from among the Apostles and preached the first evangelistic sermon to those gathered in Jerusalem to celebrate Pentecost (Acts 2:14-36). He did not say, "Look at creation and you will find God and be saved." Rather Peter boldly declared,

"Repent, and let every one of you be baptized in the name of Jesus Christ for the remission of sins; and you shall receive the gift of the Holy Spirit. For the promise is to you and to your children, and to all who are afar off, as many as the Lord our God will call" (Acts 2:38-39).

After God blinded Saul on his way to Damascus and after he regained his sight, Saul immediately preached the gospel in synagogues (Acts 9:20). In none of these cases did any of them hesitate to reach out to those who needed to hear the gospel. Paul knew it to be the *"power of God to salvation for everyone who believes"* (Romans 1:16). He also considered no other message having not only God but also His power behind it.

IMPLICATIONS FOR MISSIONS AND EVANGELISM

While God gives witness to Himself through a variety of means, only the gospel gives witness to the *"power of God to salvation to everyone who believes"* (Romans 1:17). Creation gives witness to God's glory (Psalm 19:1), invisible attributes, eternal power, and divine nature (Romans 1:20). The prophets gave witness to God's judgment, promise, faithfulness, and of things to come – including the Messiah (Hebrews 1:1). However, only in the gospel does God give witness to the saving knowledge of Jesus Christ and all that encompasses. Consequently, those who know the Savior have a mission: make the gospel known to the lost, including those who have never heard it before.

The Apostle Paul teaches a very insightful lesson concerning salvation. He writes,

"And you He made alive, who were dead in trespasses and sins, in which you once walked according to the course of this world, according to the prince of the power of the air, the spirit who now works in the sons of disobedience, among whom we also once conducted ourselves in the lusts of our flesh, fulfilling the desires of the flesh and of the mind, and were by nature children of wrath, just as the others" (Ephesians 2:1-3).

Paul included himself among those who were once *"dead in trespasses and sins."* Regardless of any religious bent or activities, only the gospel has the power to save. Paul claimed that he excelled in religious zeal beyond his contemporaries, yet he lived estranged from God and rebelled against Him. He refused to embrace the power of God but wrapped himself in his own. The power he rejected includes the initiative and active intervention of God in bringing about new life to those *"who were dead in trespasses and sins"* (Ephesians 2:1). Paul discovered this truth on his way to Damascus to round up Christians for their death sentence. He did not know the gospel and followed what he thought was the truth.

However, God intervened with Paul on his journey and sent him crashing to the ground. God insured that the gospel came to the one whom He wanted to spread the good news. This good news centered on the righteousness He demonstrated through His Son that we may *"receive abundance of grace and of the gift of righteousness"* through which we *"will reign in life through the One, Jesus Christ"* (Romans 5:17). The gospel has at its core this fundamental teaching found in the Apostle Paul's letter to the Romans.

Given this fundamental truth of the gospel, it begins with everyone who places faith in Jesus Christ to save from sins. Everyone who hears the gospel for salvation beforehand never heard it. How did each of us come to hear it? We heard the gospel when someone shared it. The Apostle Paul aptly describes the process of the gospel proclamation and answers the question about how people hear the gospel:

> *"How then shall they call on Him in whom they have not believed? And how shall they believe in Him of whom they have not heard? And how shall they hear without a preacher? And how shall they preach unless they are sent?"*
> (Romans 10:14-15)

Who sends the preacher of the gospel? Jesus gives a clear answer in His commission to His disciples,

> *"Go into the world and preach the gospel to every creature. He who believes and is baptized will be saved; but he who does not believe will be condemned"* (Mark 16:15-16).

Jesus, the Son of God and second person of the Trinity, sends the preacher. He does so by His own authority (Matthew 28:19). If He then has the authority and He does the sending, then He also possesses the power to accompany the gospel to awaken the hearts of those who hear it to respond to it. Faith is the work of God in the heart unto salvation (John 6:28). Therefore, when we came to faith in Christ, it was not of our own will (John 1:13) but of the work of God in our hearts.

IMPLICATIONS FOR MISSIONS AND EVANGELISM

This faith becomes the starting point of the commission God gives to each person who has come to know Christ. God applied the gospel to us and then gave us a commission to preach and teach the wonderful things God did for and in us concerning salvation.

THE GOSPEL: RELATING TO GOD

How do we come to know God and relate to Him? What does that relationship involve? Alister McGrath poses additional questions pertinent to this discussion:

> *"How do we enter into a relationship with God? How are we distinguished from those outside this relationship? And what obligations does this relation place on us?"*[1]

Often, when we encounter the word "obligations," our contemporary Christian mindset may automatically take us to salvation by works, because "obligation" implies or suggests works or action on our part. A biblical context frames such a word. McGrath speaks of obligation in terms of trust and not of a work, as in the case of Abraham of whom McGrath states,

> *"We can now see that the basic idea is that faith in God's promises is regarded as 'righteousness' – in other words, Abraham's relationship with God is 'right' when he puts his trust in God's promises."*[2]

From McGrath, we understand that righteousness is relational by involving God's promises and trust: the former God's commitment and the latter individual faith that incites confidence and reliance on God's righteousness. In this sense, we can view obligation from a relational stance. Marriage serves as an illustration. Marriage has the obligations each spouse brings to the relationship. Each commits to love and to submit to one another. Each devotes time to building up the other and nurturing the marital bond. Each fosters communications and understanding. Each devotes to bringing up their children and all the responsibilities for contributing to their growth toward adulthood. All of these consist of the obligations of marriage, obligations that are not burdensome but joyful and satisfying because of the mutual commitment and trust they share in the oneness of marriage.

The same principle applies to the life of faith with God. Those who are in the right with God live by faith (Romans 1:17). This relationship calls on us to trust His leading in our lives, to exercise the salvation He gave us through His grace (Philippians 2:12). Paul urges believers to *"put on the Lord Jesus Christ, and make no provision for the flesh, to fulfill its lusts"* (Romans 13:14). No application of the gospel could have more clarity. These truths point to relating to the living God.

McGrath later expands on righteousness or justification by faith when he compares a contemporary misunderstanding:

> *"...that we are justified because we believe, that it is our decision to believe that brings about our justification."*[3]

As opposed to the above statement, McGrath claims the Reformation acknowledged the biblical truth that

> *"...affirms the activity of God and the passivity of man in justification. Faith is not something human we do, but something divine that is wrought within us."*[4]

The truths of righteousness and justification by faith are essential for those who do not know Him and have never heard the gospel as well as for those who do know Him and want to know Him better. The Bible discusses being the children of God (John 1:12; Romans 8:16; 1 John 3:1, 10). It speaks of God as our Father (John 6:27; 1 Corinthians 8:6; 15:24; Galatians 1:1; 2 Peter 1:17). While God lays claim to us when He calls us to faith in Him, the life lived out of that faith is one from the

IMPLICATIONS FOR MISSIONS AND EVANGELISM

standpoint of love and not one from a burden or guided by laws as is customary in a civil society. While custom legalizes the marriage relationship and provides the legal status of marriage, marriage itself lives out from love and not from the law. In a similar manner, God's claim on us for salvation is not one from a legal standpoint but one from sons and daughters relating to a Father within a family.

THE GOSPEL AND THE FAMILY OF GOD

What does the Bible tell us about becoming part of the family of God? Is it accepting Christ as our personal Savior? Are there certain steps in a process, such as praying with someone, going forward during a church service, responding to a call, or any number of initial related activities? Must we assume a particular physical position, such as on our knees or prostrate on the ground? Must we bow our heads and close our eyes or raise our head to heaven and lift our hands?

These are helpful guides and tend toward affirming our decisions. However, we must remember that faith precedes them, and they are not in themselves faith but an expression of it. Many churches use one, many, or all of these with those who come to their churches. However, it is important to note that they are not means of becoming or being a Christian. Many go forward in churches once or several times for profession of faith. Others do so for "rededication" of their lives to Christ. Still others have offered prayers many times to God only later to see those prayers fade in their memories. These activities do not make one a Christian.

During his crusades, Billy Graham noticed that many who came forward after his preaching later fell away and went back to their former lives. This concerned Graham, and he took action to attempt to correct this situation. His organization started courses for training crusade counselors to meet with those who came forward. He also met with local church pastors and leaders. He recruited them to aid him with those who attended the crusades for encouraging them in their new faith and becoming a part of a church community.

During these training sessions, those in his organization taught these prospective counselors how to share the gospel. To their surprise, many who came for training had never placed their faith in Christ and had never before heard the gospel. While this training and network of churches provided substantial help for those who heard the gospel at crusades, many still went back to their old lives. They never embraced faith in Christ.

Such experiences in history demonstrated that human activity has no saving power. These experiences also underscored a misunderstanding of faith. An act of human will does not save. Granted, many who professed faith in Christ did remain in the faith and became leaders in their church communities. However, none of the activities they went through made them Christians. What Christian leaders learned in evangelism is that human effort or activity has no power to keep people, to sustain their faith, or even to become a Christian.

There is no power in human activity or effort for pleasing God. Becoming a Christian and a member of the family of God is not the initiative of the individual but of God. He must first disclose Himself and give understanding for one to express faith in Christ. A person exercises faith in Christ. He saves, reconciles us to God, and imparts to us new life.

Becoming and being a Christian is a spiritual issue. Consequently, it takes spiritual power to bring spiritual life to those whom the Bible pronounces *"dead in trespasses and sins"* (Ephesians 2:2). No matter how many times a person goes forward in a church, during a crusade, or at any similar event, this activity does not and cannot save anyone. It fails to bring them into a right relation with God. Through the gospel, we discover the power of God unto salvation to everyone who believes and the provision for entrance into the family of God.

IMPLICATIONS FOR MISSIONS AND EVANGELISM

THE GOSPEL AND THE TRIUNE GOD

That gospel involves the triune God. Frequently, when sharing the gospel in his letters, Paul expresses the work of the entire Trinity. One particular passage is stunning in its message about how all three persons of the Trinity wholly participate in the process of salvation. He declares,

"Therefore, having been justified by faith, we have peace with God through our Lord Jesus Christ, through whom also we have access by faith into this grace in which we stand, and rejoice in hope of the glory of God... Now hope does not disappoint, because the love of God has been poured out in our hearts by the Holy Spirit who was given to us." (Romans 5:1-2, 5).

The above is a concise statement of the gospel. It allows us to understand how the triune God becomes involved in our salvation. God the Father initiates the move toward salvation in His righteousness and love. He loved us so much that He gave His only Son to die on the cross to save us from His wrath on sin. He heightens our confidence and hope in His faithfulness to perform what He said He would do. Christ died for our sins that He might reconcile us to God our Father. We understand God's love through the indwelling Holy Spirit. Darrell Johnson brings the gospel into application in an insightful manner,

"The Son really loves the Father – another understatement. This is the secret of Jesus' existence, the driving force of his ministry. He really loves the Father; this is why he is always telling us about the Father. And the Son draws near to me in order to draw me to himself so I can love the Father the same way he does.

And the Spirit? The Spirit is totally taken up with the goodness and beauty of the Son and

the Father. And the Spirit falls upon us – a bit stronger than draws near – so we can be ravaged with his love for the Son and Father."[5]

This statement illustrates the jewel in the crown of the gospel. Paul confirms this jewel in the following statement,

"*God showed His love for us in that while we were yet sinners, Christ died for us*"
(Romans 5:8).

He saved us to love us and to join us with Himself in eternal enjoyment of all He is and did for us. No other message than the gospel discloses this powerful message and allows us to understand and experience the full purpose and power of redemption.

When Paul opened his letter to the Church at Ephesus, one of the very first truths He desired his readers to know is this full purpose. He writes about God's choice of believers from the foundations of the world according to His own will. Then he makes an astonishing statement,

"*...that we should be holy and without blame before Him in love, having predestined us to adoption as sons by Jesus Christ to Himself, according to the good pleasure of His will, to the praise of the glory of His grace, by which He made us accepted in the Beloved*"
(Ephesians 1:4-6).

In this passage, we understand how God's love threads its way from the Father through the Son. He desires us to stand before Him in love. The great truth of Paul's statement is that He places us in the position of blamelessness through His love. He does this through His grace by which we stand fully accepted in His Son.

This passage combined with the passage from Romans quoted earlier gives us a glimpse of our eternal home where we will dwell as a large family with God as our Father and Jesus as

IMPLICATIONS FOR MISSIONS AND EVANGELISM

our Brother, always secure and in complete contentment in God's grace. This gospel alone reveals the standing we have with God. No alternate message is adequate.

Have you embraced this message?

THE GOSPEL AND JUSTIFICATION BY FAITH

The message of salvation is of utmost importance in proclaiming God's plan of redemption, and the gospel is that message. Jesus sent out His disciples to preach the gospel He Himself preached (Matthew 4:23; Luke 9:6). The disciples (apostles) preached and wrote about believing the gospel. We learn from them that God's saving activity is all about content rooted in Christ's death on the cross. In this activity, God revealed His righteousness. The Apostle Paul informed us that the gospel reveals the power and righteousness of God (Romans 1:16-17). Any discussion of the gospel with someone who has never heard it must begin with the righteousness of God. Understanding of the gospel begins with understanding of the God who ordained it. The righteousness of God is foundational to understanding justification by faith or the saving message of God's acceptance of us through grace.

One might protest that this is a very broad term and somewhat abstract. Indeed, it is, because the word "righteousness" or "justification" has fallen out of widespread use. Rather, substitutes replaced these words thereby watering them down to meanings often not intended.

However, these terms remain in our Bibles, and we cannot ignore them. Substitutes often do not convey the full meaning of biblical terms due to the historical and cultural distance from their original biblical use. Additionally, they remain God's written word as the truth about our standing before God. They explain what He has done to reconcile us. He spoke through the biblical authors to convey the great truths of salvation, and His righteousness is foundational to those truths.

God's Promise, Abraham, and Justification by Faith

Revisiting their meaning with Abraham is helpful. After God gave Abraham His promise of a son, the Scriptures states of him,

> *"And he believed in the Lord, and He accounted it to him as righteousness"*
> (Genesis 15:6).

This verse connects faith and righteousness. Righteousness is not associated with any kind of behavior or something Abraham did. Rather the connection highlights God's initiative and Abraham's faith. Righteousness never indicates striving for perfection, living a moral life, or performing right acts or behavior. God's pronouncement of Abraham as righteous preceded any action on Abraham's part. God appeared to Abraham and gave him a promise (Genesis 12:1-7). Through God's revelation to him, Abraham came to know God and entrusted himself to the LORD who disclosed Himself and spoke promises (12:7). Later, God revealed Himself again to Abraham and promised a son as an offspring from his own body. Faith declares that the one who expresses it entrusts oneself to God. Righteousness informs the person with faith that one stands in the right before God.

This standing is not that of perfection but of God's acceptance of rebellious sinners whom He draws to Himself. God reconciles those who once stood alienated from Him by declaring them righteous. The charge of not guilty before Him expresses this standing. Abraham did not perform any right or moral act to gain God's favor. His standing as righteous before God simply rested with God and trust in Him for deliverance.

Understanding and applying the term *righteousness* is essential for understanding forgiveness of sin, acceptance with the Father through Christ, and blamelessness before God as His children. The righteousness of God encompasses justification by faith, the foundation of right standing with God. Such language as righteous, righteousness, justification, and related

IMPLICATIONS FOR MISSIONS AND EVANGELISM

biblical synonyms do not often appear in our vocabulary or even in many modern versions of the Bible. In fact, we rarely if ever hear these terms in everyday conversation. Yet it must be part of the discussion for a person to come to grips with what occurs in salvation.

Coming to Terms with Justification by Faith

Taking the gospel to those in our culture not accustomed to terms understood fifty, one hundred fifty, or even two-thousand years ago is a challenge. The unchurched population has grown even greater in the present generation than in the generation one hundred fifty years ago. This growth places more individuals at a greater distance from the language of the gospel than those who heard it then or in the first century. Consequently, the words of the gospel have a stranger meaning and a greater distance culturally to contemporary ears.

However, such a circumstance is not new. When Paul traveled to Athens to meet up with Silas and Timothy, the gods of the city distracted and upset him. These people knew nothing of the gospel or the terminology around it. When he began sharing the gospel, they called him a babbler and took his message as something new and strange. When he preached Christ and the resurrection, many scorned him and held him in contempt. He had to apply a strategy with a frame of reference common to both them and him – the unknown god.

While tapping into the language the Athenians associated with their stone god, he explained the real God of the universe and made the distinction between their unknown god and the Creator and Redeemer (Acts 17:22-31). He accommodated without compromising the gospel message. This event occurred only 30-40 years after Christ died. A greater distance exists between the days of Christ and us. We live among people who similarly consider biblical terminology strange to their ears or perhaps babble.

Consequently, it is easy for contemporary professing Christians to lose the path back to original biblical meaning of the righteousness of God and justification by faith. However, as messengers of the gospel, we must have a clear understanding of this essential teaching underlying the gospel for sharing it with another. The use of the term "justification by faith" could draw a blank stare from those who have never heard the gospel or the words themselves. This reaction informs us that beginning with this term may not be the best strategy. However, this hardly discounts its use.

An understanding of all justification by faith encompasses aids in reaching the heart of the hearer. People understand personal alienation, guilt, sin, debt, hopelessness, and the war of a myriad of internal conflicts and conflicts with others. Framing these conditions toward God and the war we constantly have with Him in our rebellion brings one's spiritual condition to the forefront. At this point, we present Jesus as the one who turns war with God to peace. The Apostle Paul brings together justification by faith, Jesus Christ, and peace with God in the same breath when he writes,

"Therefore, having been justified by faith, we have peace with God through our Lord Jesus Christ" (Romans 5:1)

This wonderful passage is a great place to start with sharing the gospel. People always seek peace in the world, but they may be surprised that the peace God grants the heart far surpasses their understanding of it. Peace with God means the war between God and the rebellious sinner ceases. Jesus mediated peace and caused all hostilities to terminate. Before faith in Christ, individuals had the status as enemies (Romans 5:10). Christ brought peace through His blood, not an emotional or inner peace but a peace that meant war with God ended. Emotional or inner peace turns our focus on ourselves.

Peace with God resulting from justification by faith turns our eyes to God in gratitude for bringing all hostilities to a halt. Emotional or inner peace comes and goes. That type of peace is temporary and not the peace of which Paul writes. Peace with God is permanent and does not waver, because it rests with God and His love for us through Christ. He cancelled all the debts (sin) of this war and set us free from the captivity of sin's debt

IMPLICATIONS FOR MISSIONS AND EVANGELISM

to become sons of the living God. From enemies, we became children of God.

Justification by faith through the person of Jesus counters a hopeless spiritual condition. It reveals that God is gracious, quick to forgive, no longer holding sin (debt) against the sinner. Christ sets us in the right before God. Faith embraces this truth. These acts of God bring a person face to face with the liberty of justification by faith. Sharing this message with those who have never heard the gospel gives them the knowledge of the truth the Holy Spirit uses toward faith, repentance, and conversion.

Urgency of Communicating Justification by Faith

The messenger of the gospel must have a firm grip on this core truth in the gospel. It is the gospel's heartbeat. We must bridge the cultural and generational gap with this gospel message. We must communicate an uncompromising message in a way recipients understand. This same challenge existed one hundred fifty years ago for those who were just becoming acquainted with coming forward during a church service (or the altar call).[6] They responded to the preacher's call to come to Christ.

Some could have taken responding to the plea of the altar call as that act of salvation.[7] Rather faith in Christ must preempt and void any such notion. The meaning of *righteousness* and *justification* also gets us away from the faulty thinking that we must do something for salvation rather than justification as an accounting through which God rendered us in the right before Him. This rendering makes salvation an initiative of God and not of us.

In sharing the gospel, it often reduces to *accepting Jesus as one's personal Savior*. This phrase did not exist two centuries ago. It is indeed important to know that Jesus is Savior and that it involves trusting Him by faith. However, such a description of salvation can mislead without further explanation. While faith in Christ for salvation does not require an elaborate and complex presentation or a number of rituals, faith has its grounds in certain truths that comprise its content.

Does *accepting Christ* convey these biblical truths? What are these truths? Trusting Christ emphasizes faith, God's acceptance and forgiveness of sins through grace, reconciliation, standing before Him as righteous, and the promise of hope. On what foundation does that acceptance rest? Justification by faith brings us back to the answers that underlie the meaning of *accepting Christ as one's personal Savior*.

God's righteousness serves as that acceptance, forgiveness of sin, reconciliation, and hope. That is, the acceptance of Christ is a matter of faith. That faith finds it source in God's grace and righteousness in Christ through which and through whom God accounts the believing heart in right standing before Him (2 Peter 1:1b). The Scriptures highlight Abraham as the example of this accounting when they proclaim,

"For what does the Scripture say?
"Abraham believed God, and it was accounted to
him for righteousness"" (Romans 4:3).

We must arm ourselves with this content in sharing the gospel to connect modern language to biblical terms.

As stated earlier, we find these great truths in the summary Paul wrote to the Roman church,

"Therefore, having been justified by faith, we have peace with God through our Lord Jesus Christ, through whom also we have access by faith into this grace in which we stand, and rejoice in hope of the glory of God"
(Romans 5:1-2).

We notice these truths found in justification by faith: peace with God, access to Him, grace that makes the believer in the right before Him, and hope. The gospel draws from a number of theological truths and presents them in summary form in a way for our hearts through faith to grasp them. Thankfully, the Holy Spirit works through the gospel to bring about understanding in spite of our occasional struggles to make the message clear to the hearer.

IMPLICATIONS FOR MISSIONS AND EVANGELISM

Alister McGrath cites several teachings or doctrines on which justification by faith touches of which he states,

"All these ideas [expiation, reconciliation, adoption, transformation, and consecrated] *gives flesh to the framework established by the basic idea of being right with God."*[8]

He expands on these ideas related to justification by faith or right standing with God:

a) Expiation of sin or the turning away of God's wrath through cancellation of sin (Romans 3:35)
b) Reconciliation with God and Jesus our Advocate in reconciling those in rebellion to God
c) Adoption as God's children
d) Transformation of life
e) Consecration or being set aside

All of the above come through the power of God. They make up the message of the gospel. Christ paid the penalty for sin and turned God's judgment away from us. His work on the cross reconciled us to God – those who beforehand showed disobedience. Christ made the relationship right. God then went beyond reconciliation to lay claim to us as His own children. He gave us the Holy Spirit for renewing our lives in conformity to Christ. He set us apart from a condemned world of which we used to belong. Faith in Christ grants us all of these benefits in salvation.

Salvation remains by faith alone. It is faith in the knowledge of Jesus Christ disclosed in the Scriptures: the forgiveness of sin (Matthew 26:28; Luke 1:77; Ephesians 1:7). It is knowing the God who promises and keeps His word, the God who is righteous and true not only to Himself but also to us (2 Corinthians 1:20-22). Our faith also rests on the relationship He established with us as His adopted children, set apart for a new life with an eventual resting place in a new place He prepared for us (John 14:1-2; 2 Corinthians 5:17).

He accomplishes all of the above through the power of the Holy Spirit and the provision He made through His Son.

Faith means trusting and following the reality of God's provision through Jesus and leaving behind our life of rebellion against God. No message has greater urgency. It calls upon those who live at war with and in rebellion against God to turn to Him. The renewal of the Holy Spirit and the blood of Christ changes the believer's destiny from condemnation to hope established through peace with God.

BRIDGING THE GOSPEL CULTURALLY

We live 2,000 years from the time when the Apostle Paul wrote and preached salvation and find it difficult to place ourselves in Paul's mind to grasp its significance. Our culture is not his. We need to bring his meaning into our language, timeframe, and culture without diluting the gospel and the salvation we enjoy through Jesus. We need to remain true to its original meaning. Using terms that suggest human effort not only dilutes salvation but also makes it human centered.

This is not to say we cannot use contemporary phraseology to convey the gospel, such as *accepting Jesus as our personal Savior*, *receiving Christ*, or any number of other modern phrases paraphrased from a variety of biblical passages or biblical teaching or training. We must continue to bridge contemporary language to biblical language. We must be careful also to retain the meaning the biblical authors conveyed. In so doing, the meaning of the gospel of grace through faith does not get lost.

One of the problems Christians face today is conveying a different meaning of a biblical word or passage using contemporary phrases. This is both a problem with a language barrier and theology. Modern liberal theology often departs from biblical theology and seeks modern language to convey this changed theology.

For this reason, it is important to be a student of the Bible for grasping what the message of the gospel biblical authors intended to convey. This means that our own personal understanding of biblical terms must align with those of the biblical authors. Consequently, when we use contemporary terms and phrases, we must trace the path back to the original intent of the biblical authors. Words, phrases, and analogies for conveying biblical truths change from one age to another and from one culture to another. Truth never changes.

THE BEGINNING: GOD'S SELF-REVELATION IN HISTORY

Communicating the gospel to another requires that we also understand it. We must know what it takes to be in right relationship with God. To test our understanding, we must start where the biblical authors began with the biblical witness itself. McGrath again is helpful at this point when he writes,

> *Scripture witnesses to the self-revelation of God in human history.*[9]

All that bears on salvation begins with God and not with us. So also is God's communication to us in the Bible God centered and not man centered. God discloses, and we discover. To say it in another way, God reveals through written revelation declared through those whom He chooses. We receive it by faith, embrace it, and obey it.

To apply it, we begin with God for discovering His will in salvation and not with ourselves. It is not our opinion through speculation. We are safe from error to have these truths as our starting point. All that we know of God and His redemptive plan finds their source in the Scriptures alone. The Scriptures are His disclosure to a lost humanity through the biblical authors. The more we come to grips with the intent of the biblical authors, the less we rely on speculation and our own meaning. They inform us about the meaning and means of salvation. We test our understanding and that of others by the Scriptures alone.

We do well not to depart from or revise the meaning or means according to any *"control belief"* (as Sanders and Pinnock's starting point) we impose on His word apart from what the biblical authors teach. It is God's word and message through the agency of human authors. They at times found it difficult to understand the prophetic words they themselves received from the Spirit concerning God's grace.

They remained obedient and true to God in disclosing God and His word to their audiences. God revealed to them that they did not serve themselves but all to whom the gospel came (1 Peter 1:10-12). We simply discover it, come to understand it by His Spirit, and respond to it through faith. The meaning and the message of the Bible rests with the biblical authors and the Holy Spirit who inspired them. To read our opinion into the Scriptures risks misconstruing the gospel of salvation. Inclusivism demonstrates this danger. We can trust the sufficiency of His disclosure.

INCENTIVES TO PREACH THE GOSPEL

Many of those who have heard the gospel ridicule it, suppress its message, and willfully and intentionally reject it. Others mix it with their own message for a different view of salvation. We must be aware of mixed messages foreign to the biblical one in the gospel. Our own initiative to discover God arises from our relationship with Him and motivates us to pursue His holy word with all seriousness and energy.

We recognize that the miracle He performed in us to set us right with Him through Christ cannot remain inside of us. Too much is at stake for keeping His message in the gospel under wraps. Christ died for those who placed faith in Him to live. The destiny of the lost is an eternal destiny and constrains us to share the gospel with them.

Therefore, when we hear the gospel of Christ, what do we do with it? What do we do with the messenger, the Holy Spirit? What do we do with the subject of the message – Jesus Christ? What do we do with the Author of the message – God Himself? Do we question His goodness and sovereign ability to take His word and to proclaim it to the entire world to everyone whom He saves to hear it and trust Him by faith? Does doubt about His justice bog us down and leave us distrusting the message He gave us to proclaim? Do we raise the question about only a few hearing and receiving the gospel and thereby seek alternative means of salvation for those who never hear it? Do we say, "I will stay within my little community and leave the rest to God. He will save them another way with another message."

After Paul takes his readers through humanity's condition his second letter to Corinth, he pivots to a very important issue: "Why tell others about this Christ?" He gives three important reasons. This section explores these reasons.

The Terror of the Lord

"Knowing, therefore, the terror of the Lord, we persuade men" (2 Corinthians 5:11).

The lost face a hopeless eternity, a terror of eternal separation from God. By placing ourselves in their shoes in what we know, would we not want them to hear the message that will save their lives? Jesus not only gave His disciples a mission and commission, but He also included us in it. Reaching the lost with the only remedy for escaping the judgment of God fulfills that mission. When Jesus healed people, they proclaimed the mighty power of God.

Paul made persuasion his constant means of reaching the lost with the gospel. He did not leave it up to the knowledge of what one knew from the light of creation. He realized that knowledge of the impersonal created order could not reveal the personal God's righteousness, salvation, or the great love and grace He had toward us. Paul believed and proclaimed the one and only gospel of salvation – Jesus and Him crucified (1 Corinthians 2:2; 15:1-3). He knew the urgent task before him sufficiently to take the gospel to the edges of civilization. His fearless passion for the lost drove him to persuade men. Nothing less than the saving knowledge of Christ consumed him to share the gospel of eternal life. The knowledge from the light of the created order does not command such urgency.

Crazy for God

"For if we are beside ourselves, it is for God"
(2 Corinthians 5:13).

Paul often received ridicule for standing up for His faith in Christ. Near the end of his life, he stood before King Agrippa and Festus and gave an account of compassion for Christ. During his speech before them, Festus interrupted Paul and loudly exclaimed,

"Paul, you are beside yourself! Much learning is driving you mad!" (Acts 26:24)

Many like Festus, those who do not understand God's ways attempt to dismiss or misunderstand compassion for the lost. They see God's love as an attempt to force religion down another's throat. Many also attempt to rationalize Christian compassion as a violation of church and state or infringing on the individual rights. Still others brush aside God's compassionate gospel with the statement, "That is OK for you but not for me" or "Your truth is not my truth." Some even go so far as to make fraudulent claims based on scientific method in attempts to show that Christians exhibit lower intelligence than atheists.[10] These are misguided applications and rejection of the truth. Paul declared,

"...the message of the cross is foolishness to those who are perishing" (1 Corinthians 1:18).

That is, the cross is madness to those not knowing God's love.

Regardless of how others view the gospel or us, our relationship with God compels us to bring the message of reconciliation to the lost. We know the gripping experience of knowing God so that we should also want to share that experience with others. Compassion is compelling. One desires to be around another who loves. It gives safety, security, comfort, sacrificial caring, and motivation to give in return. God's love also reveals His faithfulness and patience. From our

IMPLICATIONS FOR MISSIONS AND EVANGELISM

condition, love also demonstrates the cost it had for God, the cost of His own Son, a cost so precious that nothing could repay Him for such sacrifice. This sacrifice is God's ultimate expression of love. Would we not want others to know it?

Many think sharing the gospel with others is craziness. During the Christmas of 2013, the American Atheists resurrected a billboard in New York Times Square that had "Christ" crossed out and stated, "Who needs ~~Christ~~ during Christmas - Nobody." The irony with such signs is that those who oppose the gospel message of Christmas actually promote it by leaving Christ in the word "Christmas" and make His name known. By holding Christians in disdain and considering Christians crazy they actually promoted the name of Christ.

While the Apostle Paul claims craziness for God, He reveals that God's love expresses the normal way of living. Therefore, boldly proclaiming the gospel of love and righteousness reveals a life hard to grasp by those who do not know Christ and love God. The gospel imparts a new understanding through God's conversion of the heart and allows a person to understand God's love and righteousness is sane. Living faithfully toward God and sharing with others the life of commitment to Him is normal. Living a life of love delivers us from the insanity of alienation from God and others and the destructive nature of sin. This is the good news the gospel declares to the lost. As those who believe in Christ, we celebrate God's love in the gospel, a love many consider crazy.

For the Love of God

"For the love of Christ compels us"
(2 Corinthians 5:14).

Is there any greater reason to proclaim the gospel to the lost but to share the love we know in our relation with Him? The two most prominent words in the New Testament are righteousness and love. Both are compelling traits of God, for both exhibit His character toward humanity. We see both in the cross,

> *"For God so loved the world that He gave His only begotten Son that whoever believes in Him should not perish but have everlasting life"* (John 3:16).

The Bible teaches both righteousness and love, not as one derivative of the other or in a balance, but in an integrated whole in God. Both traits of God integrate in Him so that they are one, because God is one. Notice John's declaration about God. God loved the world. God gave up His Son to death on a cross. That is,

> *"For He made Him who knew no sin to be sin for us, that we might become the righteousness of God in Him"* (2 Corinthians 5:21).

God showed His love through His righteousness and His righteousness through His love. He judged the sins of the world through His Son on the cross *"the just for the unjust that He might bring us to God"* (1 Peter 3:18). In judgment on sin, God demonstrated righteousness. In judgment on sin, God saved and showed His love. Such faithful love demonstrates to us the same kind of love we are to exhibit toward Him and others. In his worship and prayer toward God, Augustine shares how we enjoin such righteousness and love,

> *"The problem is that You [God] have not simply commanded purity in regards to the objects of our affections. You also desire righteousness in how we bestow love upon both You and our neighbor as well. When I receive pleasing, intelligent praise, I seem to myself to be pleased with the thoughtfulness or compassion my neighbor is showing toward me. I am aggrieved when I see evil in another, when I hear him criticize what he doesn't understand or when he speaks against the good."* [11]

IMPLICATIONS FOR MISSIONS AND EVANGELISM

Notice how Augustine integrates love and righteousness toward both God and one's neighbor. Such love grieves over *"evil in another,"* because evil is unrighteous and runs cross-purposes with God's purpose and love. We have no understanding of God's love and righteousness until God reveals them to us. They are spiritually divine qualities alien to us. They require spiritual discernment from God (1 Corinthians 2:14). They are gifts from God through His Spirit. We cannot know them by any other way. When we receive them, they compel us to share them with our neighbor. This sharing is the heart of evangelism that announces the ancient biblical truth we first learned when we came to understand God's righteousness and love toward us,

"For God so loved the world that He gave His only begotten Son, that whoever believes in Him should not perish but have everlasting life" (John 3:16).

The conclusion of realizing the nature of God's love and righteousness is that we come to know Him and His ways with humanity. This knowledge of God and passionate love for Him compel us to *"pursue peace with all people, and holiness, without which no one will see the Lord"* (Hebrews 12:14). Those who are lost will never see the Lord. This causes grief. The lost are God's mission. The knowledge that arises from the light through the created order can never reveal God's righteousness and great compassion.

That light is impersonal and fails to carry God's imprint of love. Only the personal Light of the World, Jesus, carries that imprint of God's love (John 8:12; 9:5). Only the cross of Christ shines forth the unconditional love of God. It is unconditional, because we can give nothing in return for it. The lost need to look to the cross to recognize their condition so *"the light of the gospel of the glory of Christ, who is the image of God, should shine on them"* (2 Corinthians 4:6). Christ is the expressed righteousness and love of God. No substitute exists for the cross of Christ. No other message or means exists for drawing people in reconciliation with God. No message other than the gospel leads to knowing God and His love.

We are His missionaries for declaring to the lost the love and righteousness of God. Christ made the mission clear: preach the gospel. The results are also clear: *"He will save His people from their sins"* (Matthew 1:21). What God did for us motivates us to share the gospel with others – the gospel of peace with God and of holiness *"without which no one will see the Lord"* (Hebrews 12:14). Passion for the lost begins with compassion from the triune God. Being right with God begins with a righteous God and the righteous act of Christ's death on the cross. The world must know this to escape the judgment of God on sin and to experience the love of God through Christ the Lord. Therefore, *"the love of Christ compels us"* (2 Corinthians 5:14) as ministers of reconciliation.

IMPLICATIONS FOR MISSIONS AND EVANGELISM

NOTES

[1] McGrath, Alister E., *Studies in Doctrine* (Grand Rapids: Zondervan, 1998), 368.
[2] Ibid, 369.
[3] Ibid, 391.
[4] Ibid.
[5] Johnson, Darrell, 65.
[6] Sweeney, Douglas A., and Mark C. Rogers, "Walk the Aisle," *Christian History* (10/22/2008):1-2, http://www.christianitytoday.com/ch/thepastinthepresent/storybehind/walktheaisle.html, accessed September 27, 2013.
[7] Ibid, 2.
[8] McGrath, 371.
[9] Ibid, 368.
[10] Zuckerman, Miron, Jordan Silberman, and Judith A. Hall, "The Relation between Intelligence and Religiosity: A Meta-Analysis and Some Proposed Explanations," *Personality and Social Psychology Review* (Vol. 17:4, November 2013): 325-354.
[11] Augustine, *Confessions of St. Augustine: The Modern English Version* (Grand Rapids: Baker Publishing Group. Kindle Edition, 2005), Kindle locations 2424-2427.

Bibliography

BIBLIOGRAPHY

Allen, Robert A. "The Expository Sermon: Cultural or Biblical?" *Journal of Ministry and Theology* (1998).
Armstrong, John H. "The Unique Christ and the Modern Challenge." *Reformation and Revival* 2:02 (1993).
Bailey, Daniel P. "Jesus as the Mercy Seat: The Semantics and Theology of Paul's Use of "Hailasterion" in Romans 3:25." *Tyndale Bulletin* 51:1 (2000).
Baugh, S. M. "The Cloud of Witnesses in Hebrews 11:6." *Westminister Theological Journal* 68:1 (2006): 118-119.
Calvin, John. *Commentary on Romans*. Ed. John Owen. Trans. John Owen. Grand Rapids: Christia Classics Ethereal Library, n.d.
—. *Institutes of the Christian Religion*. Philadelphia: The Westminster Press, 1960.
Canady, A. B. "The Parable of the Generous Vineyard Owner (Matthew 20:1-16)." *Sourthern Baptist Journal of Theology* 13:3 (Fall 2009).
Caneday, A. B. ""Evangelical Inclusivism" and the Exclusivity of the Gospel: A Review of John Sanders's No Other Name." *Southern Baptist Journal of Theology* 01:4 (1997).
Carlson, Dwight. *Who'll Be in Heaven & Who Won't?* Amazon Kindle. Bloomington: WestBow Press, 2012.
Carson, D. A. *Exegetical Fallacies*. Second Edition. Grand Rapids: Baker Publishing Group, 1996.
—. "God's Love and God's Wrath." *Bibliotheca Sacra* 156:624 (1999).
Collmer, Rober G. "The Limitation of Mysticism." *Biblliotheca Sacra* 116:462 (April 1959).
Cook, Don. "Christian Illuminati." *Reformation and Revival* 3:4 (Fall 1994).

BIBLIOGRAPHY

Cranfield, C. E. B. *Romans: A Shorter Commentary*. Grand Rapids: William B. Eerdmans Publishing Company, 1985.

Cunningham, Harold G. ""General Equity" and the Westminster Confession of Faith." *Tyndale Bulletin* 58:2 (2007).

Elwell, Walter A., ed. *Evangelical Dictionary of Biblical Theology*. Grand Rapids: Baker Books, 1996.

Erickson, Millard. *Christian Theology, Second Edition*. Grand Rapids: Baker Books, 1998.

—. "The Fate of Those Who Never Hear." *Bibliotheca Sacra* 152:605 (1995): 5-6.

Fackre, Gabriel, Ronald H., Nash, and John Sanders. *What About Those Who Have Never Heard?: Three Views on the Destiny of the Unevagelized*. Downers Grove: InterVarsity Press, 1995.

Fruchtenbaum, Arnold G. "The Toronto Phenomenon (Part 2 of 2)." *Chafer Theological Seminary Journal* 2:2 (Fall 1996).

Geisler, Norman L. "Religious Pluralism: A Christian Response." *Christian Apologetics Journal* 4:2 (2005).

Geivett, R. Douglas. ""Misgivings" and "Opennesss": A Dialog on Inclusivism between R. Douglas Geivett and Clark Pinnock." *Southern Baptist Journal of Theology* 02:2 (1998).

Green, Joel B., Scot McKnight and I. Howard Marshall, *Dictionay of Jesus and the Gospels*. Downers Grove: InterVarsity, 1992.

Hawthorne, Gerald F., Ralph P. Martin, and Daniel G. Reid, ed. *Dictionary of Paul and His Letters*. Downers Grove: InterVarsity Press, 1993.

House, Paul R. "Biblical Theology and the Inclusivist Challenge." *Southern Baptist Journal of Theology* 2:2 (1998): 3.

—. "The Battle for the Doctrine of God." *Southern Baptist Journal of Theology* 1:1 (1997).

Johnson, Darrell W. *Experiencing the Trinity*. Vancouver: Regent Colleg Publishing, 2002.

Johnson, Phil. "What's New with the New Age? Why Christians Need to Remain on Guard Against the Threat of New Age Spirituality." *Southern Baptiat Journal of Theology* 10:4 (Winter 2006).
Kushner, Harold S. *When Bad Things Happen to Good People.* Knoph Doubleday Publishing Group, 2004.
LaSor, William Sanford, David Allen Hubbardm and Frederic Wm. Bush. *Old Testament Survey: The Message, Form, and Background of the Old Testament.* Grand Rapids: William B. Eerdmans, 1996.
Lewis, Gordon R. "The Church and the New Spirituality." *Journal of the Evangelical Theological Society* 36:4 (December 1993).
Lewis, Gordon R., and Bruce A. Demarest. *Intergrative Theology.* Grand Rapids: Zondervan, 1996.
Lightner, Robert. "A Case for Systematic Theology." *Conservative Theological Journal* (2000).
Linden, David H. "A Study on Justification." *Reformation and Revival Jouranl* 8:01 (1999).
Lucas, Sean Michael. "Christianity at the Crossroads: E. Y. Mullins, J. Gresham Machen, and the Challenge of Modernism." *Southern Baptist Journal of Theology* 3:4 (Winter 1999).
Macarthur, John. "Open Theism's Attack on the Atonement." *Master's Seminary Journal* 12:1 (2001).
Machen, J. Gresham. *Christianity and Liberalism.* Grand Rapids: Wm. B. Eerdmans Publishing Company, 1923, Reprinted 2001. Kindle Edition.
Magnum, A Todd. "Is There a Reformed Way to Get the Benefits of the Atonement to "Those Who Have Never Heard?"." *Journal of the Evangelical Theological Society* 47:1 (2004).
McGrath, Alister E. *Studies in Doctrine.* Grand Rapids: Zondervan, 1998.
Milton, John. *Paradise Lost.* New York: D. Appleton & Co., 1851.

BIBLIOGRAPHY

Montgomery, John Warwick. "Speculation Versus Factuality: An Analysis of Modern Unbelief." *Bibliotheca Sacra* 168:669 (2011).

Moo, Douglas. *Encountering the Book Of Romans*. Grand Rapids: Baker Academic, 2002.

Morgan, Christopher W., and and Robert A. Peterson. *Faith Comes by Hearing: A Response to Inclusivism*. Downers Grove: InterVarsity Press, 2008.

Newell, William R. *Romans Verse-by-Verse*. Grand Rapid: Christian Classic Ethereal Library, 2009.

Okholm, David L., and Timothy R. Phillips, ed. *More Than One Way*. Grand Rapids: Zondervan, 1995.

Osburn. "Those Who Have Never Heard: Have They No Hope." *Journal of the Evangelical Theological Society* 32:3 (1989).

Phillips, W. Gary. "Evangelical Pluralism: A Singular Problem." *Bibliotheca Sacra* 151:602 (1994).

Pinnock, Clark A. *A Wideness in God's Mercy: The Finality of Jesus Christ in the World of Religions*. Grand Rapids: Zondervan, 1998.

—. *Most Moved Mover: A Theology of God's Openness*. Grand Rapids: Baker Book House, 2001.

Pinnock, Clark. *Does Prayer Change Things? Yes, if you're an Open Theist* Homiletics Online, n.d. 6 November 2013. <http://www.homileticsonline.com/subscriber/interviews/Pinnock.asp>.

Pinnock, Clark H. "Open Theism: "What is this? A New Teaching? - and with Authority? (Mark 1:27)." *Ashland Theological Journal* 34:0 (2002).

Pinnock, Clark, Richard Rice, John Sanders, William Hasker, and David Basinger. *The Openness of God: A Biblical Challenge to the Traditional Understanding of God*. Downers Grove: InterVarsity Press, 1994.

Pyne, Robert A. "A Critique of Free-Will Theism, Part 2." *Bibliotheca Sacra* 158:632 (2001).

—. "The "Seed," the Spirit, and the Blessing of Abraham." *Bibliotheca Sacra* 152:606 (1995).

—. "The Role of the Holy Spirit in Conversion." *Bibliotheca Sacra* 150:598 (1992).
Pyne, Robert A., and Stephen R. Spencer. "A Critique of Free-will Theism - Part Two." *Bibliotheca Sacra* 158:632 (2001): 397-403.
Sanders, John. *No Other Name: An Investigation into the Destiny of the Unevangelized.* Grand Rapids: Williams B. Eerdmans, 1992.
Schaff, Philip. *Creeds of Christendom, Fourth Edition.* Prod. Christian Classics Ethereal Library. Grand Rapids, n.d. Electronic document.
Schleiermacher, Friedrich in Toon, Peter. "Ways of Describing the Holy Trinity." *Reformation and Revival* 10:3 (2001).
Schreiner, Thomas R. "Paul's View of the Law in Romans 10:4-5." *Westminster Theological Journal* 55:1 (1993).
Schultz, Carl. "Know, Knowledge." *Evangelical Dictionary of Biblical Theology.* Ed. Walter A. Elwell. Grand Rapids: Baker Books, 1996.
Seifrid, Mark. "The Near Word of Christ and the Distant Vision of N. T. Wright." *Journal of the Evangelical Theological Society* 54:2 (2011).
Strobel, Lee. *The Case for Faith: A Journalist Investigates the Toughest Objections to Christianity.* Grand Rapids: Zondervan, 2000.
Sweeney, Douglas A. and Mark C. Rogers. "Walk the Aisle." *Christian History, Christianity Today* 22 October 2008. <http://www.christianitytoday.com/ch/thepastintheprese nt/storybehind/walktheaisle.html>.
Thielman, Frank. "God's Righteousness as God's Fairness in Romans 1:17: An Ancient Perspective on a Significant Phrase." *Journal of the Evangelical Theological Society* 54:1 (2011).
Tunnicliffe, Patty. "Everything Old is New Again: Oprah Winfrey, Her Guests, and Their Spiritual Worldview: Developing Spiritual Discernment in an Undiscerning Age." *Christian Apologetics Journal* 8:2 (Fall 2009).

BIBLIOGRAPHY

Utley, Bob. *The Gospel According to Paul: Romans*. Bible Lessons International, 2013. <http://www.biblelessonsintl.com/>.

Ware, Bruce A. *Father, Son, Holy Spirit: Relationships, Roles, and Relevance*. Wheaton: Crossway Books, 2005.

—. *God's Lesser Glory: The Diminished God of Open Theism*. Wheaton: Crossways Book, 2000.

Wax, Trevin. *Inclusivism: What is "Faith" Anyway?* The Gospel Coalition: Kingdom People, Living on Earth as Citizens of Heaven, 26 July 2007. Web blog. 26 July 2013. <http://thegospelcoalition.org/blogs/trevinwax/2007/11/page2>.

Wellum, Stephen J. "An Evaluation of the Son-Spirit Relation in Clark Pinnock's Inclusivism: An Exercise in Tinitarian Reflection." *Southern Baptist Journal of Theology* 10:1 (2006).

White, James R. "The Newness of the Covenant." *Reformed Baptist Theological Review* 01:2 (2004).

Zuckerman, Miron, Jordon Silberman, and Judith A Hall. "The Relationship Between Intelligence and Religiosity: A Meta-Analysis and Some Proposed Explanations." *Personality and Social Psychology Review* November 2013.

Index

A

Apostle Paul, 15-16, 27, 30, 37, 46, 48-49, 61, 63-64, 70, 75, 81, 87-88, 93, 105, 107, 110, 179, 194, 196, 202, 210, 236-237, 244, 251, 255

Atonement, 102, 131, 134, 180, 213-214

Authority, 19, 21-22, 31-34, 39-41, 50, 56, 62, 65-66, 69-70, 78, 83, 146-147, 180, 184, 199-200, 229, 231, 237

B

Believe, 11, 15-20, 27, 29, 31, 45, 52, 64, 66, 68-70, 74-75, 91, 95, 101-102, 124, 134, 159, 179-180, 183, 202-203, 205, 229, 237, 239

Biblical interpretation, 34, 41, 50

C

Centrality of Christ, 115, 119, 120, 125, 154

Christian faith, 12, 40, 47-48, 50, 56, 71, 74, 79, 125-126, 153, 159-160

Compassion, 65, 211, 254-255, 257, 258

Compromise, 19, 37, 39, 40, 42, 44, 46, 50-51, 248

Control belief, 34, 65, 100, 108, 121, 184, 252

Created order, 26-27, 35, 48, 71, 73, 76, 78, 83, 90-93, 98-100, 124, 144, 147, 153-154, 158, 163, 171-172, 176-178, 186, 231, 254, 258

Creation, 10-11, 19-21, 27-28, 30, 32, 39-40, 48-49, 51, 53, 59, 62, 66-71, 73-78, 82-83, 89, 102-103, 107, 115, 118, 122, 124-126, 128-129, 144, 148, 150-151, 154-155, 158-159, 162-163, 166, 168-169, 176, 178-179, 207, 209, 217, 220, 229, 231, 235

Cross of Christ, 191, 258

D

Doctrine, 19, 32, 41-43, 46-50, 56, 65, 72, 148, 178

E

Eternal life, 16, 20, 37, 78, 84, 115, 200

Eternity, 12, 20, 22, 49, 69, 73, 75, 77, 83, 120, 133, 155, 169, 178, 183, 254

Evangelical, 11, 19, 25, 36, 40, 45, 47, 61, 114, 131, 181, 183, 198, 221

Evangelism, 12, 56, 65, 237-260

Exclusivism, 11, 19, 20, 25, 44-45, 61, 69, 71, 79, 89

Exclusivists, 61, 183

Explicit faith, 11, 45, 61, 127, 160, 175, 180

F

Fairness, 17, 20, 27, 35, 103, 105, 108, 110-111, 118-122, 127, 151, 183-191, 195-196, 199, 208

Faith, 9, 11-12, 16, 18-21, 25-29, 31, 33-34, 37, 40, 42, 45-48, 56, 61-62, 66-71, 74, 77, 87-90, 92-98, 100, 102, 105, 107-110, 112,

INDEX

116, 118, 125-126, 129, 133-134, 143, 145, 147-150, 153-155, 157-166, 168-169, 171, 173-180, 197, 200, 213, 216-217, 220, 229-231, 237-238, 240-242, 248, 250-254

Faith in Christ, 26, 45, 62, 87, 89, 93, 107, 110, 159, 173-174, 180, 197, 237, 241, 248, 254

Faith principle, 92, 129, 133, 145, 147-149, 154, 157, 161, 163, 173, 175, 177

Faithful, 20, 89, 127, 165, 196, 208, 232, 257

Faithfulness, 12, 15, 68, 77, 87, 97-98, 100, 196-197, 200, 202, 204-208, 210, 212, 217, 229, 232, 236, 242, 255

Father, God the, 21-22, 26, 37, 43, 49-54, 58, 67, 73-83, 87-88, 93, 114-115, 117, 121, 149, 154-155, 158-161, 164-165, 167, 181, 195, 226, 239, 242-243, 245

Fewness doctrine, 20, 25, 150, 211

Finite, 21, 28-29, 32, 54, 74, 76, 105, 108, 122, 129, 171, 176, 178-179, 185, 188, 209

Forgiveness, 89, 104, 109, 112, 143, 180, 245, 250

Free will, 39, 56, 98, 128, 169, 171-172, 195-196, 228-230

G

General revelation, 19, 21, 66-70, 74, 82, 91, 93-94, 99-100, 115, 125-126, 128-129, 157, 163-169, 172, 176, 178

Gentiles, 18, 204, 206-207, 210, 215-217, 220, 228

Gospel, 9, 11-12, 15-20, 22, 25-27, 30, 35, 37, 42, 48-49, 51-52, 55-57, 61-73, 82-84, 87-95, 98-103, 105-107, 109-111, 113, 116, 119-122, 125-126, 129, 134, 143-144, 148-153, 157, 161, 163, 166, 169, 172, 175, 179-180, 183-184, 186-191, 193-195, 199, 202, 204-208, 211-212, 216-217, 228, 232, 235-237, 239, 241-244, 246, 248, 250-258

Grace, 20, 33, 47, 61, 68, 74, 77, 93, 100, 112, 117, 153, 197, 203-204, 223-224, 237, 242-244, 251-254

H

Heaven, 21, 25, 50-51, 55, 59, 70, 77, 89, 104, 148, 156, 181, 223, 240

Holy Spirit, 21-22, 28, 36, 40-41, 43, 47-53, 57-58, 64, 72, 74, 88, 110, 114, 127, 158-161, 164, 166-167, 169, 172, 181, 188, 195, 235, 249-250, 253

Humanity, 10, 12, 20, 26, 28, 30-31, 38-39, 48-51, 53, 56, 59, 64, 66-67, 72-74, 76-78, 83, 89, 91, 99, 105, 107-113, 118-121, 124, 128, 145, 147, 161, 170, 176-180, 184, 186, 189-190, 195, 207, 209, 220, 223, 229, 231, 239, 252-254, 256, 258

I

Incarnation, 19-20, 47, 50, 52, 71, 73-74, 83, 90, 93-94, 165, 206

Injustice, 88, 119, 151, 191, 194, 196, 208, 211-212

Interpretation, 34, 41-43, 100, 204, 224, 227

J

Jesus Christ, 11, 15-16, 19-20, 23, 27, 33, 47-48, 52-53, 61, 64, 66, 69-70, 73, 79, 82, 88-92, 114-116, 120-121, 127, 129, 148-149, 152, 154, 160-161, 168, 175, 178-180, 189-190, 194, 197-198, 203, 213, 228, 235-237, 243, 250, 253, 258

Judgment, 15, 17, 25, 28-29, 35, 95, 105, 108, 113, 116, 127, 135,

144-146, 149-150, 155, 184-186, 188, 194, 197, 209, 214, 226-227, 231, 236, 250, 254, 258
Justice, 44, 48, 88, 102-103, 105, 110-111, 118-119, 121, 125, 127, 151, 183, 185-189, 191-192, 194-195, 205, 207, 209-212, 214, 223
Justification by faith, 89-90, 95, 97, 100, 109, 125, 197, 239, 244-245, 249

K

Knowledge of God, 55, 61, 87, 94-95, 108, 113, 134, 168-169, 188, 225, 232, 250, 258

L

Light of creation, 69, 115, 125, 134, 151, 158, 172, 196, 254

M

Mediate, 73, 157, 161
Mediation, 19-21, 66-67, 74, 82, 100-101, 115, 126, 148, 152, 161, 166, 168-169, 179
Mediator, 20-21, 37, 49-51, 66, 69, 74, 83, 99, 115, 126, 148, 153, 161, 165, 213
Mercy, 18, 25-26, 44, 55-56, 77, 116, 121-122, 148, 151-152, 178, 191, 204, 208-209, 211-217, 219-220, 223-224, 227-229, 232
Missions, 9, 12, 56, 63-64, 125, 134, 136, 191, 235-260

N

Nature, 10-12, 17, 19-20, 28, 34, 38-39, 43, 46-54, 56, 63-64, 77, 91, 93, 96-97, 105-106, 109, 116-118, 121-122, 125, 127-129, 133, 149, 154, 157-158, 170, 176-177, 186, 188, 191, 196, 216-217, 228, 236, 256, 258

O

Obedience, 18, 143, 180, 194
Object of faith, 27, 66, 68, 93, 95-97, 99, 102, 129, 153, 157-158, 161, 177, 179-180
Open Theism, 55-56, 131, 181

P

Pluralism, 44, 55, 61-62, 71
Power of God, 12, 15, 62, 67, 88, 109, 144, 150, 194-195, 232, 235-236, 241, 250, 254
Proclaimed gospel, 19-20, 33, 37, 48, 56, 61, 89-90, 115, 125, 143-144, 189, 197
Promise, 12-13, 20, 22, 27, 95-98, 100, 158, 164-165, 197, 207-208, 210-211, 214, 216, 220, 229-230, 235-236

R

Reconciliation, 28, 32, 37, 53, 242, 249-250, 255, 258
Redemption, 20, 33, 35, 44, 46, 49, 51, 53, 87, 93, 98, 103, 115, 154-155, 163-164, 166, 173-174, 176, 199, 204, 212, 214, 216, 225, 229, 243
Religions, 11, 19, 23, 41, 45, 55-56, 62-65, 71, 74, 78, 114, 116, 125, 129, 152, 167, 187, 198
Resurrection, 43, 46, 53, 68, 71, 78, 93, 101-102, 144, 235, 246
Revelation, 21, 32, 45, 53, 56, 62-63, 67-68, 72, 74, 77, 90-95, 99, 113, 144, 152, 157, 160-164, 168-169, 172, 177, 180, 184, 188, 190, 206, 214, 252
Righteous, 19-20, 68, 87, 89, 92, 97, 100, 106, 109, 112, 117-118, 127, 133, 150-151, 187, 190-191, 195, 197, 207, 209, 213, 217, 232, 245, 250, 258

INDEX

Righteousness of God, 20, 62, 68, 71, 87-92, 95, 99, 102-103, 109-110, 114, 121, 150, 184, 190-191, 194, 197, 204-205, 216, 232, 244-245, 256, 258

S

Salvation, 9, 11-12, 15-17, 19-21, 25, 27, 30, 32-33, 37-38, 40, 43-52, 55-56, 61-69, 71, 73-74, 81-83, 88-95, 98-102, 104-105, 107, 109-112, 115-116, 119, 125-126, 129, 133, 135, 143, 145, 147-155, 157-160, 163, 166, 168-173, 175-176, 178-180, 183-184, 189-190, 192, 194-196, 199-200, 204, 207, 210-211, 214, 223, 226, 228, 230, 232, 235-238, 241-242, 246, 248, 250-254

Scriptures, 9, 12, 18-19, 32-33, 38-39, 42-44, 46-47, 50, 55-57, 61, 65-66, 69, 72-73, 77, 81-82, 88, 93, 96, 102, 105, 108, 117-118, 133, 135-136, 154, 157-159, 161, 163, 166-167, 169, 173-175, 180, 184-185, 188, 196, 200, 215, 230-231, 235, 250, 252

Sinful, sinfulness, 73-74, 77, 83, 105-106, 108-109, 112-113, 119-120, 128, 147, 180, 186, 190, 197, 209, 219

Son of God, 26, 52, 71, 73, 77, 82-83, 144, 154, 161, 178, 237

Special revelation, 45, 67-68, 89-90, 93-94, 99, 158, 163-164, 172, 179

Speculation, 12, 29-36, 40-43, 50, 55, 66, 69-72, 94, 100, 108, 112-113, 133-135, 169, 173, 184, 188, 196

Speculative, 11, 25-26, 33-34, 40, 42, 45-46, 65-66, 171, 196, 223

T

The cross, 20, 51, 68, 92-93, 113, 117-119, 122, 125, 127, 160, 177, 184, 191, 194-195, 197, 213-214, 242, 250, 255-258

The lost, 12, 16, 19-21, 27, 30, 34-35, 51, 55, 65, 89, 102-103, 105, 109-111, 125, 143, 148, 154, 190, 199-200, 202, 211-212, 223, 236, 254-256, 258

Theology, 32, 36, 40-44, 46-47, 54-55, 58-59, 94-95, 125-126, 130-131, 134, 145, 148, 172-175, 181, 191, 198, 207, 221, 223, 228, 231, 251

Trinity, triune God, 12, 19-20, 22, 42, 47-54, 56, 58, 66, 68, 71-73, 75, 77-78, 80-81, 83-85, 87-88, 90, 102, 118, 124, 148, 158-161, 164, 166-169, 181, 237, 242, 258

U

Unbelief, 32, 36, 40, 179

Unevangelized, 15, 19, 21, 23, 26-27, 29, 32-34, 42, 58, 61, 67, 69, 70, 82, 89, 99-100, 103, 105, 108, 115, 118, 120-121, 153, 155, 179, 191, 202, 223-224

Unfair, 17, 106, 116, 118, 120, 147, 155, 190, 231

Unjust, 17, 45, 116, 120-121, 155, 184, 190, 208-209, 217, 219, 257

Unsaved, 11, 20, 28, 61, 67, 69, 154, 191, 195, 199

W

Who have never heard, 15-16, 19, 27, 30, 89, 103, 105-106, 110-111, 116, 120, 133, 148, 157, 183-184, 207-208, 235-236

Wider hope, 55, 151-153, 178, 191, 228

Word of God, 18-19, 28, 30, 61, 81, 162

About the Author

Floyd Talbot holds two Master degrees: an MBA from Pepperdine University and Master of Arts from Western Seminary in California. As a Christian for over 25 years, Floyd has encountered a number of troubling teachings contrary to the Bible that can mislead Christians and whole congregations. Many such teachings are subtle while others are outright hostile to the gospel of Christ. Such encounters led Floyd to engage in research to determine their underlying philosophy and points of departure from Scripture. He first encountered the teachings of inclusivism about ten years ago after reading Gregory Boyd's book *God of the Possible: A Biblical Introduction to the Open View of God*. That book struck Floyd as unsettling because of its portrayal of God inconsistent with Scriptures.

It was not until several years later that Floyd discovered that Boyd belonged to a view known as inclusivism. His encounter with inclusivism in a group Bible study motivated Him to write this book. This book is Floyd's confession of faith.

Floyd has been a lay leader, led small groups, taught Bible studies, and engaged in public speaking on topics in biblical exposition and interpretation, Christian growth topics, and finance. Mr. Talbot has consulted with businesses in financial and business matters over the past 13 years and has over 25 years in financial accounting and business planning.

He has published one other book through Business Expert Press in the field of finance, *Customer-Driven Budgeting: Prepare, Engage, Execute: A Small Business Guide*, arising from his years of consulting with business owners and managers in finance, strategy, and planning.

Floyd and his wife, Vickie, currently enjoy the fellowship of the Evangelical Free Church.

www.ingramcontent.com/pod-product-compliance
Lightning Source LLC
Chambersburg PA
CBHW060501090426
42735CB00011B/2067